Guilty People

Guilty People

ABBE SMITH

With original cartoons by the author

Rutgers University Press

New Brunswick, Camden, and Newark, New Jersey, and London

Library of Congress Cataloging-in-Publication Data

Names: Smith, Abbe, author.
Title: Guilty people / Abbe Smith.
Description: New Brunswick : Rutgers University Press, [2019] | Includes index.
Identifiers: LCCN 2019012320 | ISBN 9781978803398 (cloth)
Subjects: LCSH: Criminal justice, Administration of—United States. | Defense (Criminal
procedure)—United States.
Classification: LCC KF9223 .S547 2019 | DDC 345.73/03—dc23
LC record available at https://lccn.loc.gov/2019012320

♾ The paper used in this publication meets the requirements of the American National Standard for Information Sciences—Permanence of Paper for Printed Library Materials, ANSI
Z39.48-1992.

www.rutgersuniversitypress.org

Manufactured in the United States of America

To Anita Smith—
Who always looked for the good in people, usually found it,
and inspired me to do the same.

To Emmie Green—
Whose dignity, strength, and faith that we shall overcome someday
I carry in my heart.

And to all the guilty people in my life—
Friends, family, students, fellows, colleagues. Oh yes—and clients.

"But I'm not guilty," said K. "there's been a mistake. How is it even possible for someone to be guilty? We're all human beings here, one like the other."

FRANZ KAFKA, *The Trial*

Contents

Guilty People

Introduction

As I have often felt compelled to explain in the course of writing a book called *Guilty People*, this is not a history of the Jews. It is instead a book about people who run afoul of the law and end up in the criminal legal system.

Guilty People is a follow-up to a previous book, *Case of a Lifetime*, which recounts my efforts to free Patsy Kelly Jarrett, a woman who served nearly thirty years in prison for a crime she did not commit.[1] Kelly (as she is known) was convicted of murder based on the testimony of a single shaky eyewitness and sentenced to life.

This was a formative case for me. I met Kelly when I was a second-year law student. As I made my way from law student to public defender to clinical law professor in New York, Massachusetts, and Washington, DC, the injustice of Kelly's case was a benchmark against which every other injustice was measured. Any victory felt tarnished while she languished in prison. Though I did everything I could on Kelly's behalf, the best I could achieve was her release on parole. This was hardly a moment of lawyerly triumph. "Innocent client to be supervised on parole after three decades in prison" is not the kind of thing lawyers boast about on their websites.

In *Case of a Lifetime*, I describe the enormous burden of representing an innocent person: there is nothing more grueling. I acknowledge that Kelly was not a typical client—that, in fact, most criminal defendants are guilty. To quote one longtime criminal lawyer, "I am not unique in representing guilty defendants. That is what most defense attorneys do most of the time."[2] In *Case of a Lifetime*, I also wrote about the weighty responsibility of representing people accused or convicted of crime, whether or not they are actually innocent.

But perhaps not enough.

Some former clinic students and postgraduate E. Barrett Prettyman fellows—criminal defense protégés of whom I am proud—were disappointed that I wrote a book about an innocent person. "Et tu, Brute?" they seemed to be saying. They couldn't believe I had jumped on the bandwagon, joining forces with Innocence Project founder Barry Scheck, who no longer calls himself a criminal defense lawyer because he "hasn't represented a guilty person in twenty years."[3] "How could *you*, of all people, exalt the representation of the innocent when there is so much work to be done on behalf of the guilty?" they seemed to ask.

They were not unkind. They appreciated Kelly's impact on my life. But I understood their disappointment. I am a committed, dyed-in-the-wool defender. I often say I run a "Guilty Project," not an Innocence Project. Although I acknowledge the many accomplishments of the "innocence movement," I have concerns about its focus on factual innocence in a time of mass incarceration.[4]

The United States may or may not be the most punitive nation on earth, but we are undeniably the world leader in putting human beings behind bars.[5] This was so as we headed into the twenty-first century, and it remains the troubling reality now.[6] We currently incarcerate more than two million people.[7] As a proportion of its total population, the United States incarcerates five times more people than Britain, nine times more than Germany, and twelve times more than Japan.[8] Our closest competitors, Russia and Belarus, lag well behind us.[9]

Despite signs that our incarceration policies and practices might be changing,[10] the U.S. jail and prison population has hovered at the two million mark for some time, a disproportionate number of which are people of color.[11] On top of this, more than seven million people are currently under the supervision of our criminal justice system.[12] As things stand, roughly one in every one hundred adults is behind bars in America, and one in thirty-one is under the supervision of the correctional system.[13] The numbers are even higher if you count everyone under some form of government control, including drug and other specialized "treatment" courts, and immigrant detention, which seems to be on the rise.[14]

The excessive length of American prison sentences is a big part of the problem. Never in our nation's history have so many individuals been locked up for so long. More shocking still, one in nine American prisoners is currently serving a life sentence—fifty thousand of these without the possibility of parole.[15] While we talk about reducing our prison population, we seem to be increasing the time many prisoners serve, resulting in an ever-aging prison population.[16]

This is not to mention the squalid conditions of confinement in a time of private jails and prisons, where profit takes precedence and corruption prevails.[17] As one commentator observed, "Nothing illustrates the full wretchedness and twisted nature of punishment in America as graphically as the sudden and rapid growth of private institutions of incarceration."[18]

It was not always this way. After touring American penitentiaries in the early nineteenth century, French diplomat and historian Alexis de Tocqueville exalted our enlightened approach to criminal punishment. "In no country is criminal justice administered with more mildness than in the United States," he wrote in *Democracy in America*.[19] Now far from serving as a model, the United States is a cautionary tale. One British commentator calls the United States "a rogue state" when it comes to criminal justice.[20]

A focus on innocence is a problem for other reasons. First, it is hard to prove. A claim of innocence requires proving a "negative"—the accused wasn't there or didn't do it.[21] The only hard evidence is DNA, which is available in only a fraction of the criminal cases where there is testable biological evidence. Second, a focus on "actual innocence"[22] threatens to erode the abiding principle of our criminal justice system—that the accused is *presumed innocent* unless and until guilt is proven beyond a reasonable doubt. This is an important check on state power. Moreover, the problems underlying DNA exonerations—mistaken identification, police and prosecutorial misconduct, false confessions, unreliable snitch testimony, defense lawyer incompetence—are not unique to those cases and ought to be a concern whether or not an accused "did it." A conviction is "wrongful" when there is demonstrable unfairness.[23]

Even if we could identify and free all the innocent people in prison, our system would not be fixed. There would still be prisoners serving excessive sentences in brutal penal institutions,[24] and too often, they would have landed there without the meaningful assistance of counsel envisioned nearly sixty years ago in *Gideon v. Wainwright*.[25] Alas, *Gideon*'s promise— "of a vast, diverse country in which every [person] charged with crime will be capably defended, no matter what his economic circumstances, and in which the lawyer representing him will do so proudly, without resentment"—remains unmet.[26]

I agree with my former students and fellows that a focus on innocence comes at the expense of the not-so-innocent. Guilty people become the fall guys. But guilty people are not monolithic. While it is true that some people commit serious crime, others commit minor, even trivial crime. Some are guilty of something—but not what they are charged with. Others may have committed the crime charged but with significant mitigating or extenuating circumstances. Some have committed the crime, but they have never done anything like it before—they lost control in a trying situation. Others commit crime out of immaturity, imprudence, or impulse. Some are gifted criminals, others clumsy and feckless.

Some people are all but destined to live a life of crime in view of what they've suffered in their lives. Others fall into it. Some people don't mean to engage in crime at all but lack the will or resources to extricate themselves from bad company.

As Professor Paul Butler writes:

Picture the guy who works in the mailroom at your office, and the men who dry off your vehicle at the car wash, and the sweaty kids who come to your house to deliver the mattress. Think of your high school classmate, the dude who didn't quite make it to graduation but who you got to know a little bit because he sold you weed. Maybe he wouldn't be your ideal companion for lunch at the Four Seasons or your first choice to marry your daughter. But he's not exactly a menace to society. He's made some bad choices, done some stupid things, but he's still young and his life is still salvageable. Spiritual folks might say, "God is not through with him yet."[27]

This is an apt description of most people caught up in the criminal system. None of us is only the worst thing we've ever done. Most of us learn from our mistakes and are able to put them behind us. But both luck and privilege play a role in the ability to get past bad choices. As former chief of the Civil Rights Division of the Justice Department and secretary of labor Tom Perez once said, "I am ambivalent about using the term *second chance* for prisoners, because many of them never had a first chance."[28]

As part of their training, I distribute index cards to the interns who work as investigators in Georgetown's criminal and juvenile defense clinics and ask them to write down the worst, most shameful thing they've ever done. (I assure them that we will shred the cards and no one will see what they write.) Then I ask them to imagine that what they have written is all anyone thinks of them—not their sparkling personalities, their various talents, their generosity to family and friends, their otherwise good characters. The exercise is not subtle. This is how our clients feel: reduced to their crime.

The truth is, I like guilty people. I prefer people who are flawed and complicated and do bad things to those who are irreproachable and uncomplicated and do the right thing. Flawed people are more interesting.

Those we think of as "the worst" often turn out to be not so different from the rest of us. As Clarence Darrow once said, "Everybody is a potential murderer. I've never killed anyone, but I frequently get satisfaction reading the obituary notices."[29] Or, as Katherine Hepburn argues as a defense lawyer in the movie *Adam's Rib*, "Assault lies dormant in all of us. It requires only circumstance to set it in violent motion."[30] Fittingly, Hepburn objects to the characterization of a wronged wife accused of trying to kill her husband's mistress as a "criminal." This is a strange thing to call a "citizen, wife, and mother," she says.

Unfortunately, this more nuanced view of criminal conduct is difficult for many to grasp—that is, until a friend or family member is arrested. Then miraculously, "criminals" become multidimensional people.

As a criminal lawyer, I prefer a system of justice that is concerned with proof, not truth—a scheme that makes it very hard to deprive a person of liberty or life no matter what they have done. Our criminal justice system is only as good as it treats the worst—and the least—among us. These are the people on the fast train to prison or the purgatory of endless supervision. As Dostoyevsky said, "You can judge a society by how well it treats its prisoners."

I believe that reducing our disproportionately black and brown prison population is the Civil Rights Movement of the twenty-first century.[31] We need to stop discarding human beings, banishing them from society like they are "throw-away people."[32]

Through stories about my clients, their alleged crimes, and related commentary, this book offers answers to frequently asked questions about the criminal justice system. First, the questions about "criminals": Who are these people filling our nation's jails and prisons? Are the millions convicted of crime and serving time as dangerous and depraved as they are portrayed in the media? What are the crimes they commit? How did they get caught up in the system and what happens to them there? Then the questions about the lawyers who represent them, summarized by the familiar question posed to criminal defenders: How can you represent those people? This book offers an account of what it's like to be a criminal defense lawyer—what we do and why we do it.

A number of themes about the current state of crime and punishment in America run through the book: the excessively punitive nature of the criminal legal system; the hapless people caught up in it; the enormous power of police and prosecutors; the pervasive cynicism and rigidity of those in authority; and an increasingly entrenched perception that criminals are bad people, different from the rest of us, and incapable of redemption.

The guilty are not a separate species. They are just like us—though maybe not quite as upstanding, obedient, or fortunate.

This book is about them, the guilty people. My hope is that in telling some of their stories we might recognize ourselves and see that what separates us from the guilty, more often than not, are luck and circumstance. If we can see this, we might be a little less punitive and a little more forgiving.

1

Petty Criminals

Everyone is a misdemeanant.

Those who drive — no matter how carefully or short the distance — after one too many or not enough sleep.

Anyone who has smoked a little weed.

Absent-minded grocery shoplifters munching on not yet weighed grapes.

But what can we do about all these petty criminals? We can't lock up all of 'em.

How about we lock up none of 'em.

Misdemeanors are the great equalizer. People from all walks of life can end up in misdemeanor court for all kinds of reasons.

My first case as a law student in the New York University criminal defense clinic was a misdemeanor: a young man accused of "turnstile jumping" (propelling oneself over a subway turnstile without paying). Although a transit officer witnessed this theft and immediately arrested my client, making it an easy case to prove, I spent hours interviewing my client (who admitted it), investigating the facts (which were exactly what was alleged), and researching the law (which wasn't helpful). I was relieved when my client's case was ultimately "adjourned in contemplation of dismissal," giving him an opportunity to keep his record clean if he stayed out of trouble.

A few years ago, an old childhood friend, whom I'll call Lisa, was arrested for drunk driving. She had never been arrested before and was embarrassed about it. Her arrest had been videotaped. In the video she comes across as a little loopy, but not so different from her usual personality. When asked to walk a straight line, heel to toe, she complained that she could never do that in ballet class. She protested that she had only had a couple of glasses of wine, refused the breathalyzer, and declined to say anything further. She spent the night in jail.

I happened to have moved to where Lisa was living shortly after the arrest and accompanied her to meetings with her lawyer. The best way to get oriented to practicing law in a new town is to try a case, so I was pleased to help out. It was a triable case: there was no accident or injury and no forensic or medical evidence of intoxication. Plus, Lisa was an appealing defendant. She had no record and a good job. She might have been tired, inattentive, or not the best driver rather than a criminally intoxicated one.

The trial took a couple of hours. Like many misdemeanors, it was a "bench trial" before a judge sitting alone. (Contrary to what many people believe, there is a limited right to a jury in much of the country.) The trial featured the arresting officer's testimony, the arrest videotape, and Lisa's testimony. I thought Lisa was credible enough to raise a reasonable doubt. The judge did not. He found her guilty, placed her on probation, suspended her license, and ordered her to attend "drunk-driving school," a series of classes on the horrors of drunk driving. If she completed probation successfully, she could petition the court to have her record sealed.

The case is memorable only because she was my friend.

A more recent, haunting misdemeanor featured a young man in his early twenties, whom I'll call Cal. He had no prior record and was accused of physically assaulting the thirteen-year-old son of his consider-ably older girlfriend. The basic facts of the case were not in dispute. Cal was at his girlfriend's place babysitting the thirteen-year-old, whom Cal called "Little Man," and his two younger siblings. Cal often stayed with his girlfriend's kids when she went out. On this occasion, the girl-friend had been out until late. She came home intoxicated—with her older uncle in tow—and wanted to have sex with Cal. Cal told her he didn't want to have sex while the uncle was there. The girlfriend tried to cajole him, putting her hands down the front of his pants. He took her hands out. She then began to taunt him. She called him a pussy, a girl. The girlfriend said she would go have sex with Cal's brother if he wouldn't have sex with her. She began to strike him with her fists. He did not fight back. When Cal tried to stop her from hitting him by holding her arms, Little Man suddenly jumped on his back and began punching him. Cal grabbed Little Man and threw him onto the couch in a single motion. Little Man then called the police, who arrested Cal and charged him with two counts of simple assault—one for his girlfriend and one for Little Man—and one count of cruelty to children.

Cal was dismayed to be arrested and especially to be accused of being cruel to a child. He loved Little Man. He had been in a relationship with Little Man's mother since Little Man was six years old. His own mother did not approve of the relationship. She was troubled by the age gap between Cal and the much older woman. Plus, Cal had some learning disabilities that made him seem younger than his age; she feared he could easily be taken advantage of. But she also saw that he was in love.

Cal was a beautiful young man—tall, thin, and espresso-colored, with deep-set, soulful eyes and high cheekbones. He could have been a model. He wore his hair in dreadlocks, sometimes pulled back.

Cal's student attorney and I did everything we could to get the case removed from the criminal justice system to a "diversionary program" that would allow our client to maintain his clean record. There was no sugges-tion of any previous domestic violence—no restraining order against Cal for abusing the girlfriend, her kids, or anyone else. The incident was a per-fect storm of intoxication and misguided filial loyalty. But the prosecutor was unbudging. He took accusations of child abuse seriously. Cal would have been eligible for first-time-offender domestic violence diversion if he had only assaulted his girlfriend. But an assault on a child made this option inappropriate.

We kept pressing the prosecutor. This was not a case we wanted to try, largely because of the judge before whom Cal was scheduled to appear. This judge was known for being incapable of uttering the words "not guilty," no matter the evidence. In his courtroom, proof beyond a reasonable doubt was accomplished by virtually any case a prosecutor put on. He often disparaged defense arguments as "unreasonable doubt." Once a defendant was convicted, especially of an assaultive crime, he or she went to jail. The prosecutor held firm.

We prepared for trial. We investigated the case and got signed statements from the girlfriend, the uncle, and Little Man. Much of what they said corroborated what Cal had told us. The arresting officers wouldn't talk to us, but their police reports confirmed that neither Little Man nor Cal's girlfriend was injured. Cal had made statements to the police that both harmed and helped him: he admitted what he had done but said he hadn't meant to hurt anyone.

The trial lasted two days—long for a bench trial. Little Man, the chief witness for the prosecution, was smart, well-spoken, and fiercely loyal to his mom. He said Cal had no right to put his hands on him or his mom. The police acknowledged that Cal was quiet and cooperative when they arrested him. We called the uncle, the girlfriend, two witnesses who testified to Cal's good character, a student investigator who testified that Little Man had offered a slightly different account of the incident to us shortly after it had happened than he had given at trial, and Cal.

The girlfriend was a mess. She wept throughout her testimony, saying Cal was a good man who would never hurt a flea. She said she loved her son too and didn't want to be caught in the middle. It was all her fault, she said; she'd had too much to drink and had behaved badly. In the hall outside of the courtroom, when trial was not in session, she sat on Cal's lap, her legs and arms wrapped around him, his arms around her. Sometimes they made out in the courthouse hall like a couple of oblivious teenagers.

Cal was an excellent witness even though he was nervous. He described everything that happened honestly and simply. He was incapable of guile and came across that way. He said he threw Little Man off him instinctively, without thinking, because the attack took him by surprise, and had done so in self-defense. He denied striking or doing anything other than trying to restrain his girlfriend when Little Man jumped on him. He said he was sorry about the whole thing, that he would never hurt anyone. He loved his girlfriend and her kids.

We argued hard for an acquittal. The prosecution argued equally hard for a conviction. The judge found Cal guilty of simple assault on Little Man and cruelty to children and not guilty of simple assault on the girlfriend. He seemed to consider this an exceptionally fair verdict. He told Cal there was enough evidence to support a conviction for simple assault on the girlfriend but that he was giving him a break. He then sentenced Cal to two weeks in jail and ordered the marshal to take him into custody.

Cal burst out crying. He begged the judge not to send him to jail. He said he was afraid. He had learned his lesson and would never do anything wrong again. He was weeping hard, his body heaving. His mother and girlfriend were also crying, and so was the student attorney. We tried to get the judge to change his mind. This was not a case that required a jail sentence, we urged. This was not a young man who needed to be put in a cage. A conviction itself was sufficient punishment—a permanent blemish on Cal's record that would likely prevent him from ever working with kids. Certainly probation with domestic violence classes or community service would suffice. If necessary, the judge could also order a period of electronic monitoring. The judge allowed us to make our arguments and then ordered that Cal be taken away.

I can still hear the sound of his sobs. It is unusual for a twentysomething man to cry like that in court. I found it disturbing. Others seemed disturbed too—the court clerk, the marshal, people in the audience. Even the prosecutor, who had called for jail time, did not seem to derive much satisfaction from the outcome. Only the judge seemed unmoved.

Over the next few days, we visited Cal in jail and petitioned the court to modify the sentence. The client had adjusted to his sentence better than we had. We had mixed feelings about this. Although his ability to adapt to his circumstances made it less painful to see him behind bars, he should not have had to adapt to jail. He did not need to be there. The judge denied our petitions.

Such losses can be difficult, so it's a good thing we win sometimes.

Diane Brewer (not her real name) was a young mother who had graduated from high school and was planning to enroll in community college. She worked as a cashier at one of the popular Shake Shack restaurants in downtown Washington, DC. Like almost all the cashiers, clerks, and food preparers at this Shake Shack, Ms. Brewer was African American. The restaurant managers—a general manager named Amy Rogers, who oversaw several shops, and the store manager, Alan Thompson—were white.

(Again, these are not their real names.) One day, Ms. Brewer got into an altercation with Thompson. He scolded her for not wearing a belt, which was part of the Shake Shack uniform. She replied that she wasn't the only one not wearing a belt and that general manager Rogers often failed to wear a belt, allowing everyone to see her "butt crack." This angered Thompson, who was close to Rogers. He told Ms. Brewer she was rude and disrespectful and ordered her to go back to work. Later that day, Ms. Brewer and Thompson quarreled again—this time over Thompson's delay in changing a large bill for a customer at Ms. Brewer's register, which had caused a line to gather.

At the end of her shift, Thompson told Ms. Brewer to collect her belongings and meet him in the back office. She did as she was told. When she walked into the office, she found Rogers there as well—not a good sign. Together with Rogers, Thompson fired Ms. Brewer and told her to leave the store immediately. Her final paycheck would be mailed to her. According to the criminal complaint and police reports, Ms. Brewer reacted badly. She grabbed a bunch of wires attached to the office computer system and yanked them out. As she stormed out of the office, she spat at Thompson. She was arrested a couple of days later on a warrant charging her with destruction of property and simple assault.

Ms. Brewer told the postgraduate fellow appointed to represent her that the accusation was essentially true. She felt she had been unfairly fired and lost her temper. She was not proud of her behavior that day. She said there was more to the story than was in the police reports, but she hoped she could admit guilt and be placed into some kind of first-offender program so that she might avoid a criminal record. She wanted her daughter to have a college graduate as a mother, not a criminal.

The fellow tried, but his efforts went nowhere. Ever since the AIDS/HIV epidemic, prosecutors have had a thing about spitting. It's the misdemeanor version of a mass shooting—or maybe of sexual assault without a condom. Any sort of diversion is out of the question, the prosecutor said.

In a previous negotiation of a spitting case involving a first-time offender—a female graduate student who was being harassed by a man at a bar—a prosecutor declared that she would rather be punched in the face than spat on. Doesn't it matter where the spit lands, I asked her? I mean, would you rather be punched in the face than have someone spit on your leg? What about at your feet? On your shoe? Being punched in the face is pretty brutal, I offered. She did not reply. The spit in the bar case had allegedly landed on the man's shoulder. We went to trial, putting forward an argument of self-defense and/or accident (our client hadn't really meant to spit; she was sputtering in anger because the guy wouldn't back off)— and our client was found guilty. Judges generally don't like spitters either.

After some deliberation, we decided to go to trial in the Shake Shack case. It wasn't an easy decision. Spitting cases are often jail cases. Many judges would be offended by our client's conduct and identify with the two managers. We could hear a judge saying at sentencing that a manager should be able to fire an employee without the employee damaging the office computer system and spitting at her boss. But we had drawn a good judge—someone who tended to hold the prosecution to its burden of proof no matter the allegation.

A student investigator had managed to get ahold of personnel records that gave us a better picture of what had been going on at that Shake Shack. Thompson could have been a character in the movie *Horrible Bosses*. He was known for lashing out at employees and having temper tantrums. In the seven months that Thompson and Rogers had run the store together, they had fired over fifteen people. A number of others had quit. This was not a hospitable work environment. Maybe these two hadn't exactly been well behaved on the day of the incident either. Maybe they weren't entirely truthful in their account of what happened.

Moreover, Thompson was essentially on probation himself for his unpredictable behavior, which had been documented in a formal reprimand in his personnel file.

At trial, we relied mostly on cross-examination. The fellow working with me conducted a dogged and detailed cross-examination, catching both managers in inconsistencies, contradictions, and evasions. Neither prosecution witness seemed able to tell the truth about anything—that Thompson had gotten physical with Ms. Brewer in the back office before she allegedly did what she did; that he was known for having a temper; that he was on probation; that so many employees had been fired or quit. We called a Shake Shack employee who heard Ms. Brewer shout "Get off of me" while in the back office and who, in his low-key way, offered testimony about Thompson's "bad character." We also called an elderly neighbor of Ms. Brewer who testified to her good character. We did not call Ms. Brewer.

By the time both sides rested, we were in surprisingly good shape. The prosecution's case was in shambles. Although we had intended to argue a combination of self-defense (the spitting occurred after Thompson physically assaulted Ms. Brewer) and accident or lack of criminal intent in destruction of property (she had gotten caught up in the wires in her frenzy to leave the office and hadn't meant to yank out the cords), we ended up arguing that there was insufficient evidence on which to convict because the prosecution witnesses were unworthy of belief.

When the judge acquitted Ms. Brewster, our client threw her arms around us in joy. "I can't thank you enough," she said. "Now I can face my daughter." She promised she would never be in trouble again.

We went out and celebrated—at Shake Shack.

•

Though a particular case may be gripping at the time—especially if it involves a trial—misdemeanors tend to blend together for longtime criminal lawyers. Only the rare case sticks with you. This is partly because of volume, especially for public defenders and court-appointed lawyers. As a defender and clinical law teacher, I have had more misdemeanor cases than I can count. In busy urban courts, misdemeanors tend to be processed rather than tried.[1] The goal of the system is to *move* cases, not meaningfully resolve them.

The experience of one former Cook County, Illinois, prosecutor captures the atmosphere in many big-city misdemeanor courts:

> After six months in traffic court, [Locallo] was transferred to the municipal division, where he handled misdemeanor cases in police station branch courtrooms. . . . In a grimy courtroom in the police headquarters building [downtown]. . . . Locallo helped the judge rush hookers and shoplifters past the bench. "Defendant pleads guilty, found guilty, two days' time served," the judge would say over and over. Locallo soon moved on to a south-side branch where he helped process waves of accused wife-beaters, barroom brawlers, and window-breakers—defendants who paused at the bench long enough to have their cases tossed out because the complaining witness hadn't shown, or to grab conditional discharge or probation.[2]

According to the television show *The Good Wife*, things haven't changed much in Cook County. In the first episode of season seven, lead character Alicia Florrick has had a fall from grace and is representing defendants in "bond court" (arraignment court) for $135 a case. The judge initially refuses to appoint her because he doesn't believe she can handle the volume with sufficient "alacrity"—his word of choice to convey the pace required. But Alicia ultimately proves that she can handle one case every ninety seconds: standard practice in bond court.

Defendants in misdemeanor court—sometimes called "McJustice"[3]—get more than ninety seconds, but not by much. In Florida, they get three minutes.[4] According to a 2011 study by the National Association of Criminal Defense Lawyers, misdemeanor defendants in twenty-one Florida counties spent far more time driving to the courthouse, parking, and sitting in court waiting for their case to be called than actually appearing before a judge. Even defendants who waive counsel and plead guilty get no more than three minutes.[5]

One commentator describes misdemeanor court as a "meat grinder,"[6] processing guilty plea after guilty plea. Group pleas, in which a judge lines up all those who intend to plead guilty that day and conducts a collective plea colloquy—a set piece that establishes the pleas are knowing and voluntary—are routine. First, the defendants are sworn, and then the judge establishes that each knows the charge and potential penalty in the case and is pleading guilty because he or she is in fact guilty. The judge then advises the group about the various rights they give up by pleading guilty—the right to plead not guilty and have a trial, to cross-examine witnesses against them, to present evidence on their own behalf, and to file an appeal—pausing only to ask whether they understand.

As a young lawyer at the Defender Association of Philadelphia in the early 1980s, I cut my teeth on misdemeanor cases. Some days were so long it felt like I lived in misdemeanor court. Courtroom 146, an especially large courtroom in City Hall where such cases were initially scheduled, was packed with defendants, especially on Mondays. The vast majority were represented by me—the lone public defender in the room.

I would meet my clients for the first time that morning, calling out their names one at a time to introduce myself and share whatever information I had about their cases. Some had met with other lawyers from my office soon after their arrests; others were seeing a lawyer for the first time. I understood this wasn't optimal representation, but I learned to convey knowledge and concern. Clients had a critical decision to make: whether to ask for a trial date or resolve the case that day through a guilty plea or diversionary program.

Defense lawyers were allowed to conduct the guilty plea colloquy. This was good practice, and the script soon became part of my counseling spiel.

Plus, it was my first big "speech" in court: a rousing tribute to all the rights afforded to the criminally accused. I learned that a well-delivered colloquy could cause a defendant to change his or her mind about giving up those magnificent rights. This, however, is not necessarily a good thing. Once a person backs out of a plea, he or she may not be able to return to it. There is an absolute right to go to trial but not to plead guilty.

Misdemeanor trials do not generally take up much time either. As one former prosecutor writes, "Justice is processed with extreme efficiency—a good judge and prosecutor, working as a team, can get through four or five trials a day."[7]

Typical misdemeanors include theft, drunk driving, prostitution, assault, disorderly conduct, trespass, destruction of property, possession of controlled substances, and possession of certain weapons. Some sex offenses, like indecent exposure and nonconsensual touching and groping, are also usually misdemeanors.

A few years ago, a student and I represented a man accused of grabbing a woman's buttocks as the nightclubs emptied out at 2:00 a.m. in a trendy DC neighborhood. I'll call the client Jose Martinez. Mr. Martinez worked as a waiter in one of the nearby restaurants. He was arrested and charged with misdemeanor sexual assault.

The case was serious because of the charge and because Mr. Martinez, a Salvadoran immigrant, was not a citizen. If found guilty of sexual assault—a crime of "moral turpitude"—he could be deported.

We investigated the case and got statements from the complainant, who claimed to have felt the butt-grabbing, and her boyfriend, who claimed to have seen it. They were both white professionals in their twenties. They seemed credible, if a little more outraged than we thought was merited. But this often happens in a criminal prosecution. People get ramped up. The complainant and her boyfriend acknowledged that they had been drinking martinis for a couple of hours before the alleged incident, that lots of people poured onto the street when the clubs closed, that they did not know Mr. Martinez, and that Mr. Martinez had said and done nothing to them prior to the alleged assault.

Mr. Martinez was adamant that he didn't do it. He was also terrified about being deported. He said he had just gotten off work and was going home when the boyfriend started yelling at him, tackled him, and summoned the police.

At that time, Immigration and Customs Enforcement (ICE) was not much of a presence in the Superior Court of the District of Columbia, the state-level trial court in Washington, DC. The fact that our client was a noncitizen had so far gone unnoticed. But it would surely come to the attention of immigration officials if he was convicted of sexual assault. Fortunately, Mr. Martinez was free on "personal recognizance," his promise that he would appear in court.

We had a dilemma. If Mr. Martinez appeared for trial and was found guilty—which could easily happen if the two witnesses testified that our client had inappropriately touched the complainant—he would likely be taken into custody and deported. This was precisely what he did not want. But not showing up—"bail jumping"—is a criminal offense, something lawyers cannot ethically advise their clients to do.

We tried to walk a fine line. We advised Mr. Martinez that we could not tell him *not* to come to court, but if he showed up for trial, he would likely end up in ICE custody. If he did not appear, a bench warrant would be issued for his arrest, but we doubted it would be urgently pursued. He was young and working off the books. He wouldn't be easy to find. We told him to think hard about this.

He either didn't understand what we were trying to tell him or chose to disregard it. Maybe he really didn't do it and wanted vindication. He showed up for every court date. We gave him the same advice each time.

He showed up early on the morning of trial, neatly dressed in a button-down shirt and dress pants. By a stroke of luck, the judge before whom we were originally scheduled to appear was in the middle of another trial. We were sent to another judge—a much better one.

The student defender with whom I was working was ready for trial. Our theory was that the complainant and her boyfriend had been jostled on a crowded street, and because they'd been drinking, they jumped to a conclusion that something more had happened. If the complainant's butt was indeed grabbed, Mr. Martinez didn't do it. Mr. Martinez was prepared to testify if necessary.

As sometimes happens when more than one witness testifies, the complainant and her boyfriend contradicted each other in important respects—about how much they'd had to drink, where they were when the alleged assault occurred, and most importantly, how the groping occurred. The complainant claimed that Mr. Martinez managed to put his hand up her knee-length pencil skirt. The boyfriend said he saw Mr. Martinez's hand grab the complainant's buttocks over her clothing.

It was helpful that the judge, a woman, understood that a pencil skirt is close-fitting, with a straight, narrow cut. It's not easy to get a hand under it. That the incident allegedly occurred in the wee hours of the morning was also helpful. So was the fact that both prosecution witnesses acknowledged they had been drinking. We thought we were in the land of reasonable doubt.

But we weren't sure the judge was with us yet. We felt we needed to call our client, who would testify with the assistance of a Spanish-to-English interpreter. Mr. Martinez was an excellent witness, even with an interpreter, who can sometimes get in the way. He came across as humble and respectful. He was small—no taller than 5′5″—and thin. The complainant was a couple of inches taller than Mr. Martinez, and her boyfriend was a big guy, at least 6′3″ and well-built. Would this tiny guy really grab the ass of a woman who came with a giant bodyguard who could easily kick *his*?

We argued that it made no sense. Why would our client approach this complainant under these circumstances and assault her? (The fact that our client had also had a couple of drinks went unmentioned.) We outlined the many problems with the prosecution's case. We pointed out that, in contrast to the complainant and her boyfriend, Mr. Martinez had testified credibly and consistently during both direct and cross-examination. There was more than enough reasonable doubt.

The judge agreed. When she acquitted Mr. Martinez, he seemed unsurprised. "Thank you," he said in a quiet voice.

We were thrilled and stunned. Our client had apparently known something we did not—that he would be OK, that it was better to trust the system than flee.

•

In federal court and most state courts in the United States, a misdemeanor is punishable by one year of incarceration or less; a felony is punishable by more. Although misdemeanors are considered less serious than felonies, multiple misdemeanor charges can lead to a substantial sentence, and even a single misdemeanor conviction can carry significant collateral consequences—such as loss of housing and educational opportunities—in addition to jail and heavy fines. Moreover, some serious felonies—such as sexual or physical assaults—can be charged as misdemeanors when there are problems of proof.

Still, because they are considered low-level offenses, misdemeanors do not get the attention—or due process—afforded to felonies. This is so even though the vast majority of criminal cases are misdemeanors; more than thirteen million are filed every year in the United States.[8] As legal scholar Alexandra Natapoff points out, misdemeanor processing is characterized by high-volume arrests, limited screening by police and prosecutors, an overwhelmed defense bar, and high plea rates.[9] Together, these engines generate criminal convictions "in bulk," often without meaningful scrutiny of whether those convictions are supported by evidence or are the product of a lawful arrest.[10] Moreover, many misdemeanor defendants are convicted without counsel.[11]

Guilty pleas are prevalent in misdemeanor court because, contrary to conventional wisdom, the accused do not always claim to be innocent. Instead, they often want to plead guilty to "get it over with" or because they did it. Neither of these is a good reason to plead guilty. Good defense lawyers urge clients to allow them to investigate, negotiate, file motions, and make a considered decision about trial versus plea instead of rushing to take a plea.

It is especially foolish for a defendant who is out on bail to plead guilty at the first opportunity, because misdemeanors often fall apart. Time passes, rifts heal, damaged or lost property is replaced, and witnesses fail to appear. Even initially angry crime victims think twice about spending the day in criminal court for a misdemeanor. But clients do not always heed this advice.

A student and I represented a woman I'll call Shalanda Graves. Ms. Graves, who was thirty-eight years old and had never been in trouble before, was charged with simple assault and malicious destruction of property in connection with a "bad breakup." On the evening of the incident, Ms. Graves came home to the apartment she shared with her longtime girlfriend and found her belongings in plastic garbage bags, a new girlfriend installed. Ms. Graves flew into a rage, striking her now-former girlfriend and trashing the apartment.

When we met her in lockup, she said she deserved to be there for what she had done. She allowed us to obtain her release on bail but insisted she wanted to plead guilty the first chance she got. We spent hours trying to talk her out of it. We managed to persuade her to let us investigate the case and pursue diversion. We got some helpful information from the former girlfriend, who felt bad that Ms. Graves had been arrested. It turned out the girlfriend had given as good as she got; there were grounds for arguing self-defense. Moreover, DC law states that "adequate provocation"— the kind of provocation that would cause an ordinary, reasonable person to lose self-control and act without reflection—rebuts the element of "malice" in destruction of property. The District of Columbia prefers that people, when provoked, damage property rather than human beings. We thought the circumstances here—Ms. Graves suddenly finding herself cast out and replaced—were sufficiently provoking.

This was also a perfect case for diversion. Ms. Graves was in her late thirties and had no record. She was a high school graduate with a couple of years of community college and a strong work history. A conviction would affect her future employment. Moreover, there was no injury, no indication that Ms. Graves had ever been violent before, and significant mitigating circumstances. But the prosecutor refused diversion because of the amount of damage done to the apartment.

With diversion off the table, there was no downside in going to trial. Even if Ms. Graves lost, she wouldn't be going to jail in this case. Plus, my student and I desperately wanted to go to trial. We didn't want our client to end up with a criminal record. But Ms. Graves felt she had done something wrong and should pay for it. She had struck her girlfriend, someone she still loved. She wanted to plead guilty.

We found her contrition both endearing and annoying. It spoke to her good character, but it was shortsighted. She needed to get over it. She could be sorry without being *guilty*.

We did everything we could think of to persuade her to go to trial. We met with her repeatedly. We enlisted the support of her best friend and her sister. Everyone who cared about her agreed that she should not plead guilty. We obtained postponements to give her more time. The passage of time also made it less likely that the complainant would appear for trial. The new girlfriend was no longer in the picture, so she likely wouldn't be showing up either.

But Ms. Graves wouldn't change her mind.

She pled guilty and received a short period of nonreporting probation. The lenient sentence confirmed how utterly ridiculous it was for this woman to be convicted of a crime.

When a client is in custody, the counseling calculus is different. Notwithstanding the Constitution's prohibition of "excessive bail,"[12] in much of the country, "bail acts as a tool of compulsion, forcing people who would not otherwise plead guilty to do so."[13] The coercive impact of bail falls heaviest on those who cannot afford to pay it. Faced with the prospect of an indefinite jail stay for lack of money to get out, many defendants accept plea deals instead. In some places, this happens as early as arraignment, the first court appearance.[14]

Both the guilty and innocent plead guilty to get out. Sometimes the innocent feel more pressure to plead than the guilty. As legal scholar Stephen Schulhofer says:

> The major problem with plea bargaining is that it forces the party into a situation where they have to take a guess about what the evidence is, about how strong the case might be, and they have to make that guess against the background of enormously severe penalties if you guess wrong. So defendants, even if they have strong defenses, and even if they are innocent, in fact face enormous pressure to play the odds and to accept a plea. And the more likely they are to be innocent, and the . . . strong[er] their defenses are, the bigger discount and the bigger benefits the prosecutor will offer them. Eventually at some point it becomes so tempting that it might be irresistible, especially when the consequences of guessing wrong are disastrous.[15]

In misdemeanor court, even a seemingly benign offer of diversion can undermine the right to trial. The accused—innocent or guilty—has to choose between an unknown trial verdict and a virtual guarantee of no conviction (if a diversion program is completed successfully). What lawyer would counsel the vagaries of trial over a sure bet, even for an innocent person? It's a bird in the hand. Only the truly determined will insist on a trial.

Darlene Williams (not her real name), a substitute teacher with no record, refused diversion and insisted on going to trial in a threats case. She was accused of telling her landlord she would "fucking kill her" when she came home and found the landlord and two U.S. marshals removing all her possessions, pursuant to an eviction order. Ms. Williams had asked to be informed of any final order of removal so that she could make her own arrangements.

The two had been in an ongoing and rancorous landlord-tenant dispute. Ms. Williams had stopped paying rent because of uninhabitable living conditions. The landlord had filed for eviction for nonpayment of rent. The landlord had prevailed.

Ms. Williams used to be a caseworker for a child-welfare agency. She left the agency in order to adopt a baby girl born with HIV. She raised her daughter as a single mother and public-school teacher. The daughter was now sixteen and at a prestigious New England private school on a full scholarship. Ms. Williams was substitute teaching because she had recently been diagnosed with ovarian cancer and was undergoing treatment.

I understood why Ms. Williams refused diversion. This was a ludicrous prosecution. Who wouldn't become enraged upon finding all their earthly belongings in the street? This wasn't a criminal threat; our client wasn't going to kill anyone, and the landlord knew it. But the prosecutor wouldn't dismiss the case because she felt confident she could prove it with two marshals and a middle-aged female landlord. Plus, she had offered diversion; it wasn't her fault our client had rejected it.

The trial was ugly. The judge identified with the landlord. She didn't buy our argument that these were mere angry words. She slapped down every innocent analogy—an exasperated parent saying, "It'll be murder when I get you home, young man"; one rivalrous sibling saying to another, "You're dead"; a coach saying, "Let's get out there and kill." These would all be criminal threats according to the judge. She found Ms. Williams guilty.

Ms. Williams knew this was coming. "There is no justice," she declared. This angered the judge. "I was going to sentence you to probation," she said, "but perhaps you'd rather go to jail." "Fine with me," said Ms. Williams, who received a fifteen-day jail sentence and was taken into custody. We tried to tell the judge that Ms. Williams had cancer, but she wouldn't listen. She released her early when we submitted the oncology records.

•

I do not mean to tilt the balance by sharing stories of first-time offenders only. I acknowledge that their lack of record might make them more appealing. But first-timers are prevalent in misdemeanor court. One scholar calls misdemeanor court the "gateway to the criminal system, the primary door through which Americans encounter the penal process and acquire a criminal record."[16]

There are, of course, plenty of repeat offenders too. Take, for example, Walter Winston (not his real name). Mr. Winston had a long criminal record, consisting largely of petty offenses—theft, bad checks, drug possession, and disorderly conduct. On this occasion, he was accused of stealing two cans of Budweiser Lime-a-Rita (an unappealing-sounding margarita-flavored beer) from a convenience store. The store clerk testified at trial that Mr. Winston put the beer in his pockets while walking around the store. The clerk confronted him, found the beer, and called the police. The defense was that there was insufficient evidence to prove criminal intent, as our client was in the store when arrested and had never tried to leave. The judge agreed with us that there was an innocent explanation for carrying beer in a pocket, since DC had recently passed a tax on plastic shopping bags. It wasn't that Mr. Winston was innocent, she said, just that there wasn't enough evidence to prove guilt.

"Antoine Buckley" also had a bit of a rap sheet. He had been living with his girlfriend at an apartment complex when they got into an argument and she kicked him out. They were still going at it outside when a neighbor called the police. Two security guards from the complex arrived first and told him to leave. He said OK. He had a suitcase and a very shiny, bright-orange bag with a Puma logo. When the police came, Mr. Buckley fled and was seen by the police and security guards tossing the orange bag. The police caught him, retrieved the bag, searched it, and found an orange Puma shoe box containing several ounces of marijuana in a large ziplock bag, a scale, and dozens of small, empty ziplock baggies.

Mr. Buckley swore up and down that he was innocent. Those weren't his drugs. He was on parole and a conviction would mean jail for both possession with intent to distribute marijuana and violating parole. He couldn't take a plea. So we did what we could and constructed a trial theory: it was nighttime and difficult to see; this was a high crime and drug area; people often discard drugs when the police appear; the drugs could have been anyone's; police and security guards jumped to a conclusion. The problem was that this particular bag could not have been more distinctive. It wasn't a muted orange that blended into the fall foliage. It was fluorescent.

My favorite moment at trial was when Mr. Buckley passed us a note complaining that the shoe box wasn't even his size. He wanted us to argue that. We declined.

The judge had no trouble finding Mr. Buckley guilty. But Mr. Buckley was indignant at sentencing. He said he always pled guilty, but this time he wasn't and that's why he went to trial. He felt unfairly treated, wronged; *railroaded*. The judge gave him fifteen days. He was still carrying on when he was taken into custody.

Somehow, we persuaded the parole board to not give him any more time, so Mr. Buckley ended up serving only those fifteen days. He later admitted to the whole thing.

When people ask how I feel about my clients lying to me, I often say if I had a court-appointed attorney with hundreds of other clients, I'd probably claim to be innocent too. How else to motivate the lawyer? But what I really want to say is a variation on a scene from Woody Allen's classic movie *Annie Hall*[17] that shows a flashback to Alvy Singer's childhood living under the Coney Island Thunderbolt (roller coaster). In the scene, a cleaning woman is discovered stealing, and Alvy's mother fires her. Alvy's father is not happy about this. "She has no money!" he proclaims. "She's got a right to steal from us! After all, who is she gonna steal from if not us?"

I feel the same way about my clients. Who else are they gonna lie to?

Of course, some clients lie because they are ashamed—of what they've done and of having been arrested. They revisit the shame with their lawyer, no matter how nonjudgmental we try to be. They want us to think better of them.

It reminds me of a story from my friend Kathy's childhood. When she learned to write, she took a bright-red crayon and wrote her name— "Kathy, Kathy, Kathy"—all over the family's white piano. When confronted by her father, Kathy denied she had done it.

Still, many clients are painfully honest. Take, for example, a client I'll call Renee Cooper. Ms. Cooper was African American, in her midfifties, obese, toothless, and always fretting about something—how she would get to court, how she would get to the mental health clinic, the long lines at drug testing, various family problems. Ms. Cooper had been in and out of trouble much of her life. She had a long record consisting mostly of drug possession and prostitution, but she had also done time for selling drugs. She was doing well on parole when she "caught" a new prostitution charge.[18]

The facts of the case were memorable and not in dispute: Ms. Cooper had offered to perform oral sex on an undercover police officer in exchange for fried chicken. Ms. Cooper was only slightly humiliated to have been arrested under these circumstances. As far as she was concerned, she was hungry, and a blow job in exchange for dinner was not a bad trade. But the arrest was a problem. It was a violation of her parole and meant she had to go to court on the new case.

We tried hard to get her to complete mental health diversion—a thera-peutic, treatment-oriented alternative to criminal prosecution—so that Ms. Cooper might avoid a new conviction and parole violation. But she missed meetings, tested positive for drugs or "water loaded" before testing, and otherwise failed to comply with the requirements of diversion. So the mental health judge put her back on the regular criminal calendar.

This was not a triable case, and Ms. Cooper knew it. She figured she would plead guilty and throw herself on the mercy of the court. Her goal was to stay out of jail. By some miracle, her parole officer took pity on her and did not charge her with a violation for the new crime. So the only thing we had to worry about was whether the judge before whom Ms. Cooper was scheduled to appear would send her to *jail* for doing something as des-perate as offering a blow job for fried chicken—assuming she was going to continue to test "dirty" or otherwise fall short on pretrial release.

I got a kick out of Ms. Cooper. She always greeted me with a big bear hug. She called me "Ms. Abbe." She was funny and charming. She said she had heard of me, and that I was known as a great lawyer. I doubted this.

The case dragged on for a while, Ms. Cooper trying her best to comply with pretrial release conditions. She was ultimately placed on probation notwithstanding her less-than-perfect performance. The judge said the important thing was she had no new arrests. I think I wasn't the only one charmed by Ms. Cooper.

A client I'll call Lester Johnson, who was accused of shoplifting a pair of electric clippers from a CVS pharmacy, was also truthful—if challenging. Even though the crime was captured on videotape, Mr. Johnson refused to plead guilty for probation and insisted on going to trial. He was forty-nine years old. He had been in trouble when he was younger but not for years since. He did a stupid, impetuous thing but thought the store should have let him go when they recovered the clippers. He understood the system enough to know that sometimes even strong cases fall apart: witnesses fail to appear; evidence is lost. He wanted a trial or dismissal.

The trial date happened to fall on Mr. Johnson's birthday.

When the prosecution declared it was ready—the store security guard was present, videotape in hand—Mr. Johnson was unmoved. He was ready too. It was unclear to me whether this was a matter of principle—he felt the government should have to prove its case—or if he had backed himself into a corner by maintaining that he wanted a trial.

I tried to uncover exactly what his objectives were. We didn't have much time. We also didn't have much privacy; as often happens, we talked in the hall just outside the courtroom. The judge had given the case a brief recess and would recall us momentarily.

Although the original deal was off the table, Mr. Johnson still had the option of pleading guilty rather than go to trial. The judge who would hear the trial or plea was someone I'd appeared before many times. He was fair minded. If Mr. Johnson pled guilty and expressed regret, he would likely be sentenced to no more than a year of probation. But a pointless, time-consuming trial would test the judge's goodwill.

I explained this to Mr. Johnson. I told him we were prepared to go to trial if that's what he wanted but he should understand that in this case, a trial would be more like a "slow guilty plea." If Mr. Johnson's objective was to avoid jail, he should plead guilty. If his objective was to have his "day in court" no matter the consequences, he should go to trial. I acknowledged that he might still receive probation if convicted at trial.

We went back and forth. He remained adamant. In the end, I told him it was his decision and we would go to trial.

I went to check on a case in another courtroom. By the time I returned, things had changed drastically. A busload of middle-school children had suddenly descended on the courtroom where the shoplifting trial would occur. There must have been forty kids on some kind of field trip.

I grabbed Mr. Johnson and threw all that "client-centered counseling"[19] to the wind. Forget trial, I said. There's no way the judge won't make an example of you in front of all those kids. He'll use you to teach them not to shoplift. He'll talk about how we all suffer when people steal—shops have to hire security, consumers pay higher prices, there is greater surveillance. But if you plead guilty—if you "man up" and throw yourself on the mercy of the court—the judge will be generous. He will show those kids that judges have a heart when an accused takes responsibility for his actions.

I didn't give him much of a choice; he went with the plea. Mr. Johnson was so good during the plea and sentencing—he made no excuses, said he was ashamed of himself, and swore it would never happen again—that the judge gave him only six months nonreporting probation.

When it was over, he threw his arms around me. He said he couldn't thank me enough for saving his fiftieth birthday.

•

Leon Dash's *Rosa Lee* may be the best book ever written about a chronic petty offender.[20] Dash, a longtime reporter for the *Washington Post*, based the book on his Pulitzer Prize–winning series of articles about the hard life of Rosa Lee Cunningham and her children, who lived in one of the poorest neighborhoods in Washington, DC. Born into abject poverty and violence, Rosa Lee was a school dropout at thirteen, mother at fourteen, battered wife by sixteen, single mother thereafter, and ultimately a heroin addict. She had eight children by six men, supporting them first as a night-club waitress and then through prostitution, theft, and drugs. Between 1951, when she was first arrested for stealing, and 1996, when the book was published, she went to jail twelve times, serving a total of five years. In that same period, she moved eighteen times, twice to homeless shelters.

In less skilled hands, Rosa Lee could have been an ugly poster child for the "urban underclass." But Dash manages to convey the deeper context of her story: the deprivation that disproportionately affects African Americans in blighted inner cities, along with the "debilitating history of racial oppression, economic exploitation, and segregation."[21] He also conveys Rosa Lee's humanity—who she is as a person, how she makes sense of her life—notwithstanding her failings.

And she has many. She does some terrible things: introduces her children to drugs; has her children collect from her johns; prostitutes her daughter; teaches her children and grandchildren how to steal; uses a young grandson as a drug runner; does not encourage her children to go to school or work; and brazenly lies—in court, in treatment, to Dash. All but two of her children end up in the criminal system. Dash is unflinching in his depiction of Rosa Lee and is "deeply troubled by her choices."[22]

But Dash also recognizes that some of the most disturbing things about her might also be her strengths. Along with being deceitful and manipulative, she is resourceful and charming. Her ability to survive—from the abuse she suffered as a child and violence at the hands of men to the ravages of drugs and periods of incarceration—is itself remarkable. Rosa Lee is resilient. She also does some good things—she is devoted to her church, provides for her family, is a loyal friend, never physically abuses her children (managing to stop that cycle of violence), makes real efforts to stop using drugs, feels genuine remorse about the bad things she has done, and manages to raise two successful children.

For some, Rosa Lee is too extreme, too bleak. I agree that she is not the prototypical misdemeanant. But I have seen male and female versions of

Rosa Lee in courtrooms across the country—badly damaged people who seem destined to cycle in and out of the criminal justice system (and whose children follow in their footsteps). They are frequent offenders but not terribly serious ones.

One repeat client—I'll call him B. J.—had a longstanding drug problem. He was in and out of treatment, in and out of jail. His drug abuse mirrored local trends: he went from heroin to crack to PCP and back to heroin. His record consisted mostly of theft, drug possession, possession of drug paraphernalia, and failing to come to court. When he was clean, he was a sweetheart. He would come around to the clinic just to say hello and "borrow" a couple dollars for a cup of coffee. These were periods when he had stable housing through a drug treatment program or shelter. When he was using, he looked awful—unclean and unkempt. He lived on the street during those periods. He had no family; he had been abandoned as a child and placed in foster care. He was especially attached to one of my colleagues, who represented him well over the years, getting him out of a number of jams. Then B. J. stole my colleague's laptop. This pretty much ended B. J.'s relationship with my colleague—at least so far.

•

In addition to drug and alcohol addiction, mental illness is prevalent in misdemeanor court. Take, for instance, a client I will call Patrick Djumbe. Mr. Djumbe, a Congolese national, left the Democratic Republic of Congo during a period of brutal war and unrest. He and an older brother obtained asylum, settled in Chicago, and found work at a hotel. All was well until Mr. Djumbe began to behave strangely in his late twenties. He became obsessed with returning to the Congo but cut up his passport. He stopped going to work, bathing, and eating. One day he got on a Greyhound bus to Washington, DC, with just enough money to pay the fare. He went directly to the Congolese embassy and insisted on seeing an official who would send him home. They gave him papers to fill out. He tore them up and left.

He returned to the embassy the next day and made the same request. They again gave him papers to fill out, which he promptly tore up. He wanted action, not papers. He returned to the embassy the next day, and the day after, with the same results. The embassy obtained a "barring notice" prohibiting Mr. Djumbe from being on the premises. When Mr. Djumbe returned there, he was arrested.

A first-time offender, Mr. Djumbe was released on personal recognizance. The only condition of release was that he stay away from the Congolese embassy. He immediately went back and was rearrested. He was released again, with the condition that he stay away from the embassy, but he did not comply. He was arrested again and released with conditions. So far, no judge wanted to lock Mr. Djumbe up. But this would not last.

We tried to intervene, both with Mr. Djumbe and with the embassy. Perhaps we could work with Mr. Djumbe to get him back to the Congo. We assembled the paperwork for obtaining a new passport and offered to fill it out for Mr. Djumbe, explaining that this was a necessary step. Mr. Djumbe wanted no part. We inquired about whether the Congolese government might fly Mr. Djumbe home with or without a passport. He needed both a plane ticket and a passport. Mr. Djumbe allowed us to contact his brother in Chicago but refused to talk to him.

The brother was alarmed that Mr. Djumbe was in Washington, DC. He wanted him back in Chicago so he could take care of him. He understood that Mr. Djumbe needed mental health treatment; he'd had him committed to a psychiatric hospital earlier that year. But Mr. Djumbe held this against the brother. He was not mentally ill, he said, and his own brother had sent him to a mental hospital against his will.

We tried to prevent further arrests. We asked the embassy to call us, not the police, the next time Mr. Djumbe came around. We would come and escort him off the premises. This worked for a time. The people at the embassy didn't think Mr. Djumbe belonged in jail either.

Mr. Djumbe was allowed to be outside of the embassy, just not in the building. He was fine with that. He would stand on the corner across from the embassy or sit on a building ledge. I wanted to buy him a plastic chair so he could be more comfortable. He said no.

More arrests followed—but not generated by the embassy. The police arrested Mr. Djumbe for being too close to the embassy. On one occasion, they grabbed him, and he put his hands up so he wouldn't be handcuffed and tried to wriggle away. He told the police his lawyers said he could be outside. He was charged with assault on a police officer.

A judge ordered Mr. Djumbe to the public psychiatric hospital for a competency evaluation. By this time, he had eleven open cases. We demurred. Irrational conduct is not the marker of incompetency. Nor is mental illness alone. Under the U.S. Supreme Court case *Dusky v. United States*,[23] a defendant is competent if he has "sufficient present ability to consult with his lawyer with a reasonable degree of rational understanding" and a "rational as well as factual understanding of the proceedings against him." The *Dusky* standard is decidedly low: an accused must understand the charges and be able to assist counsel. Mr. Djumbe more than met this standard. He understood the charges, even though his thinking was sometimes confused. We had a good working relationship with him even though he wasn't always interested in speaking with us. We lost the argument, and Mr. Djumbe was taken to the psychiatric hospital.

He did well in the hospital, partly because of the structure there. He was more lucid. He also cleaned up. He had been in desperate need of a bath and haircut.

We were surprised when the evaluation concluded that he was incompetent. There was little factual support for this conclusion. To the contrary, the report confirmed that Mr. Djumbe understood the charges against him, the basics of a trial, and the role of counsel. Although he didn't entirely trust his lawyers, he was willing to give us a try.

But before we were able to contest this finding at a competency hearing, the hospital made a request to the court that Mr. Djumbe be involuntarily medicated. This was what Mr. Djumbe had feared most. We challenged both.

The decision to forcibly medicate Mr. Djumbe required an initial proceeding at the hospital, presided over by a panel of outside mental health professionals. A law student and I were allowed to participate. The panel questioned Mr. Djumbe's primary doctor, various hospital staff, and Mr. Djumbe. Consistent with conventional treatment for schizophrenia (Mr. Djumbe's diagnosis), Mr. Djumbe's doctor believed he would benefit from antipsychotic medications.

Mr. Djumbe did not. His reasons for not wanting to be medicated were reasonable. He told the panel that, in his country, people did not trust government doctors. Moreover, he explained, *animals* were injected in his country, not people. He told the panel that he had been medicated once before, in Chicago—strapped down and forcibly injected—and had felt brutalized and humiliated by the experience. He did not believe this had made him "better." When the doctors at the proceeding pressed him about why he would refuse a mere shot, he said, "Because I am a human being."

The student and I both found this moving. Mr. Djumbe was asserting his dignity, his personhood. The panel members voted unanimously in favor of forcible medication. We urged more talk therapy—that the hospital staff try harder to gain Mr. Djumbe's trust. We suggested they bring in a mental health professional who was African. Successful treatment required Mr. Djumbe to accept that he needed it; forcible injections were a short-term fix at best. They listened politely but didn't change their minds.

Fortunately, Mr. Djumbe's competency hearing happened soon after. Because the evaluation was easy to challenge, we prevailed, and Mr. Djumbe was released from the hospital before they could medicate him. Mr. Djumbe seemed genuinely happy. He had not thought that someone like him could prevail against the government.

Mr. Djumbe did not belong in criminal court; his conduct was the product of mental illness, not criminality. It was painful to see him behind bars after each new arrest. Unfortunately, his experience is not unique. With the deinstitutionalization of the mentally ill over the past several decades, more and more have ended up in criminal court.[24] As Sheriff Thomas Dart of the Cook County jail notes, "We've systematically shut down all the mental health facilities, so the mentally ill have nowhere else to go. We've become the de facto mental health hospital."[25]

The numbers are staggering. According to one Justice Department study, 64 percent of people in jail have a mental health problem requiring treatment, 24 percent of whom with symptoms that meet the criteria for a psychotic disorder, such as schizophrenia, major depression, or bipolar illness. Most also have substance abuse disorders.[26] In some places, the number of mentally ill defendants is even higher.[27] Sheriff Dart refers to the constant cycle of arrest and incarceration, mostly involving poor people who commit minor offenses and cannot afford bail, as "criminalizing mental illness."[28]

Although many courts now have mental health diversionary programs, they can be overly selective. Mr. Djumbe was not eligible because he had too many open cases and had been charged with the "violent offense" of assault on a police officer. Generally speaking, to qualify for a mental health diversionary program, the charge must be minor and nonviolent, the mental illness well documented, and the accused willing to receive treatment—requirements that disqualify many people who would benefit from mental health diversion.

Mr. Djumbe's cases were eventually resolved, largely through a series of trials. It was miraculous that Mr. Djumbe appeared for all his court dates. Mentally ill people often find it difficult to manage multiple court dates and end up accumulating more charges as a result. At trial, we argued that the barring notice was not sufficiently clear—Mr. Djumbe did not actually enter the barred premises, and he lacked the specific intent required for contempt of court. We won some and lost some. A couple of cases were dismissed because the prosecution wasn't ready.

Between the time he had spent in hospital and in jail, Mr. Djumbe received a "time served" sentence with no further supervision. When his last case was over, he thanked us, shook our hands, and left the courthouse. (Curiously, we had no further contact with him. Perhaps he made it back to Chicago.)

Some mentally ill clients are tough to win over no matter how hard you try. Together with a postgraduate fellow, I represented a woman accused of threats and assault on a police officer. She was African American and a devout Muslim who wore a niqab (face veil) that covered her entire face except for her eyes along with a hijab. Slightly out of sync with the veil and head scarf, she wore a multicolored Hawaiian dress with the word "Aloha" printed on it. She had a long history of hospitalizations for schizophrenia.

She was accused of assaulting two secret service agents a few blocks from the White House. Based on a report that a woman matching our client's description had discarded a "mysterious package," the two agents pursued her, tackled her, and searched her. They found nothing on her and no package anywhere. Our client was angry about what the agents had done and expressed it. She declared that the men were not allowed to touch her; they needed to get a female agent. There was a further struggle. By the time she was taken into custody, she had abrasions on her face and two sprained wrists. The agents claimed the injuries were the result of her aggressiveness. She maintained that she was injured when the two large white men had tackled her to the hard ground.

The basis for the threats charge was our client saying to the agents, "You'll get *yours*," while pointing to some pins on her Hawaiian dress, one of which featured an American eagle with a rifle.

Our client was what mental health professionals would call "labile" and ordinary people would call "unpredictable" throughout the course of our representation, which culminated in a trial. Sometimes she was docile and deferential, but other times she accused me and the fellow representing her of working with the prosecution.

Remarkably, she ended up testifying beautifully, helping to create a reasonable doubt about the testimony of the secret service agents—who, we argued, arrested our client to cover up their own excessive force. We argued that the words she said to the agents were "profanity and prophesy" (she also swore a lot in addition to telling the agents, "You'll get yours") rather than a criminal threat to do bodily injury.

When she was found not guilty of all charges, she graciously wished the judge, "Aloha."

•

So as not to suggest that misdemeanor court is essentially harmless, I want to end with a story of how frightening it can be.

Back when he was a federal prosecutor, my friend and Georgetown colleague Professor Paul Butler was arrested and charged with assault. The charges were baseless—laughably so—but that didn't make them go away. He had to hire a lawyer and go to trial. In brief, the story of his prosecution goes like this:[29]

When he left a prominent law firm to go to the Justice Department, Butler moved from an affluent neighborhood to a more affordable one. Included in his rent was a parking space. Butler didn't need the space, because he used a bike for transportation, so he decided to rent it out. But he noticed that there was often a car parked there. He figured someone had seen that the space was never used and taken advantage of the opportunity. One night he approached the guy who parked there and explained that, though it had been vacant for a while, it was his space and he'd be using it from now on.

But the man told Butler that he rented the space from a lady in the apartment complex named "Detroit." Detroit was in her late thirties, short, stout, and never without her two German shepherds. She also turned out to be a police informant (that's how she got the name Detroit). Butler knocked on Detroit's door and told her that he owned the space and he needed it. She replied that it was hers. He showed her his lease, with space number nine clearly marked as belonging to his apartment. She slammed the door in his face.

The conflict played out with Butler renting out the space to a young social worker who was then harassed by Detroit. The harassment included Detroit physically accosting the young woman and leaving threatening notes on her car. Then one morning, sawdust left by the workmen who were refinishing Butler's floors was dumped on the social worker's car. Butler went to confront Detroit. Upon observing her sweeping telltale sawdust from her porch, he told her he was calling the police.

But before Butler could make the call, three police cars careened into the parking lot, sirens blaring, and arrested him. Detroit had beaten him to the punch. She told the police that someone had put sawdust on her porch and, as she was sweeping it up, her neighbor Butler had run up to her and pushed her down, causing a back injury.

It made no difference that this was a complete fabrication, that Butler was a federal prosecutor, or that the social worker to whom Butler had rented his parking space would corroborate that the sawdust incident had Detroit's name all over it. Butler was handcuffed, put in the back of a squad car, and taken to the police station.

From there, Butler was transported to court, where he was arraigned on a misdemeanor charge of simple assault and released on his own recognizance. He retained one of the best criminal lawyers in town, Michele Roberts. Some months later, Roberts tried the case and obtained an acquittal in ten minutes—the shortest jury deliberation in the history of the DC Superior Court.[30]

Roberts and Butler prevailed because Detroit was "belligerent, confused, and occasionally incoherent"[31] on the witness stand and the police got caught up in their own lies. Butler was acquitted notwithstanding his own belligerence as a witness:

> I look each jury member in the eye and I tell them the story. The apartment, the rented parking space, Detroit, the sawdust. With all my heart I resent being in this position, but it's not the jury's fault. It's the goddamned prosecutors' fault. When it is time for their stupid cross-examination, I let them have it. I am angry and self-righteous and I spit my answers. The U.S. attorney's office has devoted two lawyers to my case, including a senior black prosecutor. I hate him the most. I am just getting going when the judge announces a recess for lunch.[32]

Thankfully, over lunch Roberts gave Butler a talking-to about his attitude and he managed to turn things around: "That afternoon I am meek as a lamb. This seems to go over well."[33]

Butler understands that the system worked for him—"to the extent that you can describe a system as 'working' when a man is arrested and made to stand trial for a crime he did not commit"—chiefly because of his money, social status, knowledge of the legal system, and excellent defense counsel.[34]

Butler's innocence is not really the point of the story. The point is its utter mundaneness. This is not the tale of a death row exoneration, a wrongful felony conviction, a hideous hate crime, or even a driving-while-black, being-on-one's-own-porch-while-black,[35] or sitting-in-a-Starbucks-while-black[36] case. It's a "little misdemeanor" case that had enormous consequences for Butler—just as most misdemeanor cases have enormous consequences for the person charged. It shows how much power a single accuser can have, no matter how incredible. It shows how easy it is for the entire criminal legal system to come down on an individual. It took fifteen months before Butler was tried and acquitted.[37]

A key difference between Butler's case and most misdemeanors is that Butler's was heard by a jury. A few years after his case was tried, the District of Columbia did away with jury trials for most misdemeanors by limiting the maximum sentence to 180 days (just below the number that triggers the right to a jury trial).[38] As Butler accurately notes, "Judges, you see, are more likely to convict than juries."[39]

I cannot begin to calculate how many bench trials with essentially the same features as Butler's result in convictions. I am talking about one-witness cases with little or no corroboration (like other wounds, Detroit's supposed back injury could have happened in nonnefarious ways) where the defense offers a plausible competing account and maybe even testimony from character witnesses, as happened in Butler's case. Sadly, I can name many judges who might have found Butler guilty at a bench trial.

Notwithstanding Butler's impressive academic pedigree—Yale undergraduate and Harvard Law—and the fact that he was a federal prosecutor, he was reduced to a criminal defendant. It was demoralizing. As Butler writes: "It sounds silly, but what I remember most about my own case is how mean some people were. The police officer who lied on the stand. The guy who threw the lunch bag at me inside my cell."[40]

Plus, initially mild punishment for a misdemeanor conviction can turn harsh when clients are less than perfect. Missed appointments, relapse into drug and alcohol abuse, failure to comply with mental health treatment, and failure to pay fines can lead to revocation of probation or diversion. There doesn't need to be a new crime. This is how many petty offenders end up in jail and prison.[41]

•

With the exception of Paul Butler, this chapter has recounted stories of guilty (though sometimes not very) criminals. These are not the kind of cases that end up on the evening news, receive attention on the internet, or are considered by the Supreme Court. They are too petty to spark that kind of interest. Still, they illustrate what we are mostly talking about when we speak of "guilty criminals" in the United States.

The thirteen million U.S. misdemeanor cases previously noted is probably a low number. In Florida alone, a half-million misdemeanors are filed every year, meaning that 3 percent of the state's adults come through its misdemeanor courts each year.[42] An astonishing number of people experience the criminal justice system in misdemeanor court.

By and large, these are not fearsome criminals who pose a threat to public safety. No one would lose sleep over them being out on the streets. Most have done things that many of us could have done in a bad moment. Even the chronic offenders are more of a nuisance than a danger.

Yet "justice" is sometimes needlessly harsh in the lower criminal courts, the place where misdemeanors are processed. At the very least, justice has a random quality there. Much of the randomness has to do with the luck of the draw: the prosecutor, judge, and defense counsel can have more impact on the outcome of a case than the facts.[43]

I should point out that the judges and prosecutors in the above stories were black and white, male and female, young and old. This is disappointing but not surprising.

The presence or absence of witnesses also has an outsized effect on prosecution for petty crimes. For instance, it was not a coincidence that a prosecutor with two U.S. marshals as witnesses would choose to go forward against Ms. Williams, the woman with no record who yelled at her landlord. And yet, a prosecutor's ability to prove a case or to "win" is not supposed to be the chief impetus for the decision to prosecute.[44]

Although this is not a book about policy, I can't help arguing what should be obvious from this handful of fairly typical stories: defendants, their families and communities, and taxpayers would be better served if we removed many minor offenses from the criminal justice system and created broad and effective pretrial diversion programs for more serious misdemeanors. So too would the notion of justice.

2

Ordinary Felons

───────────────────────◄O►──────

You need to plead guilty and cut your losses.

I ain't taking no plea.

The crime was captured on videotape — with you in it.

I ain't taking no plea.

You were found with stolen goods, identified by witnesses, and made an incriminating statement.

I ain't taking no plea.

Okay, we'll go to trial. But what would you have me do in the face of overwhelming evidence?

Win!

37

Macy Clark (not her real name) was adamant. She did not assault, rob, or kidnap anyone: Kia White (not her real name either) was lying when she accused Ms. Clark and two others of attacking her with a pipe. It did not happen. All that had happened was she and Kia had argued, Kia had thrown ice tea in her face, and then the two had fought. She had gotten the better of Kia, but it had been a fair fight.

Ms. Clark admitted there was bad blood between her and Kia White. They had been in a Twitter war for months. The feud was prompted by jealousy; they both had babies with the same man. Lately, the trash talk had escalated from insults about each other to insults about Ms. Clark's daughter and Ms. White's son. Things had reached a boiling point when Ms. Clark came upon Ms. White walking down the street with her little boy.

Ms. Clark was driving home from the DMV with her teenage niece and a childhood friend when she saw Ms. White walking with her son. She told the friend to pull over so she could give Ms. White a piece of her mind about her latest tweet. She had barely gotten a word out when the other woman threw the drink.

The two tussled in broad daylight, each throwing punches. The friend and niece both got out of the car and watched. One held Ms. White's son's hand to make sure he didn't wander into the street.

The fight was over almost as soon as it had begun. But someone had called the police. In addition to assault with a dangerous weapon (though no weapon was found), kidnapping (Ms. Clark's friend restraining Ms. White's toddler), and armed robbery (Ms. White's purse had gone missing), Ms. Clark was charged with assault with significant bodily injury, cruelty to children, and simple assault.

When the police questioned Ms. Clark, she denied knowing Kia White or fighting her. This was not helpful.

Ms. Clark had a hard time believing she was facing these charges. She had never been arrested before, was employed as a nurse's aide, and was a devoted mother. She said she would consider a diversionary program that would keep her record clean. But diversion wasn't on the table for these felony charges.

The fellow working with me knew he was lucky to keep Ms. Clark out of jail pending trial. Ms. White had been badly beaten. But he also knew the girl-on-girl nature of the incident was helpful; it was seen as a mere "cat fight." Sometimes sexism has its rewards.

We spent a lot of time investigating and negotiating the case. The investigation was not fruitful. Ms. White told a credible story of being jumped by three women, including Ms. Clark, whom she named. She was struck by something she alternately described as a pipe or a pole. She was not vindictive, which made her more credible. She was ashamed of her own childish behavior on Twitter and did not want Ms. Clark to go to prison. But she didn't back down from what she said happened and believed Ms. Clark should be held accountable. It had *not* been a fair fight: it had been three against one. What's worse, she had been beaten up in the presence of her little boy.

We pressed Ms. Clark for the names and addresses of her friend and niece, but she didn't want to involve them. This was *her* problem, she said, not theirs. We explained that we needed to speak to these witnesses even if they didn't end up testifying. Ms. Clark was impassive. We pointed out that her untruthful statement to the police—even if made out of fear—suggested she had something to hide. We needed to back up her account with at least one other. She refused.

Her niece was young, barely sixteen, she said. And her friend had only acted on Ms. Clark's behalf. She would handle this business on her own.

We focused on the government witnesses. One was a professional clown. He lived in an apartment building that overlooked the site of the fight and had seen the tail end. By the time he got downstairs, the three women were gone. The complainant was bruised and crying and said her purse was gone. He never saw anyone with a pipe or pole. The other witnesses—an older couple coming from church—saw several women grabbing and shoving each other, with one getting the worst of it. The wife said one of the women was hitting another with a stick. The husband said one of the women had a stick, but he didn't see her use it. Neither saw anyone take a purse.

Our efforts to negotiate a lesser charge were not productive. We wanted a misdemeanor plea to simple assault. The prosecutor said no. He liked his case, which consisted of a sympathetic complainant and three innocent bystanders, each of whom saw at least part of the incident. "This was an armed felony assault," he said. "I won't have trouble proving the elements of kidnapping and robbery, as well." He was right about the law in DC. According to the kidnapping statute, the crime—a Class A felony punishable by up to thirty years—includes seizing, confining, or detaining another. Likewise, if one of the women grabbed the complainant's purse in the course of an armed assault, that is armed robbery, also punishable by up to thirty years in prison. The charges seemed overblown under the circumstances, which is why Ms. Clark was having trouble accepting the gravity of her situation. Yet the prosecutor had reason to be confident. Jury instructions don't distinguish between a more serious armed robbery—like getting held up at knifepoint—and having something taken from you during a fight with a stick.

Meanwhile, Ms. Clark was facing a lot of jail time, we had no defense witnesses to contradict the government's case, and Ms. Clark wasn't concerned.

•

I can remember only random details of my very first felony jury trial. It was an alleged strong-arm robbery in the Philadelphia subway involving three codefendants, two men and a woman. I represented the woman, whom I'll call Monique Barnes. I don't recall the exact allegations (it might have been a gold chain snatch) or the nature of the defense (it might have been that my client was "merely present," or this was an argument during which a chain was accidentally damaged or lost).

My cocounsel—both court-appointed—were older than I was, but both were happy to defer to me in witness examinations, objections, and arguments. Maybe they did so because they were incompetent. This would ordinarily be an arrogant thing for a young lawyer to say, but one of the lawyers did not seem prepared. He had an anxious look on his face as he rifled through the police report and preliminary hearing transcript. He didn't have much to say for his client. The other lawyer rode a bike to court, something I surmised from the rubber bands on the bottom of his pants. Inexplicably, he kept them on in the courtroom. I thought this was an oversight and suggested he might want to take the rubber bands off before we picked a jury. "Nah, no one will notice," he said.

The thing I have always liked best about felony representation is the jury. I still remember what a great feeling it was—scary at first, but ultimately exhilarating—to try a case before twelve citizens rather than a single judge. At last I was talking to ordinary people who had common sense and life experience and would understand the importance of standing between a fellow citizen and the power of the state. Here was a chance to make an impassioned argument and not have a judge say, "Tone it down, counsel; there is no jury here."

But effective persuasion consists of both reason and passion, no matter who the audience is. The ability to engage in logical reasoning—to identify and explain the flaws in the prosecution's case that create reasonable doubt—is essential for criminal trial lawyers. Yet it is impossible to move jurors (or judges) with reason alone. The central challenge in criminal defense is persuading factfinders to do what they are loath to: free someone who might in fact be guilty simply because it hasn't been proven. You have to embolden and move people to do this. A little well-placed emotion can make a difference.

My heart was pounding when I gave my first closing argument to a jury. They were out for a long time before returning a compromise verdict—guilty of a lesser degree of robbery. My client, Ms. Barnes, received a short jail sentence. I remember my supervisor being pleased.

•

We seemed to be headed for trial in Ms. Clark's case. She didn't want to plead to a felony, and the prosecution wasn't offering anything less. We continued to urge her to bring her friend and niece, but she resisted.

We prepared for trial with misgivings. We would claim self-defense: Ms. White had struck the first blow. We would point out inconsistencies in the government's case and the fact that none of the witnesses had seen how the fight started. We would also prepare Ms. Clark to testify. But the stakes were high, and our defense uninspired.

We made a plan to meet Ms. Clark near her workplace at lunchtime. She had missed several scheduled meetings at the clinic, and we needed to discuss the wisdom of going to trial. We picked her up and drove to a nearby Subway restaurant.

We described what the trial would consist of and showed her a sentencing chart. Without witnesses to back up her account of a fair fight, prison was a real possibility. We were before a judge who would understand the difference between someone whose temper got the better of her and a dangerous criminal but who would be more generous if Ms. Clark owned up. A pointless trial would test his patience. We urged Ms. Clark to plead guilty so we could build the strongest possible case for no jail time at sentencing.

Ms. Clark cried. It was the first time she had shown any real emotion. She didn't want to plead guilty, but she didn't want to go to trial either. She was scared of both. We understood this was a big decision. We suggested we meet with her family and arranged to meet at a church where her mother worked.

It was nearly Christmas. The fellow and I—a pair of Jews—had a laugh when we arrived at the church. Jesus was everywhere—white Jesus, black Jesus, Jesus on the cross, Jesus in the crèche, Jesus at the Last Supper. The meeting was more or less an "audition" so the family would see we were able lawyers. The mother had her doubts and talked about getting a "paid lawyer." Ms. Clark's brother—a well-dressed guy with a big personality—liked us. He told his sister to bring the friend and niece. He'd had his own experience in the criminal system and understood that sometimes it's best to cut your losses.

We talked with the niece and friend. As usual, the truth probably fell somewhere between the complainant's version and our client's. According to the witnesses, the fight had begun as Ms. Clark described—an angry confrontation and a tossed drink. The niece had held the little boy's hand. But the friend might have thrown a punch or two and might have kicked Ms. White when she was on the ground. As for the pipe or pole or stick, it turned out Ms. Clark had grabbed from her car a miniature baseball bat—something she had bought at a fair a couple of weeks before. But they swore no one hit Ms. White with the bat.

We persuaded the prosecutor to let Ms. Clark plead to one count of felony assault and dismiss the other charges. We put together a sentencing memorandum describing the context of the crime and setting out Ms. Clark's acceptance of responsibility, her lack of any criminal history, and the significant consequences of a felony conviction. The fellow made a forceful argument at sentencing, deftly noting that Ms. Clark was a single mom whose child would suffer if she were incarcerated, without prompting the usual judicial response—that Ms. Clark should have thought of that when she assaulted Ms. White. The judge suspended a nine-month prison sentence and placed Ms. Clark on probation with the condition that she attend anger management classes and maintain employment.

It is now more than five years later, and she has never been in trouble again.

•

A first felony conviction is a serious event. It can affect employment, housing, student loans, the ability to serve in the military, and more. I am especially protective of clients who have never been in trouble before, whether charged with a misdemeanor or felony. I don't like anyone getting a criminal record on my watch.

I once represented a woman—let's call her Mary Alice Murphy—who was facing three counts of felony assault for an alleged attack on a school principal, a vice principal, and a police officer. She had no criminal record and was somewhere on the spectrum of developmental disability. She was diffident and unsophisticated. She was married to a trying man whose chronic pain prevented him from working but not from constantly hectoring his wife. They had two children: an eleven-year-old daughter and a son a couple of years younger. Ms. Murphy kept up the house, took care of her husband and children, and looked after other neighborhood children to supplement the government assistance the husband received.

The daughter was being bullied at school; some older boys were extorting her lunch money. She came home crying nearly every day. Ms. Murphy had reached out to her child's teacher and the school's vice principal. The teacher tried to intervene, but the shakedowns continued. The vice principal unhelpfully suggested the girl take boxing lessons. Ms. Murphy contacted the principal, who agreed to a meeting.

On the scheduled day, Ms. Murphy dropped her husband and daughter off at the school and parked the car. She then joined her family in the principal's office. When she asked the principal to "please do something to make the situation stop," he laughed. According to Ms. Murphy, she "lost it." She swept everything off the principal's desk, grabbed him by the collar, and clocked him in the face, breaking his glasses and fracturing the bridge of his nose.

Unfortunately, the incident escalated when the principal pressed a panic button on his desk, prompting the vice principal to rush in. When the vice principal grabbed Ms. Murphy around the chest from behind, she bit him. A police officer then burst in with a billy club, which Ms. Murphy managed to grab in order to strike him once in the head.

In Pennsylvania, where the incident occurred, assault on a schoolteacher or police officer is a felony in the second degree, punishable by up to ten years in prison, even if the assault would have been a misdemeanor if committed against someone other than a teacher or cop. If the assault causes serious bodily injury, it is punishable by up to twenty years.

Ms. Murphy was released on bail. When we met to discuss her case, her husband accompanied her, dominating the discussion and turning it to his own suffering over the incident. The prosecution offered to drop one of the charges if Ms. Murphy pled guilty to two felony assaults, but they would go no lower. We decided to go to trial.

I was sanguine about our prospects, something I would later regret. I figured most jurors—especially if they were parents—would be able to relate to Ms. Murphy. She was a woman with no record who had tried to stop her child's bullying at school by reaching out to teachers and administrators. Her efforts had been especially impressive given her limited intellectual and other resources. Her loss of control was not unprovoked: she had been shouldering her daughter's distress, the school had done nothing to help, and finally the principal—her last resort—had *laughed* at her. I was hoping the jury might "nullify" (or disregard) the strict letter of the law and find Ms. Murphy not guilty because she wasn't a criminal. Surely I could persuade at least one juror, resulting in a hung jury.

Heeding my advice on proper courtroom attire, Ms. Murphy wore a dress to court. Alas, this turned out to be her wedding dress, something she had last worn more than a decade before, when she was at least thirty pounds thinner. She teetered unsteadily in sparkly stilettos, her wedding shoes.

I picked a jury consisting largely of parents. Most were white women, like my client. The judge was a mean-spirited tyrant who always poured on the charm with jurors, coming down from the bench to talk with them during voir dire (jury selection) like a television talk-show host. He proclaimed his deep belief in our system of justice. Meanwhile, he was known for unfair and irrational rulings during trial—generally on behalf of the prosecution—and harsh sentences. I think some jurors saw through him, but most seemed to like him.

On top of this, his wife was a member of the Philadelphia school board. I raised this conflict of interest at the start of the trial, asking the judge to recuse himself because of the nature of the case and his wife's position. Citing the Code of Judicial Conduct, I argued that the court's impartiality "might reasonably be questioned" based on his spouse being "an officer . . . of a party" with an interest in the proceeding.[1] The judge refused.

The trial was relatively uneventful, except for the judge inserting himself in bizarre ways. He was solicitous of prosecution witnesses but would look bored, make faces, and turn his back on defense witnesses.

The testimony of prosecution witnesses was mostly consistent with their accounts in police reports. I pointed out any embellishments on cross-examination. I also pointed out that after Ms. Murphy's encounter with the principal, she had been attacked from behind first by one man and then another and had reacted instinctively to protect herself.

When it came time to put on the defense case, the judge called me and the prosecutor to the bench. He turned to the court reporter and told her to not record what he was about to say. Then he said, "Ms. Smith, if you put your client's daughter on the stand and your client is convicted, I will sentence her to the maximum." After a moment of stunned silence, I pulled myself together and said to the court reporter, "Let the record reflect that the judge just threatened to give my client the max if the defense calls an eyewitness. Moreover, he ordered that this threat not be transcribed."

I did not call my client's daughter, not because of the judge's threat, but because it wasn't in my client's interest to do so. The girl would not be allowed to testify about having been bullied and how awful that was, and her account of what happened in the principal's office was basically the same as what had been testified to. Moreover, the girl felt it was her fault that her mom was in trouble and often burst into tears. If she did that on the witness stand, the jury might feel manipulated and blame her mother.

Ms. Murphy testified about how upset she had been about her daughter's abuse. She was apologetic about "flying off the handle" in the principal's office. But she said she had acted on instinct when attacked from behind. We also called a couple of character witnesses to testify to Ms. Murphy's truthfulness, peacefulness, and law-abidingness. A member of her church said she was a "gentle soul" who "wouldn't hurt a fly." A neighbor said this incident was "contrary to her character."

The jury was out for a few hours. They acquitted Ms. Murphy of assaulting the vice principal (maybe they bought her claim of self-defense or didn't like his boxing lesson advice) but convicted her of felony assault on the principal and police officer. The judge ordered her taken into custody.

All hell broke loose. Ms. Murphy's daughter was wailing. Her son joined in. (For some reason they were both in court.) The husband was in shock and did nothing to calm the children. Ms. Murphy was in shackles when her daughter leapt past the court staff and grabbed ahold of her mother's leg, crying, "Don't take my mommy." She was dragged along until the bailiffs pried her hands free.

I begged the judge to allow Ms. Murphy to remain free pending sentencing. There was no evidence she posed any danger or risk of flight.

This was a situational offense—an unusual occurrence based on particular circumstances—and she was an essential caregiver to her children and disabled husband. The judge wouldn't budge.

I was disappointed in the jury—and in my own miscalculation about how jurors might regard this case. The white jurors said afterward they identified with the various (white) officials and considered Ms. Murphy "poor white trash."[2] The African American jurors were kinder. They saw Ms. Murphy as a good mom in a bad moment; some had had their own experiences with unfeeling school and law enforcement officials. Still, no one was willing to stick their neck out and hang the jury.

It was hard for me to get rid of the image of Ms. Murphy being taken away in shackles. It was hard to imagine her in jail—this simple woman in her wedding dress. How would she cope?

I went to see her the next day. She was happy to see me and did not seem the least bit troubled. She was wearing a loose-fitting jail-issued dress and sneakers; she was comfortable for the first time in days. "People have been so kind to me here," she said. "They've given me these nice clothes, and I only have to do a little sweeping and mopping." Her jail life might have been easier than her home life.

But she was worried about her kids. I assured her I would immediately file a motion for her release. We would get a psychological evaluation of her. I would keep filing motions until the judge relented.

He did, but only after two weeks of repeated motions, reports, and letters to the court. Ms. Murphy ultimately received a time-served sentence and probation.

It has now been many years, and to my knowledge, Ms. Murphy has never again been in trouble.

•

Ms. Clark, Ms. Barnes, and Ms. Murphy are all convicted felons—indeed, convicted *violent* felons. It is unusual—but not terribly so—that they are women. According to the Sentencing Project, more than a million women are currently under the supervision of the criminal justice system in the United States. Nearly two-hundred thousand are in prison or jail. There has been a 404 percent rise in incarceration of women over the past thirty years, nearly double the rate of men.[3] According to the Bureau of Justice Statistics, even as the number of incarcerated men has started to decline—by 4.2 percent between 2010 and 2013—the number of incarcerated women increased by nearly 11 percent.[4]

The popular Netflix series *Orange Is the New Black*, based on Piper Kerman's memoir about the time she served in the women's federal prison in Danbury, Connecticut,[5] comes close to capturing who is locked up in women's prisons—with a little dramatic license. All kinds of women are in prison: wise and foolish; charming and tiresome; resourceful and inept; old and young; lesbian, bisexual, transgender, and straight; every race and ethnicity. Women make friends, and sometimes *family*, in prison.

Most women in prison are white, nearly a third are black, and 16 percent are Hispanic.[6] In federal prison, most women are locked up for drug offenses or some form of theft or fraud. (Kerman was convicted of drug-related money laundering.) In state prisons and jails, women's crimes run the gamut from drug offenses to murder, but most are locked up for public order offenses (drugs and prostitution) and property offenses.[7] Like the three women whose stories I shared above, many violent female offenders are first-time offenders.[8] Many women prisoners have children. Most have experienced sexual or physical abuse. Nearly three-fourths have a mental health problem.[9]

Violent felons, even relatively harmless first-time female offenders, are not the poster children for prison reform. Instead, the call to reduce our prison population tends to focus on nonviolent drug offenders. As of October 2016, President Obama's much-heralded clemency drive resulted in commuted sentences for 774 federal prisoners, most of whom were nonviolent drug offenders.[10] Focusing on drug offenders was a fine idea in the federal system, where nearly half of all inmates are serving time for drugs, but federal prisoners account for only 14 percent of the U.S. prison population.[11]

As Professor John Pfaff and others have argued, we will never significantly scale back incarceration if we focus solely on nonviolent offenders.[12] The widely held view that locking up more nonviolent offenders for longer periods of time is responsible for mass incarceration is wrong. Not only do most drug offenders tend to serve relatively short sentences in both state and federal prison, but even in federal prisons, violent offenders serve the longest sentences. In state prisons, where the overwhelming majority of prisoners are confined, half have been convicted of violent offenses and only 17 percent of nonviolent drug offenses. As Pfaff documents, since 1990, 60 percent of growth in the state prison population has come from locking up violent offenders.[13] In other words, if we really want to shrink our shocking prison population, we are going to have to reduce the punishment faced by violent offenders.

This reality is what made the president's commutations—and even his impassioned speeches about criminal justice—disappointing. On July 14, 2015, at the NAACP convention in Philadelphia, President Obama gave a rousing speech about our "broken system" of criminal justice that "has locked up too many Americans for too long, especially a whole generation of young black and Hispanic men."[14] He laudably referred to the criminal justice system as a "pipeline from underfunded, inadequate schools to overcrowded jails" and used the phrase "mass incarceration." He connected racially charged upheaval in places like Ferguson, Missouri, and Baltimore, Maryland, after police shootings of young black men to systemic bias in the criminal justice system. He called for sweeping bipartisan reform. He even acknowledged that although some "murderers, predators, rapists, gang leaders [and] drug kingpins" needed to be "behind bars," it is possible to lock even these people up for too long, leading to "diminishing returns."[15]

But the only group he pledged to help was nonviolent offenders.

People who kill, no matter the circumstance, are too hot to touch, even though homicide has the lowest recidivism rate.[16] Sex offenders of all kinds might be even more politically dangerous, especially in the current #Me Too climate—even though sexual assault and rape also have low recidivism rates.[17] A six-month sentence and lifetime sex offender registration for an intoxicated Stanford University freshman who digitally penetrated a woman intoxicated to the point of unconsciousness prompted public outcry and a successful petition to recall the sentencing judge.[18] This was so even though the probation department recommended the same sentence for the young man.[19]

Politicians won't take up the cause of ordinary "violent felons" either, like the three women with whom I began this chapter. It's a political third rail that no one seems willing to touch.[20] Almost all reform proposals from across the ideological spectrum call for reducing punishment for nonviolent, nonserious, nonsexual offenders—what scholar Marie Gottschalk calls the "non, non, nons."[21]

•

I have represented a lot of drug offenders in cases with every conceivable drug: heroin, crack cocaine, powder cocaine, marijuana, PCP, methamphetamine, Ecstasy, quaaludes, Suboxone (used to treat opiate addiction), and more. Clients have been charged with simple possession (a felony in some jurisdictions), possession of drug paraphernalia, possession with intent to distribute, and distribution. Some were dealers, many were a combination of user and dealer, and most were just trying to make a buck. Because my clients were charged in state criminal systems, most didn't end up serving an unduly long sentence (compared to federal time).

Drug cases are not especially memorable, but if not resolved through a guilty plea or some sort of diversion, they can be interesting when they go to trial. There is plenty to litigate: suppression motions, challenges to laboratory reports, challenges to so-called drug experts, trials based on whether the quantity of drugs was enough to prove intent to distribute (as opposed to personal use), and trials based on police or informant credibility.

One memorable case was a jury trial in which our client (I'll call him Deshawn Tibbs) was charged with distribution of crack based on his presence in a courtyard known for drugs, a brief "transaction" with one young man, a conversation with another, being found with "marked money" (money prerecorded by the police before being used in an undercover transaction), and the discovery of a "stash" of drugs nearby. I tried the case with a fellow. Mr. Tibbs was nineteen years old but looked much younger. He wore glasses. He swore he wasn't selling drugs and was at the apartment complex because his mother, who had recently died of cancer, used to live there. He said he got the marked $20 from a guy who owed him money.

It was a two-codefendant case. A young public defender, supervised by a more senior one, represented the alleged accomplice. The prosecution maintained that Mr. Tibbs was in charge and the codefendant worked for him. We argued it was a weak circumstantial case, Mr. Tibbs was not found with drugs or observed selling drugs, and there was an innocent explanation for the marked money. We were in pretty good shape when the prosecution rested, but we decided it was important for Mr. Tibbs to explain how he came to possess the marked money. Though he wasn't terribly articulate—he had a nervous stutter—we believed he would come across as sympathetic.

He turned out to be a terrific witness. He told his story better on the witness stand than he had during practice sessions. Between his stammer and glasses, he was the opposite of a drug kingpin. We were pleased. The public defender supervisor had a different view. He grabbed me during recess and said, "You had that case won until you called your client." This is among the most annoying things anyone has ever said to me. Every defense lawyer knows the decision whether to call a client is difficult and fraught.

The jury acquitted Mr. Tibbs and convicted the codefendant. I felt vindicated but did not rub the supervisor's nose in it. The jury did that for me. It said our client's testimony had made all the difference: no one believed he was a drug dealer.

A sadly memorable felony drug case involved a client I'll call Alvin Jones, who refused a plea that would have resulted in a one-year prison sentence. He was out on bail and couldn't tolerate the idea of willingly going to prison—a criminal defendant version of Dylan Thomas's call to "not go gentle into that good night."[22] A fellow and I did everything we could to convince him to take the plea. The officers had testified credibly at a suppression hearing that they had seen our client exchange an off-white substance for money and had subsequently found crack in his sock. At trial, we would have to make the cops out to be liars based on small, inconsequential inconsistencies.

We fought hard, but Mr. Jones was convicted and sentenced to ten years in prison. This was painful and pointless. He was a good guy who was getting out of the drug business to focus on his career as a DJ. He lost a decade of his life for small-time drug dealing.

I might be less judgmental about drug dealers than many people. After emigrating from Russia, my paternal grandfather and his brothers made their way from Boston to Chicago and from the livery stable business to the liquor business. They established a wholesale wine and liquor distributorship before Prohibition, kept it going illegally during the thirteen-year alcohol ban, and reestablished it legally when Prohibition was repealed. My great-uncle Nate—a dapper dresser and the brains of the operation, according to family lore—did some jail time for bootlegging. I can only imagine the shady company my grandfather and his brothers kept during that time and some of the things they must have done to protect their business.

My Jewish ancestors believed in the American Dream; they wanted to make it in this country and give their children a better life. In this respect, they were not unlike the Chambers brothers, four African American brothers who migrated from a small town in Arkansas to Detroit in the 1980s to pursue their big-city dreams. William Adler's 1995 book, *Land of Opportunity*, tells the story of Billy Joe, Larry, Willie, and Otis Chambers, who came north for automobile jobs but saw an opportunity to capitalize on the crack cocaine epidemic by developing one of the first retail crack distribution networks in the nation, which grew into a multimillion-dollar drug empire. Unlike my grandfather and great uncles, the Chambers brothers were sent to prison for many years.[23]

Crack cocaine may be worse than booze. I witnessed the devastation wrought by the crack epidemic in the 1980s, 1990s, and early 2000s to families, neighborhoods, and entire cities. But the motivations behind the illegal booze trade and illegal drug trade are not so different. As a result of his success in business, my grandfather could afford to send my dad to college—the first in his family to attend. The Chambers brothers sent money back home to their struggling family in Arkansas.

•

Wilton Marley (not his real name) was not exactly inconspicuous. He was heavyset, ungainly, and openly gay. He often wore a loud, wide-striped polo shirt and a bright-pink, flowered bucket hat.

Mr. Marley was a latter-day Fagin. In Charles Dickens's *Oliver Twist*, Fagin is described as a "receiver of stolen goods" who teaches children to pickpocket in exchange for food and shelter.[24] Mr. Marley was more of a solo actor but, like Fagin, made a living by thievery. He had a lengthy record of theft-related offenses. He had done time in prison and been on long periods of not exactly successful probation and parole.

He was charged with two counts of robbery, two counts of theft, and three counts of credit card fraud. Robbery in Washington, DC, includes three basic elements: (1) there must be "force or violence," including by "sudden or stealthy seizure or snatching"; (2) something of value must be taken; and (3) the thing of value must be taken either directly from a person or from the person's possession. According to case law, "possession" includes items within arm's reach; a purse sitting next to a woman on a park bench is in her possession, as is a purse hanging on a chair in a restaurant. Unarmed robbery is a felony punishable by up to fifteen years' imprisonment. If armed, it's thirty years.

Mr. Marley was captured on videotape lumbering into a restaurant in one of DC's up-and-coming neighborhoods wearing his fuchsia bucket hat and wide-striped polo shirt and carrying a backpack. On the tape, he can be seen sidling up to a table of young women who are laughing, talking, and sharing a bottle of wine. He sits next to them and reaches into two handbags hanging on the back of their chairs, takes two wallets, and puts them in his backpack. He is drinking a glass of water and pretending to look at a menu as he does this. Suddenly, he looks at his watch as if he is late for something, says something to the waiter, and departs.

After leaving the restaurant, Mr. Marley went to a nearby CVS pharmacy and used stolen credit cards to purchase three CVS gift cards for $250 each, essentially engaging in money laundering (and credit card fraud). The CVS clerk became suspicious of the different names on the credit cards and called the police.

Mr. Marley was not an easy client. He might have had a personality disorder. He fired his first two lawyers. A fellow and I were appointed to represent Mr. Marley with a warning that we were his final lawyers. At first, he insisted it wasn't him on the tape. We told him it was definitely him—and, more importantly, no juror would think it was anybody else. He wasn't happy with this. He maintained he was a victim of mistaken identification and the tape was "grainy." "Not so grainy," we told him. He wanted to fire us too.

We said we would investigate the case and see what we could come up with. At the same time, we would negotiate a plea just to have some options. He told us not to bother. "I'm fighting this case," he said. We told him we understood how he felt, but the crime was *videotaped*. He declared he would never plead to robbery: "I am a thief, not a robber," he said. He had his principles.

The truth is, we agreed with him on this point. The robbery statute in DC—and in a growing number of jurisdictions—is so broad it includes conduct that used to be considered theft as a matter of common law. When I was a public defender, pickpocketing, which involves at least some bodily contact, was considered theft from a person, not robbery. We understood why Mr. Marley felt that stealing without force or any touching at all wasn't robbery.

We made this pitch to the prosecutor. "But that happens to be the law," he said. "And your client has done this before. He is a menace." We pointed out that Mr. Marley hadn't hurt anyone. The prosecutor rolled his eyes. "Mr. Marley can plead to one count of robbery, one count of theft, and one count of credit card fraud—that's the best I can do." We thought reducing a seven-count indictment to three counts wasn't bad. Our client was unimpressed.

We researched the law, looking for some way out of "possession" and "stealthy snatching." But the law appeared to be well-settled. We watched the videotape a dozen times trying to find a way to craft a misidentification theory. But we couldn't make that argument with a straight face. We tracked down the women whose wallets had been taken. One agreed to talk to us. She said she felt "violated" by what had happened and vulnerable whenever she went to a restaurant. She now keeps her purse on her lap and is wary of anyone sitting close to her. The other initially refused to answer the door. When she finally appeared, she said she would do her talking in court and had no sympathy whatsoever for the "man who robbed her."

We were at wit's end. There was nothing to try here. We urged our client to think hard about the plea. He wouldn't. He didn't trust us and was considering representing himself. We tried to assure him we were on his side and would represent him well, whether he pled guilty or went to trial. During one court appearance, the judge spoke up on our behalf. "These are two excellent lawyers," he said. "You'd be foolish not to make use of their services." The judge tried to explain the benefits of the plea offer to Mr. Marley (without inappropriately inserting himself into plea bargaining).

Our client was mollified about us—for the moment—but refused to plead. We went to trial.

We came up with a defense we could live with: there was nothing "stealthy" about this bucket-hatted, hulking, effeminate man sticking his hand in women's purses. Under the facts of this case, Mr. Marley's conduct did not amount to robbery by stealthy snatching, and he should be convicted of theft instead. We would argue the prosecution had overcharged Mr. Marley—he was accused of seven separate criminal charges, including two counts of robbery, one of the most serious crimes on the books—for what was properly a misdemeanor. Mr. Marley signed on to this defense.

We carefully picked a jury, though it hardly mattered who the jurors were in view of the evidence. The fellow working with me tried the case well. He won a motion for judgment of acquittal on one of the credit card charges when the prosecution failed to present sufficient evidence. He made an impassioned closing. It was a victory that the jury was out for a couple of hours before convicting on the remaining six counts.

Mr. Marley was not happy. I guess he thought we would pull a rabbit out of a hat. I had thought so, too, for a moment. This is called "trial psychosis." In between trial and sentencing—as we were retaining an expert to help us identify something in Mr. Marley that might explain and mitigate his criminal conduct—he fired us, filed a claim alleging that we had provided ineffective assistance of counsel (IAC) under the Sixth Amendment, and for good measure, sued us for malpractice. He claimed that we failed to find a critical defense witness—to what purpose we had no idea—and had chosen a defense he hadn't agreed to.

These things happen. Criminal defendants are not always the most well-balanced people. You learn to take an IAC and malpractice claim in stride. What is more, I'm willing to fall on my sword and acknowledge there are things I could have done better when a client calls me incompetent. I'm glad it doesn't happen too often.

•

There are robberies and then there are *robberies*. A client I represented as a public defender developed a drug problem after his wife left him. One day, high on cocaine and wearing no disguise, he took his father's revolver and robbed a man walking on his parents' street in broad daylight. He was immediately arrested and charged with gunpoint robbery, which carried a maximum sentence of twenty years in prison and a mandatory minimum of five.

I did not do much for this client; there wasn't much I could do. He was found with the gun and the victim's wallet a block away from the crime scene, was identified by the victim, and gave a full statement to the police admitting what he had done. He knew he had no choice but to plead guilty.

My only real task was to persuade the judge to sentence him to no more than the mandatory five years. I had plenty of material. My client was a good man who had done a bad thing while high on a very potent drug. He was a high school graduate with a solid work history and minimal contact with the criminal justice system. He had been badly shaken by the breakup of his marriage. He acknowledged the seriousness of the crime and was ashamed. His parents were hardworking people who came to court to show their support.

I argued that this was a situation in which the mandatory minimum was unduly harsh, and this man was not someone who needed to be removed from society for so long. I pointed out that my client's conduct was plainly self-destructive; he must have wanted to get caught. He needed treatment, not prison. I did what I could to get the judge to see my client as a person and not another criminal.

The judge sentenced him to the mandatory minimum only.

During the five years the man was in prison, I never heard from him. This wasn't surprising. A criminal case is not exactly a happy memory, and most clients don't stay in touch. Frankly, it wasn't an especially memorable case for me either; it was a quick guilty plea. All told, I probably spent a couple of hours with this client. When I received a letter from him a few months after he got out of prison, I was pleasantly surprised. His letter remains one of my very favorites:

Dear Ms. Smith,

I want to thank you for everything you did for me. I still remember the words you said in court. Your kind words helped me during some of the low times I had in prison. I am now a grown man who is living with his parents again. I don't mean to sound ungrateful. I love my parents and don't know what I would have done without them these past years. Plus, having a home to go to was important to the parole board. But I am putting away money every week so I can move out and get my own place.

I work for a laundry. I make deliveries and carry heavy boxes of shirts up and down flights of stairs every day. Sometimes I carry seven boxes at a time. It is hard work and my legs ache at the end of the day. But I'm lucky to have a job.

I'm thinking about going back to school to become a plumber or maybe an electrician. I think I could make a good living with those skills.

I would like to meet someone nice and raise a family. I hope I have the chance. I will teach my kids about the importance of going to school and getting a job and staying away from drugs.

I just wanted you to know I'm doing okay.[25]

•

There are many kinds of felonies. In one jurisdiction or another, I've handled all of them: homicide, arson, rape, kidnapping, carjacking, robbery, burglary, aggravated assault, perjury, obstruction of justice, car theft, gun possession, drug dealing, theft above a certain statutory value, forgery, and others.

Gun cases are a lot like drug cases—interesting to litigate but troubling to jurors who don't like guns. Every once in a while, there is a sympathetic gun case. Once, I helped represent a corrections officer (CO) who had been laid off when the Lorton correctional complex—the Virginia facility where DC state prisoners were sent—was closed. The CO was licensed to carry a gun in Virginia but not in DC. He had absent-mindedly left his handgun in the car when he went into the District to go to a club. When he got lost and went the wrong way on a one-way street, a police officer pulled him over. He remembered the gun and alerted the officer so as not to cause alarm (the CO was African American and did not want to be a "black man with a gun"). He showed the officer his work ID and said he had meant to leave his gun at home in Virginia but had forgotten to. He was arrested for unlawful possession of a firearm.

A fellow tried the case with me when we failed to persuade the prosecutor to dismiss it. We thought the prosecutor was making a mistake—that a DC jury would think hard before giving a corrections officer a criminal record. After all, our client wasn't using the gun to commit a crime and was licensed to carry it in a neighboring state. We cobbled together a defense: our client did not knowingly possess a gun in the District of Columbia, so he lacked the requisite criminal intent.

The jury was not out long before acquitting. They were annoyed that their time was wasted with this case. "Aren't there more serious criminals to prosecute?" they asked the assistant U.S. attorney.

Another somewhat sympathetic—or at least entertaining—gun case involved a client who was accused of shooting her boyfriend. The two could have been played by Whoopi Goldberg and Dennis Hopper, so I'll refer to them as such. They both maintained that the shooting was an accident that occurred in the course of an argument over Dennis's insistence that Whoopi learn how to use a gun. Still, it was charged as an assault while armed—a mandatory minimum five-year sentence with the prospect of much more time—and unlawful gun and ammunition possession.

Dennis accompanied Whoopi every time she came to my office. He wore a raccoon hat like a latter-day Davy Crockett. He was a nervous wreck about what was going to happen to Whoopi. He said he wouldn't be able to live with himself if she went to prison. "This whole thing was my fault," he said. "She would never hurt me."

The case is memorable partly because I was accused of unethical conduct in the course of it. The circumstance was a question that comes up often in criminal practice: What should a defense lawyer say to a complainant who doesn't want to testify in court and asks the lawyer what to do? I have a set piece that comports with the ethical rules. I tell the complainant that (1) I represent the accused; (2) I cannot give you legal advice; (3) what I am about to say should *not* be construed as legal advice; (4) a subpoena is a court order; and (5) in my experience, when complainants fail to appear, there are three possibilities—the case is continued to give the prosecution another chance to bring the complainant in, a bench warrant is issued for the complainant's arrest, or the case is dismissed. I make sure that I repeat "This is not legal advice" throughout.

On the day of Whoopi's trial, Dennis didn't appear. Various other matters were called while the prosecutor tried to locate Dennis and decide what to do with the case. Suddenly, just before the lunch recess, Dennis walked into the courtroom. When the prosecutor confronted him about his tardiness, threatening some sort of reprisal, Dennis pointed at me and said, "She told me not to come."

The prosecutor was furious and accused me of a catalog of misconduct, including obstruction of justice. I denied doing anything improper. The trial judge convened a hearing and called Dennis to the stand. He told the judge that it was his gun and that Whoopi didn't mean it, and he asked if Whoopi could please just come home. When asked why he was late to court, Dennis said he didn't want to testify but was afraid of getting in trouble if he didn't. The judge found the allegation that I had told a witness to disobey a subpoena, or had obstructed justice in any way, unfounded.

After the hearing, the clerk approached me and said, "That must have made you nervous." I admitted it had. He smiled and said, "You never had anything to worry about." "Why not?" I asked. It turns out that before Dennis took the stand, the clerk had taken his raccoon hat from him along with a large grocery bag. I hadn't noticed that he was carrying anything. The clerk asked if I wanted to know what was in the grocery bag. "Sure," I said. "Kittens," the clerk said. "Several live baby kittens." The clerk had made sure the judge knew this before Dennis began his testimony.

Most gun cases are not sympathetic. First, there is the horrifying and seemingly constant occurrence of mass shootings in this country. Then there is the nature of firearms these days. Increasingly, gun cases involve semiautomatic weapons, whether a relatively small Glock, a more potent-looking TEC-9, or any number of other assault pistols or rifles. One of the challenges in these cases is to defuse the scariness of the weapon so the jury can focus instead on whether the prosecution proved that the accused had it.

One client charged with possessing a sinister-looking gun came to court on the day of jury selection wearing what can only be described as *Annie Hall* glasses. He had never worn glasses in all the time I had known him. I understood what he was trying to do. He was good-looking and was hoping to look innocent as well. I told the fellow I was working with to advise the client to get rid of the phony glasses.

•

The ordinariness of an alleged felony is no guarantee that punishment will be ordinary. A man named Lenny Singleton (his real name), who was not my client, developed a crack cocaine addiction in the mid-1990s. To fuel his habit, he walked into thirteen stores in Norfolk, Virginia, over an eight-day period and committed "grab-and-dash" robberies—either distracting the clerk or pretending to have a concealed gun before stealing from the cash register. On one occasion, he was armed with a kitchen knife, but he never physically hurt anyone. Before each robbery he would smoke crack and drink a twelve-pack of beer. He stole about $500 in total.

He was twenty-eight at the time, a college graduate who had served in the navy. He knew he was in serious trouble when he was caught and charged with multiple counts of robbery. He accepted a plea deal that got rid of some of the charges but provided no assurance about the sentence he would receive. He knew he would do some time. He ended up before one of the toughest judges in Virginia, who gave him two life sentences plus one hundred years.

Mr. Singleton has now served more than twenty years. He is called "Pops" by other inmates. He has never committed a single disciplinary infraction and is in the Honors Dorm. He works every day in the furniture plant at the Nottoway Correctional Center in central Virginia. He earns eighty cents an hour building furniture used in Virginia's universities. A percentage of his pay is taken for court costs and fines. He still owes nearly $2,000. He recently married a high school classmate with whom he had lost touch, but they got to know each other again through letters. Since his incarceration, Singleton has seen prisoners convicted of more serious crimes come and go. "I was out of my mind on drugs, but I wasn't going to hurt anybody," he said. "I was just after the money." His only hope for not dying in prison is a conditional pardon from the governor.[26]

There are many Mr. Singletons in prisons across the country. They do not profess to be innocent but have been incarcerated for so long they can barely even remember their crimes. They are no longer dangerous criminals even if they once were. They are old and expensive to house and often have medical conditions.

•

When I was a public defender, burglary and car theft were among the most commonly charged felonies where I practiced. By burglary, I mean the common law definition: illegal entry into a building for the purposes of committing an offense, usually theft. Burglary is a classic "specific intent" crime. Illegal entry without specific intent to commit a crime is a mere trespass. Although the object of burglary is usually theft, it can also be physical assault, sexual assault, kidnapping, robbery, or arson.

Perhaps the most famous burglary was the 1970s Watergate break-in. On June 17, 1972, after midnight, five men connected to the effort to reelect President Richard Nixon were arrested for breaking into the Democratic National Committee (DNC) headquarters at the Watergate office building in Washington, DC. They were there to photograph campaign documents and install listening devices in telephones. A security guard became suspicious when he noticed tape covering the latches on doors leading from the underground parking garage to several offices (allowing the doors to close but remain unlocked) and called the police. The five men were tried by a jury and convicted of conspiracy, burglary, and violation of federal wiretapping laws.

It is a common mistake for people to say they were "robbed" when they were *burgled*. If you happen to be home when a burglar appears and the intruder takes something from you by force, then you have been robbed as well as burgled. But if you aren't present, it is a burglary, not a robbery.

I lived in an apartment in a large Victorian house in Philadelphia my first few years in the public defender's office. One day after work, I came home to find a hole in my door where the doorknob was supposed to be. I prayed my landlord was replacing the doorknobs for some reason, but I knew otherwise. When I entered the apartment, I saw the clear signs of a burglary: my stereo system was gone and a bunch of dirty clothes that had been in the laundry bag were strewn on the floor. This second thing seemed odd: did the burglar have a dirty underwear fetish? When I couldn't find the laundry bag, I realized the burglar had used it to carry off the stereo equipment.

The police officers who responded to my 911 call mocked me when they learned I was a public defender. They said they had seen a guy walking down the street carrying what looked like stereo components in a bright-red laundry bag. But they lacked probable cause to stop and search him.

In my day, the Philadelphia public defender's office represented all defendants at arraignment. Lawyers would be assigned weekend arraignment duty every eight months or so. It was the luck of the draw whether you worked 8:00 a.m. to 4:00 p.m., 4:00 p.m. to midnight, or midnight to 8:00 a.m. A colleague was home taking a nap before working the dreaded midnight shift when she was awakened by the sound of an intruder. She managed to grab and hold the young man who had broken in until the police came. She went back to sleep after they took him into custody. She was interviewing clients and making bail arguments when the young man appeared in the next group of defendants. She told the judge she had a conflict of interest. The judge was uncomprehending. "What are you talking about?" he asked. "This is *my* burglar," she said. "I think he probably ought to have someone else represent him."

Even if nothing is stolen, the act of breaking and entering with the intent to commit a crime is a burglary. Depending on the jurisdiction, the "buildings" that can be subject to a burglary include sheds, barns, warehouses, boats, trucks, and cars. There are caught-inside burglaries (the Watergate burglary is an example; so was my colleague's burglary), caught-nearby burglaries, and caught-with-recently-stolen-property burglaries. Caught-inside burglaries tend to result in guilty pleas. The others are more triable.

I once represented a young man whose friends decided to break into an elderly neighbor's house. She was a former suffragist with a huge collection of Susan B. Anthony silver dollars, which my client's friends stole. When my client, who had refused to participate in the burglary, made the mistake of asking his friends what they had taken, they tossed him a silver dollar. That was the basis for his initial prosecution as a coconspirator in a burglary—which we managed to get the prosecution to dismiss—and ultimately for receiving stolen property. Luckily, we were before a good judge who was willing to throw out the misdemeanor charge as "de minimis"—too trivial to merit a criminal conviction—under all the facts and circumstances.

When I first moved to Washington, DC, and was taking serious felony appointments to try more complex cases with fellows, there were virtually no burglaries. This seemed strange to me. I wondered whether, as a matter of "culture," people didn't commit burglaries in the District. Instead, it turned out that the Metropolitan Police Department had an extraordinarily low "clearance rate" for burglaries—they were lousy at solving them. Or maybe the burglars were especially skilled.

I have since represented a handful of clients accused of burglary. Most cases were connected to domestic violence, such as a break-in to beat up a girlfriend. A few were break-ins to steal money and electronics. I have represented more than one intoxicated person who believed he was entering his own home when he broke into someone else's. One client was caught on a ladder leading to a second-floor window of his neighbor's house in broad daylight. The neighbor had just bought a new big-screen TV for his bedroom.

•

A fellow and I represented a woman who had fled a war-torn West African country and obtained asylum in the United States. I'll call the woman Kadiatu Okori. She was employed as a nurse's aide and was caring for a well-to-do elderly woman I'll call Lois Rosenthal when she was charged with felony theft and related offenses. Ms. Okori was alleged to have written and signed six checks totaling nearly $25,000 to herself from Ms. Rosenthal's checking account.

It was a serious case because of Ms. Rosenthal's age: crimes against the elderly carry additional penalties. Plus, there were a lot of charges. Ms. Okori was charged with six counts of first-degree theft from a senior citizen, six counts of identity theft in the first degree of a senior citizen, and three counts of first-degree fraud of a senior citizen—fifteen charges in all.

Ms. Okori denied doing anything wrong and insisted that Ms. Rosenthal had given her the money. She didn't know why Ms. Rosenthal would say otherwise. She maintained her innocence in spite of compelling evidence to the contrary: Ms. Rosenthal never wrote checks to individual caregivers, as they were employed by a service; the checks were not in Ms. Rosenthal's handwriting or signed "Lois P. Rosenthal," as she always signed her name (the P was for her maiden name, Pollakoff); the checks appeared to be in Ms. Okori's handwriting; and the checks were deposited by Ms. Okori into her own bank account the same day they were written.

We filed a motion for a handwriting expert because of our client's strong denial that she had written those checks. But I doubted we needed one. I brought copies of the checks and samples of Ms. Rosenthal's and Ms. Okori's handwriting home to my then fifteen-year-old son, Joe. I often ran trial theories by him; he was a good stand-in for a juror. He took one look at the checks and the handwriting and said, "Mom, your client wrote the checks."

But Ms. Okori wouldn't relent. She was adamant that Ms. Rosenthal gave her that money because she was an excellent and devoted caregiver.

We conducted an investigation. We spoke to Ms. Rosenthal's other caregivers, the bank clerks who had processed the checks, and Ms. Rosenthal's son and daughter. When we tried to speak to Ms. Rosenthal, we heard from her lawyer. He was well known in DC and a bit of a character. He said he appreciated our efforts on behalf of our client but Ms. Rosenthal would not be available for questioning. The language he used was saltier.

We also met with Ms. Okori's family. We learned more about her than she had shared. She was young when her country's war was at its most brutal. When rebels took over her village, they committed acts of unspeakable cruelty. Ms. Okori's father and uncle were killed before her eyes, their throats slashed. Her mother was raped while Ms. Okori hid in another room. She managed to escape and was ultimately reunited with surviving family in America.

We met with the prosecutor to see if there was an alternative to trial. We were concerned about Ms. Okori's citizenship status. She was a legal resident but not a citizen. Theft from an elderly person is a classic crime of "moral turpitude." If she were convicted, she could be deported. We thought Ms. Rosenthal and her family might prefer a nontrial disposition of the case so that she would be spared having to appear in court and that her family might be satisfied with restitution and probation rather than prison and deportation.

The prosecutor was tough but fair. He preferred a felony plea because of the vulnerability of the victim. He told us Ms. Rosenthal felt betrayed by what Ms. Okori had done. We pointed out the nonviolent nature of the offense, Ms. Okori's lack of a record, her traumatic history, and the very harsh prospect of deportation for a woman whose only family was in the United States. He came around and offered a plea to misdemeanor theft, which would be less likely to come to the attention of U.S. Immigration and Customs Enforcement (ICE). We couldn't have been more pleased.

But Ms. Okori would not even consider the misdemeanor plea. "I would rather have my eyes plucked out than plead guilty to something I did not do," she said. We urged her to think about the advantage of a conviction for misdemeanor theft—a rather commonplace crime—to many counts of felony theft and fraud. We described what the trial would look like and how easy it would be for the government to prove its case. We had no evidence to prove the money was a gift—only Ms. Okori's word. We shared our concerns about calling her as a witness; she came across as defensive and detached.

With her permission, we brought in her mother, sister, brother, and minister to discuss the plea offer. They were not helpful. They were angry at Ms. Okori for bringing shame upon the family.

We wondered whether Ms. Okori was so damaged from what she had endured that she was not competent to make this important decision or to stand trial. Had a finding of incompetency ever been based on post-traumatic stress disorder (PTSD)? Ms. Okori also showed signs of dissociation; she seemed to truly believe she did not write those checks. Had a finding of incompetency ever been based on a dissociative disorder? We discussed the idea of mounting a competency challenge with Ms. Okori, explaining that this would put off the trial for a while and, if we prevailed, might put it off forever. When she learned she would have to be examined by mental health professionals, she balked. She didn't want to be found incompetent, she said. There was nothing wrong with her mind. She was innocent.

One of the sad things about the case was how close Ms. Okori and Ms. Rosenthal had been. Caregiving is intimate. Although Ms. Rosenthal could be demanding—she insisted that Ms. Okori warm her clothes in the dryer before dressing her and was very particular about food preparation—Ms. Okori had come to regard Ms. Rosenthal as a grandmother. She recounted holding Ms. Rosenthal at night to keep her warm. When Ms. Rosenthal couldn't sleep, Ms. Okori would sit up with her and share stories.

We continued to counsel Ms. Okori to take the misdemeanor plea. We did this every chance we got until one day she said, "Are you prosecuting or defending me?" This was a watershed moment. We were losing her trust. We told her we would abide by her wishes and do everything in our power to defend her at trial.

The trial was excruciating. We cobbled together a defense that Ms. Rosenthal was not trustworthy because of age and diminished cognition and that she had accused Ms. Okori when her children threatened to put her in a nursing home because of her inability to handle her finances. At the same time, we would show that Ms. Okori was an exemplary caregiver—Ms. Rosenthal's favorite—in order to argue that Ms. Rosenthal had expressed her gratitude in cash.

But Ms. Rosenthal was sharp as a tack on the witness stand. It was painful when she turned to Ms. Okori and said, "I loved you and trusted you. How could you have done this?" Ms. Okori seemed to not have heard her.

There was one comical moment when the judge was instructing Ms. Okori about the conditions of her release during trial and Ms. Okori looked up and said, "Yes, Your Highness." To her credit, the judge laughed.

Ms. Okori did not testify at trial.

The jury was not out long. They found Ms. Okori not guilty of a couple of counts—the handwriting on one of the checks might have been Ms. Rosenthal's even if the signature was not—but Ms. Okori was convicted of the thirteen others. She sat stone-faced as the verdict was read.

We prepared hard for sentencing. Ms. Okori allowed us to retain a mental health professional to conduct a psychological evaluation in the hope of persuading the judge not to send her to prison. He agreed with us about her PTSD and dissociative disorder and said they explained a lot about the crime and Ms. Okori's inability to grasp the misdemeanor plea. He believed prison would be traumatic for Ms. Okori and that the shame of the conviction was already hard for her to bear.

The judge sentenced Ms. Okori to a year in federal prison.

Ms. Okori survived the year. A few days before she was to be released, ICE notified her that she would be transported to a detention facility, where she would be held pending deportation proceedings. She was detained there for several months. To everyone's surprise, she was not ultimately deported. The United States couldn't find a country to take her, and she could not be sent back to her country of origin after having been granted asylum.

You can't always predict what will happen, no matter how diligent the lawyer or unambiguous the law. We were glad about that in this case.

•

With or without the threat of deportation, felony punishment doesn't end when a person is released from prison. In addition to restrictions on employment, housing, student loans, public assistance, and the ability to serve in the military, convicted felons often lose the right to vote even after they have served their time. Close to six million Americans—one in every forty voting-age adults—are denied the right to participate in elections because of a past or current felony conviction. One of every thirteen African Americans of voting age is disenfranchised, a rate more than four times greater than non–African Americans. In several American states, one in five African American men cannot vote due to a felony conviction.[27]

Another example of the "civil death" of convicted felons[28] is exclusion from jury service. Unfortunately, this has received little attention, even though lifetime exclusion of felons from jury service is the majority rule in the United States, with thirty-one states and the federal courts prohibiting felons from being jurors. The result is that more than 6 percent of the adult population is barred from jury service, including nearly a third of African American men. This exclusion has a significant impact on the racial makeup of the jury pool in many communities.[29]

The laws vary from state to state, but restrictions on employment opportunities of convicted felons can range from not being able to hold public office to not being allowed to work at an airport, from not being able to work in a nursing home or day care facility to ineligibility to obtain a barber license.[30]

Being a *convicted felon* by itself conveys substantial stigma and shame: such a person poses a threat to the social order, and the rest of us should beware. A person's motivations and circumstances are less important than the fact that he or she is a felon.

•

It is hard to know for certain what motivated Ms. Okori, a woman with strongly held scruples who had never been in trouble before. Perhaps she suffered from trauma-borne mental illness. Perhaps she acted out of temptation or greed, the usual motivation for theft. Maybe Ms. Okori, a minimum-wage worker, believed she was entitled to extra money because of her hard work and that her well-to-do charge would not miss it. She must have convinced herself she was doing nothing wrong, otherwise the dissonance of being a good and moral person and stealing from an old lady would have been too great. She must have put out of her mind the very real possibility of being caught and the disgrace it would bring.

Ms. Okori will never work again as a nurse's aide.

What distinguishes these ordinary felons from the rest of us? Although a romantic rival has never made nasty remarks about my child, I imagine this might get under my skin. I have never physically struck a high-handed authority figure, though I have wanted to. Robbing people goes too far for me, but I understand the temptation and thrill of getting something for nothing if no one is hurt. Stealing from an elderly person seems inconceivable unless you have ever been tempted to take a dollar or two from your mom's purse. I have already pointed out the lure of drug dealing as a matter of economics. Firearms hold no interest for me, but they appeal to many Americans.

Mr. Marley—the Fagin-like thief—might be incorrigible. He seemed to feel that *he* was the aggrieved party, not those from whom he had stolen. This is not a good sign for his future prospects. But the others acted badly for reasons that are more situational than characterological: loss of temper or control, impetuousness, immaturity, peer pressure, greed or temptation, or drug or alcohol addiction. Most will learn from their mistakes and make better choices next time. The vast majority of felons do not need to be in a cage for ten, twenty, or thirty years.

3

Rapists

—◄O►—

They call me a
monster.

It doesn't matter how
young or how sorry I
am, or whether I can
change.

"Sex Offender"
might as well be
branded on my
forehead.

They will cage
me, shame me,
and banish me.

There will be no hope,
no redemption, no
future.

Now who's the
monster?

"Jamal" was barely fifteen when he was charged with armed robbery and rape. Small and baby-faced, with smooth brown skin, he looked more like he was twelve. He tried to sound cocky about the charges. "I ain't do nothin'," he said. But it was easy to see he was scared.

He had been in the juvenile system since he was ten. His misconduct ranged from truancy and shoplifting to running drugs for older boys. His school attendance had been dismal since he was put in special education classes—like he was some kind of *retard*, he complained. Disruptive behavior got him sent from elementary school to a disciplinary school and then to a nearby residential treatment program. He ran away from the program the first chance he got—straight back to his mother's house.

Yet home was hardly a sanctuary. His mother was volatile. She would fly into a rage for no reason and beat Jamal with a belt, hairbrush, shoe, or electrical cord. She had poor sexual boundaries. She would tease Jamal about the size of his penis, told him he had "titties" like a girl, and made him share a bed with her into adolescence.

Still, Jamal loved his mom.

When probation and a handful of stays in "juvey" didn't curb his misbehavior, he was sent to an out-of-state residential program. There was no place to run this time; he was hundreds of miles away. Or maybe he had grown up a little. He stayed there the full nine months, long enough to obtain a diploma—a photocopied certificate saying he had completed the program. Jamal was proud of this accomplishment. He liked it when everybody stood up and applauded. No one had ever done that for him before.

He had only been home for a couple of weeks when he "caught" the new case.[1]

The crime was vicious. Jamal was accused of grabbing a young African American woman off the street at gunpoint, dragging her behind a vacant house, and raping her repeatedly. Although the victim was the only eyewitness and her attacker was unknown to her, the evidence against Jamal was overwhelming. Not only was Jamal's DNA found in and on the victim, but the woman gave a detailed description that matched Jamal, immediately picked him out of a photo spread, and positively identified him at a lineup. Worse still, Jamal had left behind a spent condom full of his semen. To top it off, he made incriminating statements to the police. At his juvenile court arraignment, the prosecution filed notice that they would seek to prosecute Jamal as an adult.

When a fellow and I shared the police reports with Jamal, he backed off of his initial denial. He said he was high on dippers—marijuana dipped in PCP—and made a pretty girl have sex with him. He was ashamed of the charge and didn't want to talk about the details.

He was most concerned about being charged as an adult and didn't understand how that could happen. "My case will be in juvenile court because I'm a kid," he insisted. We explained the juvenile transfer statute, which set out the procedures for trying children as adults and made it pretty easy to do so. "I'll take juvenile life," he said, meaning that he would remain in the juvenile system until he was twenty-one. "They're not offering juvenile life," we told him.

Jamal often seemed high when we visited him. He probably was. Street drugs were freely available at the juvenile jail where he was being held; the guards were apparently "on the take." Jamal would shuffle out to see us in oversized slippers and baggy pajama bottoms—he was small even for juvey—a hoodie pulled low over his forehead and his eyes vacant. Sometimes he was sullen and would give us the silent treatment. Other times, he was delighted to see us—especially if we bought him a candy bar.

The fellow and I didn't mind any of this. Jamal was appealing, even in a foul mood. He seemed weary for someone so young, like life had already worn him out. His tough talk was all show.

We had to keep reminding ourselves about the seriousness of the crime. The victim described her rapist as cunning and cruel. She believed he was going to kill her. PCP can produce dissociation and aggression, so this description was plausible. This scared boy was probably very scary at the time of the crime. If convicted as an adult, Jamal was looking at a long prison sentence.

The goal was to avoid going to trial and keep the case in juvenile court. This would not be easy, even though Jamal was young and this was his first serious charge. The prosecution was determined to get an adult conviction. The burden was on us to avoid adult criminal prosecution by demonstrating either that Jamal was incompetent[2] to proceed to a transfer hearing or trial or that he could be rehabilitated as a juvenile notwithstanding the seriousness of the crime.[3]

We got a break when a court-ordered psychological evaluation raised questions about Jamal's competency to proceed due to cognitive problems. The court psychologist was concerned about Jamal's ability to understand and participate in a complex transfer hearing, which would deal with abstract concepts like Jamal's "amenability to treatment." The psychologist we retained agreed, citing Jamal's impaired ability to process language, understand abstract thought, or weigh competing factors in order to make decisions—all of which are essential to the ability to consult with counsel. She also noted how developmentally delayed and emotionally immature he was, partly due to childhood trauma.

We got another break when a fair-minded judge was assigned the case. After a lengthy and hotly contested competency hearing, the judge found Jamal incompetent and sent him to a secure juvenile institution in northern Minnesota. The institution would treat him until his competency was "restored"—through education, counseling, and special training on court proceedings.

Even better was the judge's later willingness to allow Jamal to undergo sex offender treatment as part of "competency restoration." We argued that Jamal was so ashamed of the nature of the charges, he was unable to talk about them in any meaningful way, which prevented him from participating in his own defense. The court psychologist and our expert had experienced the same difficulty in eliciting meaningful responses from Jamal and helped persuade the judge.

All of this could ultimately assist us in demonstrating that Jamal could be effectively rehabilitated in a juvenile setting. Maybe, just maybe, we could save this child from adult punishment.

•

Alleged rapists are among the most reviled criminal defendants. When a woman lawyer represents an alleged rapist, she inevitably faces an offshoot of the constant query made of criminal defenders, "How can you represent those people?" This is alternately expressed as "How can you be a woman and represent a rapist?" or, more broadly, "How can you be a feminist and a criminal defense lawyer?"[4]

Of course, women are not the only ones who find representing alleged rapists difficult. Many men do too.

I am a criminal defense lawyer, woman, and feminist who has represented many men accused or convicted of sexual assault. Although these cases are not my favorite part of the job, I intend to keep doing so. When I focus on the client—who he is, where he came from, the punishment he is facing—it is not much different from representing any client facing serious charges. There is a connection to the client that goes along with advocacy on his behalf: I am my client's confidante, counselor, and champion. Sometimes I am the only person on his side. But when I also consider the rape victim, there is a kind of dread.

Some of the dread comes from identification with the victims.

The very first woman I ever cross-examined in a rape case was young, white, and could have been me. I was a public defender in my midtwenties. She was a graduate student. She lived only a few blocks away from me, in a second-floor apartment in a house in the Germantown neighborhood of Philadelphia. I lived in a second-floor apartment in a house in Germantown. She was in bed asleep when an intruder came into her bedroom. She tried to grab her tennis racket to ward him off, but he overpowered her. I am a tennis player too. She seemed nice, someone I might be friends with. She also seemed afraid—of both my client and me.

It was a preliminary hearing, not a trial. The question was whether there was probable cause to believe an offense had been committed and my client committed it. My goal was to obtain "discovery"—to find out everything about the prosecution's case through careful questioning. Generally speaking, the defense does not offer evidence at a preliminary hearing, so as not to show our hand so early in the case. Instead, we confine ourselves to cross-examining prosecution witnesses. The witnesses' answers—memorialized in a transcript—become grist for later "impeachment" in the event there are inconsistencies.

The hearing is an adversarial proceeding that usually occurs only a few days after the crime. In addition to defense counsel, there is a judge, a prosecutor, and a court reporter transcribing the testimony. Depending on the jurisdiction, the testimony at the hearing is either of alleged victims (or other witnesses) or of police officers testifying about what victims and witnesses have told them. Some jurisdictions avoid preliminary hearings in favor of nonadversarial grand jury proceedings.

I did not ultimately try the case and don't remember the outcome. But I can still recall the shock of recognition as the complainant testified.

It doesn't matter that, as an indigent criminal defense lawyer, most of the rape complainants I have encountered have been poor, nonwhite girls and women with neither graduate degrees nor tennis rackets. No matter who the victim is, I can't help seeing part of myself in them.

I once represented a man accused of child sexual abuse who had admitted his guilt to me. When there was no reasonable alternative—no reduced sentence in exchange for a guilty plea—we went to trial. I cross-examined the child complainant in accordance with the defense theory: the child's mother's boyfriend, not my client, had sexually assaulted her. (There was some support for this theory in a police report. The girl told an officer that when she was awakened by an intruder climbing into her bed, she'd thought it was her mom's boyfriend.)

The child was around eleven. Because my client told me he did it, I knew she was telling the truth. Moreover, the child's explicit account of what happened matched my client's, even though he had been high on cocaine and Ecstasy at the time.

The tone of my cross-examination was soft and reassuring. I like kids and know how to talk to them. She agreed that she had mentioned her mom's boyfriend to the police officer who questioned her after the incident and said that he sometimes came into her room. We talked about how attached her mom was to the boyfriend and how hard it was to say anything bad about him because of that attachment. She agreed that life was much better before the boyfriend came to live with her and her mom.

She trusted me. I seemed to understand her and wasn't out to get her. I didn't make her talk about the details of what had happened like the prosecutor did. As a result, the cross-examination went smoothly, and I made the points I needed to make.

During recess she came to find me in the hallway. She told me she was going to camp that summer and wondered if I had ever been. She said she liked to play softball and was good at it, especially fielding. She asked me if I had any kids.

I gently discouraged this contact. I didn't want to hurt her feelings, but I also didn't want her to think I was her *friend*. Still, she kept coming back to me.

I felt like a terrible person. This child had been raped by my client. And now she trusted and liked her rapist's lawyer. She didn't understand the argument I had constructed through my cross-examination, that I was calling her a liar. I would make this abundantly clear in my closing while offering a sympathetic reason for her false accusation.

Here's the other problem: I liked her, too, and would have been happy to talk about camp, softball, or whatever else she wanted to talk about. I wanted to show up the next day with my spare infielder's mitt (I played third base in a local women's softball league). I wanted to tell her how sorry I was about what had happened to her, what my client had done, and what I was doing now. I wanted to tell her she was going to be OK, that she would get through this and have a good life, that she was strong and resilient.

I would have done all this if only I was not the *lawyer on the other side*. But under these particular circumstances, to say or do any of it would have been an even greater betrayal than what I had done at trial. Defense lawyers do not get to apologize—no matter how much we may want to. To do so would be vain and narcissistic. Victims of serious crime get to hate us. It is the least we can do for them.

My client was acquitted.

I still think about that little girl. I wonder what became of her. I hope she got past what had happened to her. I hope she has no memory of me.

•

Despite initial misgivings—Jamal did not see why being "incompetent" was a good thing and was frightened of being sent to such a far-off place as Minnesota—he adapted remarkably well to the institution. In some ways, he thrived. The smaller classes, tutoring, and reward system seemed to work for Jamal. His reading and math improved. His behavior was so positive that staff members described him as a peer leader. He was opening up to his various counselors—something he had never done before.

He didn't even seem to mind the cold weather. Maybe this was because he was seldom allowed outside. His alleged crimes and record of running away meant he was under very strict supervision. He was allowed to shoot baskets in a fenced-in outdoor area when it wasn't covered in snow.

He didn't care that he was one of only a couple of black kids in the institution. "I don't think about white and black," he said. "People here are nice." I was surprised by this. Jamal grew up in an impoverished, racially segregated urban neighborhood. Outside of the court system and related agencies, he did not know any white people. He had never lived among or gone to school with white kids. He had rarely had a white teacher. And yet the overwhelming whiteness of his new home didn't bother him at all. After the initial novelty wore off, he didn't even notice it.

But Jamal might have been an object of interest to people there because of his race, and he might have had some cachet in the institution because he was different—an East Coast city boy. With the exception of a small handful of out-of-staters, the residents and staff of this facility were all from Minnesota, most from the Iron Range—a very white place. Most of the staff were young—in their twenties or thirties. In a youth culture dominated by hip-hop, Jamal probably seemed glamorous. With his braids, low-slung pants, and untied shoes, he looked like a version of some of the popular musical artists of the day. He talked like them too.

Jamal preferred the way the locals talked. "Nobody says curse words," he said. "People act like they respect you and respect themselves." He was trying to talk that way too.

By the time Jamal was seventeen, he had turned his life around. He was doing well on every front: academic, therapeutic, social. He had begun to honestly grapple with some of the problems underlying his crimes. His was the rare success story. Everyone was pleased. We were building a record to keep Jamal in the juvenile system.

I visited Jamal a number of times during this period. After the first visit, the staff received me warmly, like I was one of them. They were happy to share their thoughts about Jamal's progress and their pride in him. We were all committed to turning this young man's life around; we were on the same team.

I enjoyed these visits, though travel to the institution was difficult. There were no direct flights, weather-related delays were routine, the climate was either glacial (the very long winter) or scorching (the relatively short but intense summer), and accommodations were limited. Jamal was delighted to see me and whoever else I brought along. Once it was an investigator. Another time it was our mental health expert. We talked for hours. We went over his excellent progress reports. We played Ping Pong.

In the meantime, I was getting to know the area. The Minnesota Iron Range, with its jagged red stone and earth, is oddly beautiful. "The Range," as locals call it, is a storied part of American labor history. No work was tougher or more dangerous than mining iron ore. Many workers—largely Eastern European immigrants—lost their lives mining iron in the nineteenth and twentieth centuries. The hundred-foot-high "Iron Man" statue, one of the largest freestanding statues in the United States, was built as a tribute to the miners who worked and died there.

Diversity is a thin concept in this part of the country. I didn't see a single African American or Jew. There were a lot of obese white people. Everyone sounded like Frances McDormand's police chief Marge Gunderson in the movie *Fargo*.

I was starting to feel cheerful. Our plan was working. Jamal was doing everything right. We just might beat this thing and save a child. As it says in the Talmud, the ancient Jewish text on law, "If you save one life it is as if you saved the entire world."

Then Jamal was accused of raping a young female staff member.

•

Most defense lawyers agree that it's easier to defend a murder than a rape, because in a murder case, the chief prosecution witness is conveniently *unavailable*. Meanwhile, in a rape case, you must inevitably confront the chief witness. This can be challenging and sometimes painful.

Consider Atticus Finch's cross-examination of Mayella Ewell, the troubled white woman who accused Tom Robinson, an innocent black man, of rape in Harper Lee's *To Kill a Mockingbird*.[5] Atticus was defending his client against a false charge of interracial rape in the Jim Crow South, a capital offense at that time. Still, it "gave him no pleasure" to confront the lying complainant and "hit her hard." As his daughter Scout recounts, Atticus "sat with his head down" when the cross-examination was over. And Scout "never saw anybody glare at anyone with the hatred Mayella showed when she left the stand and walked by Atticus's table."[6]

If cross-examining untruthful witnesses is unpleasant, cross-examining truthful ones can be truly unpleasant. The testimony is often disturbing. But defense lawyers must listen unblinkingly and coolly dismantle what victims say. The listening part is tough enough.

And yet criminal lawyers generally love cross-examination. Although John Henry Wigmore's famous characterization of cross-examination as the "greatest legal engine ever invented for the discovery of the truth"[7] may be hyperbolic, criminal lawyers regard cross-examination as an essential tool for testing the prosecution's proof and exposing problems with it. At their best, skilled criminal lawyers can "do anything with cross-examination," including "make the truth appear like falsehood."[8]

But this ability to subvert the truth is also what makes cross-examination hard. It is one thing to "cross" a police officer, jailhouse snitch, rival gang member, phony expert, or officious neighbor with a penchant for exaggeration; these are fun. It is another thing to cross a truthful and sympathetic rape or child sex abuse complainant in order to suggest she is lying.

This is not because there is anything wrong with such a cross-examination as a matter of ethics or constitutional criminal procedure. It is well settled that criminal lawyers must vigorously cross-examine witnesses at trial no matter how truthful they may be and no matter the alleged crime. U.S. Supreme Court justice Byron White offered the best explanation for this:

> Law enforcement officers have the obligation to convict the guilty and to make sure they do not convict the innocent. . . . But defense counsel has no comparable obligation to ascertain or present the truth. Our system assigns him a different mission. He must be and is interested in preventing the conviction of the innocent, but, absent a voluntary plea of guilty, we also insist that he defend his client whether he is innocent or guilty. . . . If he can confuse a witness, even a truthful one, or make him appear at a disadvantage, unsure or indecisive, that will be his normal course. Our interest in not convicting the innocent permits counsel to put the State to its proof, to put the State's case in the worst possible light, regardless of what he thinks or knows to be the truth. Undoubtedly there are some limits which defense counsel must observe but more often than not, defense counsel will cross-examine a prosecution witness, and impeach him if he can, even if he thinks the witness is telling the truth, just as he will attempt to destroy a witness who he thinks is lying.[9]

Still, the ethical and constitutional justifications are a separate matter from how it actually feels to confront and cross-examine alleged victims of sexual assault, knowing—or strongly believing—that they are telling the truth, and coming to terms with those feelings.

Sexual violence is pervasive. According to the FBI, a sexual assault occurs every six minutes in the United States.[10] According to the United Nations, one in three women worldwide has experienced physical or sexual violence, mostly from an intimate partner.[11] Given these figures, I am fortunate to have remained unscathed so far.

Nevertheless, I have the same fear of rape that many women have—perhaps ratcheted up by what I have seen in criminal court. It is hard to not be affected by the testimony of women and children who have been sexually assaulted. This may be an occupational hazard for a female criminal defense lawyer.

Most of the rape complainants I have confronted—like that graduate student from my neighborhood in Philadelphia—were at preliminary hearings. You cannot make a mistake at a preliminary hearing by asking too many questions or the "wrong question." You want it all—damaging as well as helpful testimony—in order to later counsel the client about his options and because you never know what you might uncover. It is an archeological dig: no detail is too small, no moment of *no moment*. Because a preliminary hearing is early in the case (too early for investigation), I know virtually nothing—except what my client is saying. Most clients accused of sexual assault deny it—at least initially. The charge is grave. But this denial means you have even less to go on as a lawyer.

Once, relying on my client's adamant denial of forcible sex—he claimed he and the complainant had engaged in consensual and mutually satisfying sex—I asked the complainant about her sexual response during the alleged incident. She immediately rejected the suggestion that what had happened was anything other than a vicious sexual assault. She was taken aback by the question and credibly slapped it down. This was important information in subsequent counseling about whether we should go to trial.

Later that day, I got a call from someone who worked at Women Organized Against Rape, a local feminist organization with the mission of ending sexual violence. They often staffed the rape preliminary hearing courtrooms and had been there during my client's hearing. (I was always acutely aware of their presence in the first row; I knew some of them from the progressive, feminist circles I traveled in.) They were not happy with my performance and wanted me to know it.

I felt a mixture of regret and indignation. It hadn't been my proudest moment. But I also hadn't done anything improper. I cross-examined the complainant "vigorously but with courtesy and respect."[12] I had accepted her answer to this particular question—as I had to other questions—and moved on. Although the complainant may have been embarrassed by my query, she was also emphatic.

Atticus Finch and Mayella Ewell again come to mind. Atticus did his best to confront and confound Mayella. He used all his skills and talents to undermine her testimony and expose her as a liar. He was good at it. This isn't surprising—he was an affluent, well-educated, experienced trial lawyer, while Mayella was poor, probably illiterate, and had never been in court before. Nevertheless, Mayella defiantly refused to answer many of Atticus's questions and exhorted the jury to take her side unless they were nothing but "yellow stinkin' cowards." She was so feisty on the witness stand that the judge overruled the prosecutor's objection that Atticus was "browbeating" her, saying, "If anything, the witness's browbeating Atticus."[13]

Writer Alice Sebold, who was raped as a young college student, writes about court proceedings as a "hostile battle." She writes about defense lawyers, "They may have been earning a paycheck, or randomly assigned to the case, had children they loved or a terminally ill mother to take care of. I didn't care. They were there to destroy me. I was there to fight back."[14]

•

It was difficult for Jamal to accept his changed circumstances. The institution that had been so good to him was ejecting him from the premises and handing him over to the authorities. He managed to call me before he was taken to the local jail to say it was consensual sex, not rape. I told him not to say anything more; the phones were not secure, and anything he said could be used against him. I advised him to tell those who tried to question him—the police or anyone else—that he had a lawyer and was asserting his right not to say anything. I told him to blame me if they pressed him; he wasn't allowed to speak to anyone, and his lawyer would be angry if he did.

The state of Minnesota charged Jamal with first-degree sexual assault and moved to try him as an adult.

I traveled to northern Minnesota as soon as I could and made my way to the St. Louis County Jail. It was heartbreaking to see Jamal behind bars even at this jail, which was oddly hospitable—at least by comparison to East Coast jails. The corrections officer at the entrance couldn't have been friendlier. He took my identification and waved me through with no wait. This had never happened to me before in any jail or prison on the East Coast, nor has it happened since.

And there was Jamal in jail clothes and a correctional system armband. Apparently, it was fine for him to be in an adult jail instead of a juvenile lockup even though he was only seventeen. Maybe this was because his eighteenth birthday was only a few weeks away. Perhaps they also knew something I didn't—that there would be no more juvenile jail for Jamal.

I was reminded of the Bob Dylan song "The Walls of Red Wing," which is about a notorious Minnesota juvenile correctional facility that has been in existence since 1889. Dylan, a Minnesota native, probably grew up hearing about Red Wing and captures the despair of those held there. Still, it would have been better for Jamal to go to what is now called Minnesota Correctional Facility–Red Wing than the adult St. Cloud Prison, where he seemed to be headed.

In addition to making a plan to see Jamal, I had called the institution as soon as I heard about the allegations. I wanted to talk to some of the staff members and residents before they were told not to talk. But the previously receptive staff was no longer happy to hear from me. No one returned my calls.

Finally, one counselor did. He was shaken up by what had happened. He had been close to Jamal. But he also knew the alleged victim. She had been visibly distraught when she reported the assault and had described it in detail. According to her, the attack happened in a secluded part of the institution. She was escorting Jamal to retrieve a personal belonging that was in storage. When they entered the storage area, Jamal started to "come on" to her. She told him to cut it out and get his stuff. Jamal then grabbed her, choked her, threatened to hurt her, and sexually assaulted her. She tried to get away, but he was too strong. After the assault, Jamal told her that she "better not fucking tell anybody."

She had bruises on her neck from being choked. The staff member didn't think the alleged victim had any reason to lie. She was also married and had a small child.

He told me I was free to contact whomever I wanted at the institution, but he doubted anyone would talk to me.

Jamal had a very different account. When he was finally able to share his story with me, it came pouring out of him. He said the woman had flirted with him for weeks. She volunteered to escort him up to the third floor to get a jacket that was in a locker there. When they got to the room, they began to make out, and one thing led to another. He said it was quick because they didn't want to get caught, and a little rough because they did it on the floor. He said the staff member freaked out and cried rape when another staff member came upon them. "You have to believe me," Jamal said. "She came on to me. I didn't do what they are saying." He sounded scared and indignant. "Oh, Jamal," I said. "It doesn't matter what I believe."

It mattered to him. He wanted to know I was in his corner. But I was in his corner whether I believed him or not. I was bound to him—to advocate for him, be loyal to him, and keep his confidences—as a matter of professional ethics and because I had become attached. I didn't want to feel attached—no one wants to be on a sinking ship—but I couldn't help it. He was in a terrible situation. I wasn't going to cut and run now.

Still, I couldn't help questioning Jamal's account, even if he genuinely believed it to be true. Was it possible that a young mother was so enthralled with Jamal that she had sex with him in a barren storage area? And when caught in the act, that she had blamed Jamal rather than lose her job over it? Even though it wasn't the most far-fetched story I'd ever heard, it seemed unlikely.

Whatever had happened in that storage area, I felt frustrated, angry, and heartbroken. Why would a secure institution for juvenile offenders allow a female staff member to escort an alleged rapist to a secluded place? It was like leaving an untreated drug addict alone with a bag of cocaine. We had come so close to accomplishing something extraordinary. Jamal had demonstrated that he could grow and change. Now everything had come to a grinding halt.

A young man already charged with rape was alleged to have raped again. By his own account, he had engaged in prohibited sexual conduct, this time in a treatment facility. There are second acts for people caught up in the criminal adult or juvenile systems, but seldom third acts.

•

Why not just give up on Jamal? Why even consider his version of events? Back when I first met Jamal, I had warned the female fellow with whom I was working not to be careless. Jamal was young and appealing but also damaged and dangerous. I cautioned her against being alone with him. This was not because I had any special powers of intuition. It was because he had already raped once.

I don't like to think the worst of people—especially clients. But I also don't want to be naïve. You can fight hard for a client but still keep your wits about you.

These new allegations against Jamal were disturbing. Whether or not they were true, they had the ring of truth. Together with Jamal's previous case—armed rape of a pretty young woman on the street—his behavior reminded me of the young rapist in Alice Sebold's poignant 1999 memoir, *Lucky*. The book is about Sebold's attack by a stranger during her freshman year at Syracuse University. Sebold, who went on to write the acclaimed novel *The Lovely Bones*,[15] is a gifted writer. She captures what happened to her, and the aftermath, in brutal detail.

Sebold was dragged at knifepoint into a tunnel near the campus, where she was then beaten and raped. As she wrote in the *New York Times Magazine* around the time her book was published, "When I was raped I lost my virginity and almost lost my life."[16] The man who raped her hurt her so badly—with his hands, fist, and penis—she was torn and bleeding both inside and out. Before raping her vaginally, he thrust his penis into her mouth, jammed his entire hand into her vagina, and urinated on her face. At the trial, the pants she had worn that night—preserved in plastic—were almost entirely red from blood.

Sebold's rapist, a man in his early twenties who looked younger, was by turns bullying and contrite. It seemed to enrage him that Sebold didn't know how to follow his instructions—how to "get wet," how to "suck dick," where to put her legs. "You're the worst bitch I ever done this to,'" he told her. But after the assault he apologized, helped Sebold get dressed, and asked whether she was OK. Then he became hostile again, then once again apologetic. He even cried as he said he was "so sorry." In the end, he acted as if what happened had been a "date." "Come here," he said. "Kiss me good-bye." When he finally walked away, he told Sebold to take care of herself. He asked her what her name was. "I couldn't lie," Sebold writes. So her attacker's parting words were, "Nice knowing you, Alice.... See you around sometime."[17]

Some five months after the rape, Sebold saw her attacker on the street. He greeted her with the words, "Hey, girl.... Don't I know you from somewhere?"[18] This chance encounter led to his arrest.

This sounds a lot like a young man I once represented who, after breaking into a single mother's home and raping her while her two-year-old baby slept in the next room, went to the refrigerator, grabbed a beer, and asked his victim if she wanted to join him. Apparently, this is not unusual behavior. Writer Patricia Weaver Francisco was raped by an intruder who asked for a beer as a prelude to assaulting her:

> He wants a beer. I feel the relief of the hostess that I have some on hand, the relief of the prisoner that we're in the realm of food and drink. It's an odd domestic moment....
>
> He sits next to me on the bed, close, near my head and drinks his beer. He also smokes a cigarette, possibly a joint. The police found burnt matches on the floor, but I have no memory of smell. He is silent for so long that I become terrified. Not the panic or the adrenaline clarity of the first terror, but a slow, frozen, cynical knowing, an engulfing certainty that now is as good a time as any for killing. But I understand in the long silence that he will rape me first. Until this moment, I have not considered the possibility. I feel foolish, a little slow or stupid. Of course, I say to myself in the quiet.[19]

I have represented boys and men who apologized for being "rough," or who seemed to come to after the rape, get ahold of themselves, and become ashamed. I have represented some men who asked for their victim's phone number so they could "go out" again. One client said to his victim, "That wasn't so bad, was it?"

Jamal may have truly believed he and the alleged victim had "hooked up"—that what had happened between them was mutual, if a little rough. He may have thought to himself, *She is angry right now, but she'll get over it.* He may have been counting on another hookup when things quieted down. But maybe he knew he had screwed up and couldn't admit it. He had misread the cues and lost control. He wanted what he wanted. The alleged victim said he had put her in a choke hold.

Many people think rape is a horrible but fluid act: the victim is seized, sexually attacked, and then discarded. Most don't really think about what happened during the attack or after. As Alice Sebold told a reporter, "For some reason, (people think) rape is like a thud. . . . 'She was raped.' End of story."[20]

But there is no "thud." There is nothing seamless, fluid, or formulaic about rape. It is often messy, awkward, prolonged, and bizarre. The act of penetration is sometimes the most awkward aspect. I once represented a man who was alleged to have raped a menstruating girl, who was wearing a sanitary napkin that had to be shoved out of the way. The girl—for whom menstruation was a relatively new occurrence—was mortified to share this fact in court. I have represented several men who, according to the complainant, were unable to obtain or maintain an erection.

This last is very much a part of Sebold's story:

"Please don't do this, please," I said. . . .

"Lie down."

I did. Shaking, I crawled over and lay face up against the cold ground. He pulled my underpants off me roughly and bundled them into his hand. He threw them away from me and into a corner where I lost sight of them.

I watched him as he unzipped his pants and let them fall around his ankles.

He lay down on top of me and started humping. . . .

He worked away on me, reaching down to work with his penis.

I stared right into his eyes. I was too afraid not to. If I shut my eyes, I believed, I would disappear. To make it through, I had to be present the whole time.

He called me bitch. He told me I was dry.

"I'm sorry," I said—I never stopped apologizing. . . .

"Stop looking at me," he said. "Shut your eyes. Stop shaking."

"I can't."

"Stop it or you'll be sorry."

I did. My focus became acute. I stared harder than ever at him. He began to knead his fist against the opening of my vagina. Inserted his fingers into it, three or four at a time. Something tore. I began to bleed there. I was wet now.

It made him excited. He was intrigued. As he worked his whole fist up into my vagina and pumped it, I went into my brain. Waiting there were poems for me, poems I'd learned in class: Olga Cabral had a poem I haven't found since, "Lillian's Chair," and a poem called "Dog Hospital," by Peter Wild. I tried, as a sort of prickly numbness took over my lower half, to recite the poems in my head. I moved my lips.

"Stop staring at me," he said.

"I'm sorry," I said. "You're strong," I tried.

He liked this. He started humping me again, wildly. The base of my spine was crushed into the ground. Glass cut me on my back and behind. But something still wasn't working for him. . . .[21]

Not only is there no single thud, but there is an excruciating intimacy. It is reductionist to say that rape is violence, not sex. Of course rape is violence, but it is *sexual* violence. As one woman who was raped as a girl explains, "It's also sex. You can't get around that. . . . He didn't run me over with a car. He had sex with me. You're not supposed to do that. You're not supposed to have sex with an eighth-grader. You're not supposed to have sex when you're in eighth grade. It was very intimate."[22]

Sebold, who is white, was raped by a young black man. Rape of a white woman by a black man is an especially problematic paradigm,[23] something Sebold understood immediately. She writes about a black schoolmate who wanted to hug her when he learned she'd been raped:

"I don't think I can," I said to Victor.

"He was black, wasn't he?" Victor asked. He was trying to get me to look at him, look right at him.

"Yes."

"I'm sorry," he said. He was crying. The tears ran slowly down the outside of his cheeks. "I'm so sorry."

I don't know whether I hugged him because I could not stand to see him crying . . . or because I was prompted further by those around us. He held me until I had to pull away and then he let me go. He was miserable, and I cannot even now imagine what was going on inside his head. Perhaps he already knew that both relatives and strangers would say things to me like "I bet he was black," and so he wanted to give me something to counter this, some experience in the same twenty-four hours that would make me resist placing people in categories and aiming at them my full-on hate.[24]

At trial, Sebold acknowledges that the defendant is the only black person in the courtroom. She feels guilty about this. She confesses that "this wasn't the first time, or the last, that I wished my rapist had been white."[25]

The women and children whom I have confronted in court run the gamut in age, position, personality. The vast majority have been poor and black. This is a reflection of indigent criminal defense in an urban setting. Most of my clients are poor and black as well.

•

My efforts to speak to staff about what had happened at the Minnesota institution came to nothing. I went office to office. They had clearly been instructed not to meet with me.

A Hibbing, Minnesota, lawyer who served as the county's part-time public defender was appointed to represent Jamal in the new case. I had no trouble setting up a meeting with him. I saw the lawyer on a holiday weekend at his home. He was cordial even though he was in the middle of a backyard barbecue.

An experienced criminal lawyer around my age, he seemed to know what he was talking about. He didn't pull any punches about how bleak the case looked. On top of everything else, the state of Minnesota was in the middle of a budget crisis, and indigent defense was one of the first things to be slashed. Some public defenders had already been laid off. There was little money for investigation and even less to hire any expert witnesses.

Moreover, the specifics of Jamal's case made it hard to argue for such an expense. Even a stable of distinguished defense experts was unlikely to turn things around for a young man who was competent to stand trial by most measures and who would be eighteen by the time of the hearing—all but ensuring that he would be sent to adult criminal court. Under the circumstances, that kind of money was better spent on a more promising case.

The lawyer and I talked about how I might be helpful. I gave him a list of contacts at the juvenile institution—people who might raise some questions about the complainant's credibility or have something positive to say about Jamal. I offered to try to obtain money from a nonprofit juvenile defense organization to pay Jamal's DC mental health expert to testify in Minnesota. The lawyer liked this idea. Neither of us wanted to go down without a fight.

I went back to see Jamal once more before leaving town. He was hoping for good news, and I had none. I told him I had met his Minnesota counsel and that he seemed like a good lawyer and a good guy. I urged Jamal to work closely with his new attorney. I explained that I would do what I could to be helpful, but I was not his lawyer on this case. When we said good-bye, Jamal suddenly looked old to me.

Back home, I raised money for the mental health expert, briefed the expert on what was happening in Minnesota, made sure the Minnesota lawyer had a complete set of Jamal's records, and made myself available for consultation. But mostly it was out of my hands.

Another fellow and I went to Minnesota for the competency and transfer hearings. (The fellow who had previously worked on Jamal's case had graduated by this time.) The hearings took most of a week. The Minnesota lawyer gave us tasks: we picked up the defense expert at the airport, prepared the defense expert to testify, got ahold of an obscure article the prosecution's expert had written, prepared a cross-examination of the prosecution's expert, prepared Jamal to testify, and took copious notes in court.

We struggled with a feeling of a foregone conclusion. What was the point of so much effort for a lost cause?

We had no illusions. No judge—no matter how courageous—would rule in Jamal's favor. His progress at the juvenile institution would now be used against him. His intellectual and emotional growth made the competency decision easy. His serious offense while in a juvenile setting made the transfer decision easy. The state did not have to prove the crime beyond a reasonable doubt, only that it probably happened. The one argument we could make was that the institution had been negligent in allowing an untreated and cognitively impaired young sex offender to be alone with a young woman. The incident could have been prevented and wasn't a fair demonstration of Jamal's capacity for rehabilitation.

We knew the judge wouldn't buy it.

No one from Jamal's family came to these proceedings—not his mother, who had spent most of his childhood high, nor his father, who had spent most of his childhood incarcerated. The fellow and I were the only "family" Jamal had there. He needed us to be upbeat, so we tried.

But the hearing was excruciating. Jamal had to sit quietly at counsel table while a parade of witnesses from the institution testified that he was fully competent to be tried in adult court and should be prosecuted there. They said they had been wrong to think Jamal could change; he had betrayed their trust on every level.

It was hard to tell what Jamal made of the testimony. Sometimes he seemed angry, sometimes hurt, and sometimes in his own world. Probably it was all too much for him. The people who had been his friends—and who had been his last, best chance of avoiding a lengthy prison sentence—were saying he was not fit to be among them.

Jamal was found competent and sent to adult criminal court. Although his local counsel worked hard—conducting the investigation, filing pretrial motions, contesting everything he could—within a few months, Jamal was convicted of rape and given the maximum sentence. He would serve more than a decade in a Minnesota prison. He would ultimately receive three times that sentence when later convicted of rape in Washington, DC.

•

I have given a lot of thought to and written much about the question of feminism and criminal defense, especially in the context of rape.[26] Although these cases are challenging, I have found a way to defend rapists and child abusers and feel good about it. I believe that criminal defense can be consonant with feminism if one embraces what I call a "feminist defense ethos." This is a way of thinking—and an *attitude*—built on two things: skepticism of the reflexive and punitive power of the state and a commitment to individual human dignity. I am lucky that there is a corps of feminist defenders who share this ethos; it would be lonely without them, the dissonance more pronounced.

Let me explain more fully.

The current context of criminal justice is important—in particular, the devastation that mass incarceration has wrought. Prison has become the policy of first, not last, resort for our most vexing social problems. In some impoverished nonwhite communities, huge numbers of young men have been swallowed up by the criminal legal system.

Yet even against a backdrop of excessive punishment, we pile on punishment when it comes to sex offenders.[27] All fifty states, the District of Columbia, and the five principle U.S. territories have enacted sex offender registration statutes—which require a broad swath of offenders to register or face criminal penalties for failing to do so—in addition to the sentence imposed. Most states also have residency and work restrictions. Indefinite civil commitment of sex offenders—beyond any criminal sentence imposed—has been found constitutional by the United States Supreme Court.[28]

Political scientist Marie Gottschalk has called sex offenders "the new untouchables."[29] News stories about convicted sex offenders forced to live under bridges, highways, and other remote areas bear this out. Not all are dangerous criminals. Sex offenders in the United States range from rapists and pedophiles to young people in consensual relationships with minors nearly their age, public urinators, indecent exposers, "sexters," and downloaders of child pornography. All are made into pariahs. As one forty-year-old man forced to live under a Florida highway for inappropriate conduct with a fifteen-year-old relative bemoaned, "I am not a monster. I am not a leper."[30]

Sarah Stillman wrote a haunting article for the *New Yorker* about juveniles who end up on the sex offender registry for "playing doctor" with siblings, pulling down the pants of a classmate on the playground, having a relationship with a willing partner several years younger, and sending a sex video to a girlfriend. Even when these juveniles are supposed to be off the registry, they are forever labeled sex offenders on the internet.[31]

The name of one young woman, now in college, can be found on the internet with the caption "Criminal Sexual Conduct" for play-acting sex with her younger stepbrothers when she was ten. The girl had been a happy child and an excellent student. When her parents divorced, she went to live with her father and his new wife, who had four children, including three sons. The boys were a novelty to the ten-year-old; she had a younger sister but no brother. One afternoon, after watching a movie with her new stepsiblings, the girl mimicked having sex with them, like they'd seen in the movie, and showed them her vagina. When one of the boys told an adult, the girl was charged with eight counts of felony criminal sexual conduct. On the advice of a court-appointed attorney with whom she met briefly, she pleaded guilty to two counts of criminal sexual conduct. When she was twelve, she was sent to a residential juvenile sex offender treatment facility for two years. She was the youngest in the program.[32]

Our hysteria-driven, hyperpunitive response to the broad category of those we call "sex offenders" is not only ineffective but counterproductive. Lengthy sentences combined with harsh postsentence regulation may actually be criminogenic.[33]

The feminist defender ethos incorporates a more nuanced sense of justice. Some offenders are dangerous and need to be off the streets. But many are not dangerous or can be treated. Feminist defenders also understand that many perpetrators have been victimized themselves—that there is a cycle of sexual abuse. Some offenders are so damaged they are mentally ill. Indeed, studies show a higher rate of mental illness among sex offenders than among other offenders.[34]

The threat of harsh punishment for sex offenders—harsher still because of the way they are treated in prison—creates an additional motivation for defenders. The stakes are higher, the urgency greater. A conviction generally means a long sentence followed by perpetual shaming and banishment.

Because the sentences are so harsh, defending alleged rapists is comparable to defending noncapital homicide. But a rape or child sex abuse conviction is worse in some ways. There is no "homicide registry." There are no residency restrictions for convicted killers. There are no civil commitment statutes specifically for homicidally dangerous persons—just "sexually dangerous ones."[35]

Some might say, "So what? We are talking about *sex offenders*: the more punishment the better." Others might say, "Come on. Be a *feminist*. Pick a side." Most people understand that rape is harrowing and deeply destructive. Rape victims often feel that a part of them has died; the sense of physical autonomy central to identity has been destroyed.[36]

Some will question whether the combination of ideology and advocacy I am trying to describe are enough to persuade a lawyer to defend these particular criminals. Doesn't there have to be a deeper, more personal commitment—something that makes a lawyer actually *care*?

It is helpful when that happens. It is best to feel a connection to the client—to like him, want to help him, share his fear. This happened with Jamal. But some clients are harder to like; some are so damaged it is hard to find their humanity. This may happen more with sex offenders than other clients.

•

Aside from preliminary hearings and trials, lawyers also confront rape or child sexual assault victims during "victim impact" statements at sentencing—when victims talk about how the crime has affected them. Generally speaking, defense lawyers ask no questions here. There would be nothing gained from doing so.

At their most powerful, victim impact statements are heart wrenching. One client I represented postconviction pled guilty to a home invasion, rape, and robbery. The victims were a couple in their midtwenties who worked on Capitol Hill. My client was sixteen. He and an older boy had been smoking marijuana dipped in PCP when they decided to rob someone. The two boys saw the couple about to enter their home and forced their way in at gunpoint. Once inside, they ransacked the place looking for something of value. Finding nothing, they forced the couple to undress, tried to make them have sex with each other, and then raped the woman in the presence of her boyfriend, a gun to his head. Both victims begged for their lives. They thought they were going to die.

It was hard to get the written victim impact statements out of my head. The victims had been happy living in a diverse urban neighborhood. Now they were fearful of their neighbors. They described how their lives had been forever altered—as individuals, as a couple, and as members of the community.

There was also testimony by the boyfriend. The transcript reveals a heroic effort to speak without breaking down. He asked the court not to be swayed by the young age of the defendant. He called him a "monster."

Being questioned at a hearing or trial must be worse than giving a statement. This is what causes people to say that rape victims are "victimized twice"—first during the crime and then in court.

But is this really further *victimization*, or simply what it means to have a rigorous adversarial system—one that holds the government to a high burden before denouncing a fellow citizen as a criminal and casting him out?

The experience of being raped is inevitably complicated by legal proceedings (that is, if proceedings happen—a rare occurrence in sexual assault cases).[37] The ability to perceive, recall, and recount is required of any witness at trial. But the trauma of a sexual assault can compromise these abilities. Here is what author and terrorism expert Jessica Stern, raped by an intruder when she was fifteen, writes about the incident, some thirty years after the fact:

The police asked my sister and me to write down what had occurred. We did this, the report states, between 11:30 pm and 1:45 am. Those words are before me now. I read the words I know I wrote in a penmanship I barely recognize. My notes from 1973 are written in italics below:

—sitting doing homework
—man walked in....
—showed us gun, don't scream...

I do recall "man walked in": I can see a kind of apparition in my mind's eye. I do recall the threat to kill us if we spoke. But now I am lost. My mind cannot focus. An apparition of cold flits across my heart but is gone so soon I wonder if I imagined it. I am annoyed with this little girl whom I'm struggling to hold in my mind's eye, who wants me to understand how she suffered. You will be fine, I want to tell her. I feel anger at her, even more than "man walked in." I do not want to hear about her fear or her pain.

It wasn't that bad.[38]

Although Stern's recollection occurs years later—after much more time than the days or months in a hearing or trial—it is probably not so different from how most victims feel. The pull of a terrible memory competes with a desire to turn away. Fear, anger, distress, and shame challenge the ability to remember. Getting close to the memory means reliving it; distancing oneself is easier—even if it leads to disconnection and denial. This is what defense lawyers mean to exploit: the challenges, vagaries, and uncertainties of memory itself. Stern was not able to picture her attacker immediately after the rape and still cannot do so. "I simply cannot force my brain to recollect my rapist's face."[39]

One thoughtful observer of criminal trials describes cross-examination as a devastating test of memory and self-possession:

The whole point is to make the witness's story look shaky, to pepper the jury with doubt. So you get a grip on her basic observations, and you chop away and chop away, and squeeze and shout and pull her here and push her there, you cast aspersions on her memory and her good faith and her intelligence till you make her hesitate or stumble. She starts to feel self-conscious, then she gets an urge to add things and buttress and emphasize and maybe embroider, because she knows what she saw and she wants to be believed, but she's not allowed to tell it her way. You're in charge. All she can do is answer your questions. And then you slide away from the central thing she's come forward with, and you try to catch her out on the peripheral stuff—"Did you see his chin?"—then she starts to get rattled, and you provoke her with a smart crack. . . . She tries to put her foot down—"Oh, don't be ridiculous"—and the judge gives her a dirty look and she sees she's gone too far, so she tries to recoup, she tries to get back to the place she started from, where she really does remember seeing something and knows what she saw—but that place of certainty no longer exists, because you've destroyed it. And now she's floating in the abyss with her legs dangling . . . and the next thing you put to her she'll agree to, just to stop the torture. And then you thank her politely and sit down.[40]

When I read the above passage to a criminal defense colleague, she said she *wished* this was what cross-examination was like. Her reaction reflects her modesty (she is a very able trial lawyer) as well as the reality that most cross-examinations have relatively narrow aims and are best executed in a low-key, methodical fashion. But the passage reflects how cross-examination feels to the witness as well as to an observer.

It might be that rape victims have an especially difficult time holding on to a memory they would rather not have. This makes these witnesses more vulnerable during cross-examination. Philosophy professor Susan Brison, who was raped and nearly murdered in the south of France when she was thirty-five, felt anxious about "keeping her story straight" and "keeping alive in [her] mind . . . the narrative [she] remembered, rehearsed, and finally, delivered to the court." This was so even though the defense at trial was insanity and the crime itself uncontested. Brison felt "there was something deadening about the requirement for truth" and "it took some conscious effort to *will the true story* to stay straight in order to reproduce it at trial."[41]

Alice Sebold, too, had trouble speaking at trial. On direct examination, she began a sentence only to "trail off" and begin again. "He told me to—that he was—well, I figured out by that time that he was—didn't want my money." She faltered not because she didn't know exactly what had happened to her. "It was saying the words out loud, knowing it was *how* I said them that could win or lose the case."[42]

The truth is difficult enough under ordinary circumstances. As writer Janet Malcolm has noted, "The truth is messy, incoherent, aimless, boring, absurd. The truth does not make a good story; that's why we have art."⁴³ At trial, truth is especially malleable. It is the lawyer's job to bend what purports to be the truth to the lawyer's own purpose. As Malcolm writes, "Trials are won by attorneys whose stories fit, and lost by those whose stories are like the shapeless housecoat that truth, in her disdain for appearances, has chosen as her uniform."⁴⁴

Alice Sebold was keenly aware of the shabbiness of truth. When members of the grand jury hearing her case asked her why she did not immediately contact the police after the attack, why she was coming through a park late at night by herself, and why she failed to identify the defendant at a lineup (the defendant had brought along a "filler" who could have been his twin and who glared menacingly at Sebold through the one-way mirror to "psych her out"), she answered "patiently" even though she felt the jurors just didn't "get it," and tailored the truth to her audience. She writes:

> On television and in the movies, the lawyer often says to the victim before they take the stand, "Just tell the truth." What it was left up to me to figure out was that if you do that and nothing else, you lose. So I told them I was stupid, that I shouldn't have walked through the park. I said I intended to do something to warn girls at the university about the park. And I was so good, so willing to accept blame, that I hoped to be judged innocent by them.⁴⁵

It is important to note that no defense lawyer is ever present in the grand jury room. A jury of ordinary citizens was blaming the victim here, not defense counsel.

But Sebold had reason to be careful about how she packaged the truth. While researching her book, she came upon the original police paperwork. The detective overseeing her case had written in a police report shortly after seeing Sebold in the hospital that he did not believe her, that "it is this writer's opinion, after interview of the victim, that this case, as presented by the victim, is not completely factual." Notwithstanding that Sebold's face was swollen from being beaten and her internal injuries required stitches, the detective recommended that the case be referred to the "inactive file."⁴⁶

Cross-examination is an especially powerful tool with a faltering, wavering, "wordless" witness. If conducted properly, it is not really *questioning* at all—at least not in the sense of wanting real answers. If the lawyer is in charge, as a cross-examiner should be, the witness won't have to (or get to) speak. All the witness will do is agree (or disagree) with the lawyer's assertions. If the witness is more confident or voluble, the lawyer will need to be even more controlling.[47]

In unraveling the truth of a witness's account, defense lawyers inevitably exploit cultural understandings and misunderstandings about sex. As Professor Stephen Schulhofer notes, sex is not always straightforward. He writes, "For most women, most of the time, 'no' does mean no. But sometimes it means maybe or 'try harder to talk me into it.' Sometimes, for some women, it means 'get physical.'"[48]

Sexism is inextricably connected to this familiar, conventional advocacy strategy, which continues to be used in acquaintance rape cases, where consent (or a combination of consent and fabrication) is typically the defense. It is not unusual for defense lawyers to play into sexism, racism, or other biases when it is advantageous to do so.[49] Exploiting prejudice is part of advocacy; indeed, the ability to persuade often relies on the ability to recognize and make use of biases and stereotypes. Exploiting fairly obvious gender stereotypes in a "date rape" case—pointing out the use of drugs or alcohol, the fact that there was flirting and/or consensual sexual activity short of intercourse, the time of day, the fact that the woman invited the man to her home or went willingly to his, what the woman wore—doesn't feel especially insidious to me. They are predictable defense tacks—standard sexist canards at trial—that any decent prosecutor would anticipate and rebut.

Of course, there are aspects of sexual assault cases that raise questions about witness credibility or reliability and are not inextricably connected to sexism: evidence of motive or bias, impaired opportunity or ability to observe, implausibility, inconsistency, poor or odd witness demeanor. But being grilled about these matters is not pleasant for alleged victims either. To Alice Sebold, the cross-examination itself—the intense interrogation, the form of the questions and their "rapid fire" deliveries, the quick jumps from subject to subject with the aim of "muddy[ing] the water" and "dragging this out"—is the strategy.[50] To Sebold, it was all "meant to imply that I was really a bit insane, wasn't I?"[51]

How does all this feel to the defense lawyer? In truth, sometimes it feels bad. But when the dust settles, it shouldn't feel so bad. First, if a witness feels terribly beaten up and outmatched on cross-examination, perhaps they weren't properly prepared by the prosecution. It is not that difficult to anticipate the issues that will come up on cross. Most prosecution offices have victim-witness advocates as well as experienced trial prosecutors who ought to prepare alleged rape victims for trial. It is not fair for blame to be laid at the feet of defense counsel rather than feckless or overly confident prosecutors.

Second, testing the "truth" of a criminal charge is the key function of a defense lawyer and is essential to the proper working of the adversary system. If we fail to engage in thorough testing, we run the risk of deferring too much to law enforcement officers "engaged in the often competitive enterprise of ferreting out crime."[52] Especially in serious, high profile cases, where emotions run high, law enforcement officers have been known to take a less faithful, more *instrumental* approach to the truth.[53] As the nearly four-hundred DNA exonerations by the Innocence Project have shown, "In far too many cases, the very people who are responsible for ensuring truth and justice—law enforcement officials and prosecutors—lose sight of these obligations and instead focus solely on securing convictions."[54] Nearly three-quarters of all DNA exonerations have been in rape cases.[55] Too often, these cases prompt a rush to judgment by government actors who, either consciously or unconsciously, end up subverting the truth.

Putting the government to the test is a key motivation for defense lawyers even when the lawyer knows he or she is defending a rapist. Okay, says the lawyer, my client may have committed the crime. But has the government played fair? Have they exercised restraint in charging, been scrupulously truthful in their pleadings and representations to the court, and comported with their obligation to disclose favorable evidence? The government's constitutional and ethical obligations are the same, whether or not my client is guilty. Have they met them?[56]

This stance is part of the craft of defending. It includes an abiding skepticism—no matter the truth of the allegations—and an ability to vigorously test prosecution witnesses—no matter how sympathetic. You learn how to do it early on, and with practice, it becomes more or less automatic, part of the job.

But again, this does not mean it is enjoyable for me to cross-examine rape complainants. The systemic and political justifications are helpful, but the dissonance doesn't necessarily disappear. Especially when the defense is that the complainant is lying—as it often is in rape cases—you have to go *at* the witness. There is no way around this fact. Effective cross-examination means exploiting every uncertainty, inconsistency, and implausibility. More than that, it means attacking the witness's integrity. As Janet Malcolm has written, "Jurors sit there presumably weighing evidence but in actuality they are studying character."[57] So without mincing words, what defense lawyers do at trial on behalf of factually guilty rapists is impugn *the very character of a truthful person who has been badly victimized*.

•

How then, knowing what I know—and admitting it out loud—can I do what is required of defense lawyers on behalf of a factually guilty client in a rape case? Why choose to do it, and how to live with it?

Jamal provides one answer. Aside from his youth, developmental and cognitive issues, and abuse of a highly addictive hallucinogenic dissociative drug at a very young age, Jamal had been physically and sexually abused since before he could talk. It doesn't take much to see a connection between what happened to him and what he later repeated with others—or why he turned to drugs.

Investigation into his family history revealed that he was the product of intergenerational, intrafamily physical and sexual abuse. His mother had repeated what had been done to her. She also turned to drugs to mask the pain. She was likely mentally ill or at least suffering from a mental disorder. She may have been the most narcissistically wounded person I ever met. She was certainly one of the worst parents. If one could transform an innocent child into a rapist, Jamal's mother seems to have had the formula.

At first, Jamal had been fiercely protective of his mother. He didn't want a harsh word said about her—not even if it helped him in court. But as we got to know and trust each other and as he got some emotional distance from home, he would lament, "Why did I have to be born to my mom? Why couldn't I have had a different mom?"

The other thing Jamal would say is, "I'm a good person. I didn't mean to hurt anyone."

I suggested earlier that sex offender clients are not always easy to like, that sometimes it is hard to connect with their humanity. Let me explain what I mean. It is not true that all these clients are unlikeable. Aside from Jamal, I also like another teen (now well into adulthood and serving a long sentence) who forced his way into the home of his victim and raped her in front of her boyfriend. Maybe they are made more sympathetic by their youth at the time of the crime, the length of time I have known them, or the fact that I have genuinely gotten to know them.

I've liked other sex offenders as well. But in thirty-plus years of defending the accused and convicted, I have also found that this group of clients might be more flawed, damaged, or "broken" than other types of clients—and are, as a result, harder to connect with.

Over the years, I have felt frightened by only a very small handful of clients. Most of these have been accused or convicted of violent offenses, often of a sexual nature. Usually, I can get past these feelings and establish some level of trust and rapport. But not always. I once represented a man accused of an especially brutal child sexual assault. He was so angry and hostile—especially toward women—it was hard to find something to talk about that might make him appear less so in front of the jury. I finally hit on fishing—something I had never done and had no interest in—but it seemed to stir a pleasant memory for him, softening his facial expression. I confess that I derived some pleasure from the fact that the prosecutor, defense lawyer, and judge were all women.

I don't mean to suggest that these clients lack humanity. But I might have to seek out their humanity more deliberately, make a study of it. Sometimes this requires substantial digging: What happened to this person to so damage him? How did he become a rapist? Who else is he?

My feminist stance—if it has not been made clear so far—includes recognition of the complexity of the entire issue. As Professor Paul Butler has written in a somewhat related context, "All I am saying is that the shit's complex."[58] As Professor Elizabeth Schneider has urged, feminism should account for the true complexity of women's lives and choices; it should reject simplistic narratives and dichotomies and "learn to accept contradiction, ambiguity, and ambivalence in women's lives, and explore more 'grays' in our conceptions of women's experience."[59]

I am deliberately not aligning myself with any particular feminist camp or theory. My commitment to feminism in this context is decidedly "big tent." My hope is that the feminism I have in mind is better revealed through an honest account of my criminal defense experience than through an elaborate, heavily theorized feminist criminal defense claim. One can be a feminist—in a deep and broad sense—and zealously defend people who are accused or convicted of sex crimes.

I am not suggesting that it is better for women and girls who have been sexually assaulted to have me, a woman and feminist, defending the accused. I do not see myself as some kind of "undercover sister" making the process better for women. I acknowledge that my gender and feminism are helpful to my clients in these cases, adding a certain credibility.

On the other hand, it is not always an either/or proposition. I recently tried a child rape case with a postgraduate fellow. The complainant was a thirteen-year-old girl; the accused was the twenty-year-old brother of the complainant's maternal uncle by marriage. The girl liked to spend time at her aunt and uncle's house playing the military-themed video game *Call of Duty*, often with our client. He was accused of climbing on top of her as she slept on the living room floor, touching her breasts, pulling down her pants, and having anal intercourse with her. There were no threats or other physical violence. Neither the complainant nor our client made a sound except for "heavy breathing." Afterward, he got up, washed himself, and went to sleep. She did the same. She remained in the same room as our client, who slept on the couch, even though her aunt was upstairs. A few days later she gave her mother a note in which she wrote, "I think I was raped." A few days after that, she and her mother went to the police station.

A colleague who stopped in to watch the trial thought the complainant was not especially appealing. She was heavy and wore her hair in small, tight dreadlocks in plaits around her head like a bowl. She didn't come across as fragile or vulnerable. Her account of what happened was peculiar.

The fellow and I found the complainant credible and compelling. She had an earnest, likeable personality. She put effort into her testimony, thinking hard before she spoke. She said that what our client did to her hurt—like she was being "stabbed in the butt"—and made her feel "dirty" and "nasty." When asked by the prosecutor what she thought of the defendant now, she said she had "no respect for him."

Our client denied he had done it. He did not know why the complainant was accusing him. Our defense was that the complainant was troubled: the eldest of eight children born to a single mother, she barely attended school and was often dumped either at her aunt's house to babysit the aunt's small children or at other relatives' houses. She had made up the story for attention; our client was the fall guy. (We would have liked to have blamed the uncle, but he was away at the time of the alleged incident.)

The case was triable because the complainant had given several different accounts of what happened, different enough to be called inconsistent. There were no physical injuries to corroborate forcible anal penetration. There was no change in her behavior to suggest something traumatic had happened. Some of her actions seemed implausible: staying in the same room with her assailant, not telling anyone right away, remaining in the house for several nights thereafter. The mother's delay in contacting the police and taking her to the hospital seemed to convey her own skepticism of her daughter's account.

Our client had a minimal criminal record and was out on bail. The prosecution had been unwilling to offer a plea to anything less than sexual assault requiring registration as a sex offender. Our client wanted to go to trial.

When it came time for closing arguments—at which we were going to argue strongly that the complaining witness had made the whole thing up and was unworthy of belief—the girl returned to the courtroom. The prosecutor did nothing. We approached the bench to request the court's intervention. We said that we understood the public's right to attend the proceedings but thought it would be needlessly hurtful for the complainant to hear the defense argument. The judge called the girl's mother up. She explained what the defense argument would entail and suggested it might be better for the complainant to return for the verdict instead. The mom agreed.

I worried later that I might have stepped too far outside my role. Was I an ambivalent feminist defense lawyer unnerved by a girl whom I believed to have been sexually victimized? Had I spent too much time reading rape memoirs? Was I being hypersensitive? My professional obligation was to my client, not to the complainant. Did I betray my client by looking after the complainant too?

I hope that I was motivated by simple humanity and that any thoughtful lawyer—defense or prosecutor, whether a complainant is lying or telling the truth—would protect a child from hearing a lawyer call her a troubled liar in court. I might have been protecting the fellow who was about to make that argument too.

Our client cried when he was convicted and was immediately taken into custody. He asked whether this meant he had to register as a "child molester." This was not a case where I took comfort in a conviction, even though I found the complainant credible. It is a terrible feeling for a client to come to court free and leave *not*. Moreover, I regarded the whole case as a tragedy that could have been prevented. If our client did it, it was a crime of opportunity and impulse. He looked younger than his age, was quiet and shy, and didn't seem to have much of a life outside of his brother's family. His parents were both dead. He should never have been sleeping in a room with a teenage girl. If *anal* sex actually occurred, I am not even convinced this was what our sexually inexperienced client had intended. Nor am I convinced that our client posed any danger of raping again.

This was a difficult case on many levels.

I doubt I'll get to Feminist Heaven.

•

Rape and race are deeply interconnected in the American criminal justice system. It is hard to talk about rape without contemplating the history of racism in the enforcement of rape law.

For much of this nation's history, it was not a crime to rape a black woman. As the property of white men, enslaved black women were essentially "unrapable"; they were objects of pleasure and profit. In the post–Civil War period and up until fairly recently, black women were still largely seen as sexual objects—incapable of refusing sex, promiscuous, up for grabs.[60]

Meanwhile, black men were seen as sexual predators—especially of white women. Black men's supposed propensity to rape white women became the pretext for thousands of brutal lynchings in the South.[61] The violent black male rapist remains an iconic image in the public imagination and popular culture. One need look no further than the so-called Willie Horton case, in which a black man was convicted of rape while on a prison furlough. The case—and the way it was exploited—cost Democratic candidate Michael Dukakis the presidency in 1988.[62]

Until the latter part of the twentieth century, the rape of a white woman by a black man was considered a capital offense in many states, while the rape of a black woman was hardly punished. Black men convicted of raping white women still receive the harshest sentences and media attention, while men convicted of raping black women typically receive more lenient sentences.[63]

This too is a feminist motivation for defending an accused sex offender, the best example of which is the amicus brief filed by a number of feminist organizations in *Coker v. Georgia*, the U.S. Supreme Court case that barred the death penalty for rape.[64] The organizations on the brief were the American Civil Liberties Union, the Center for Constitutional Rights, the National Organization for Women Legal Defense and Education Fund, the Women's Law Project, the Center for Women Policy Studies, the Women's Legal Defense Fund, and Equal Rights Advocates, Inc. The first-listed author is current United States Supreme Court justice Ruth Bader Ginsburg. The brief acknowledges the history of rape prosecutions as both racist and sexist in arguing against capital punishment in rape cases.[65]

The fact that Jamal is black and the Minnesota victim white might have played a role in his prosecution, conviction, and sentence. Jamal was no longer a troubled child in need of treatment, but a sexually violent adult black man (who was tried before an all-white jury, reflecting the demographics of the upper Midwest). But there were other factors at play as well—chief among them that Jamal had done this before. The prior DC crime—an armed rape of a stranger—was arguably more serious than the Minnesota crime, notwithstanding the fact that the former was "black on black." Not surprisingly, Jamal received a heavy sentence for that offense. He will not be a free man until he is well into middle age.

•

Jamal's story isn't really about guilt or innocence. It isn't really about the system. One could argue that the criminal justice system worked in Jamal's case because he was well represented in both DC and Minnesota. He had a meaningful "day in court."

Jamal's case is complex and tragic for reasons that are difficult to capture. I knew Jamal about as well as anyone when he was a boy. He did some dreadful things. But there was more to him than his criminal conduct, more than a prosecutor's angry exhortation at sentencing. He always greeted me with a hug. He could be funny even under dire circumstances. He was generous and forgiving no matter how people failed him—his mother, his lawyers, the staff at the residential program in Minnesota.

Jamal was not born to be a rapist. Something terrible happened to him.

Minnesota has an inmate locating system on the internet. It features current photographs of prisoners and basic information about their crimes, sentences, and release dates. You type in the inmate's name and date of birth—and suddenly a face appears.

I was stunned the first time I saw Jamal on my computer screen. I hadn't seen him in a few years. He was no longer a boy. He had filled out and had facial hair. A tattoo of a teardrop was under each eye.

I try not to go on that website. I prefer to remember him young and hopeful.

4

Murderers

———————————————◆○▶

Here in prison you quickly learn you can't judge a person by their crime.

Things happen. Bad circumstances lead to bad choices.

Plus, it turns out that the most unscrupulous and unlikable people sometimes commit the least serious crime...

While decent and likable people sometimes commit the most serious crime.

All of which explains why you can't judge a person by their crime:

Some of my best friends are murderers.

© auuuu 7/29/16

"Ronnie" was sixteen when he got kicked out of school for the second time. First, the local public school had given him the boot and now the private Christian school. His father would be furious. He had forked over a lot of tuition just for Ronnie to be expelled yet again.

Ronnie had to get away. He grabbed his dad's hunting rifle and headed next door. The neighbor's car was in the driveway. He figured she'd give up the keys when she saw the gun. When she refused, Ronnie shot her. He pulled the trigger again and again. The mother of two died instantly. Her five-year-old daughter saw the whole thing and ran to her bedroom to hide. Ronnie followed her and shot twice at her door.

When the girl thought it was over, she managed to call 911. "Please come," she said. "My mommy is dead."

Ronnie was caught several hours later at his grandfather's house, some two hundred miles away. Several shotguns, a camouflage outfit, a metal helmet, an iron cross, a swastika pin, and a copy of William Shirer's *The Rise and Fall of the Third Reich* were found in the car. When the police asked why he had done it, Ronnie said, "She laughed at me."

His trial lasted only a few days. The jury wept when the little girl testified. She held her father's hand as she recounted what happened. Ronnie's parents sat just outside the courtroom during the trial. They held hands and read the Bible with other family members.

The jury rejected an insanity defense. They convicted Ronnie of murder, attempted murder, and car theft and sentenced him to life in prison.

•

At fifteen, "Tamika" was immature, impetuous, and in love. When her mother teased her that she wasn't old enough to be in love, she shot back, "I'm plenty old." Besides, she pointed out, her mother had had a baby at fourteen. Tamika knew she and Tyrone could have a baby too if they weren't careful.

When Tamika saw Tyrone coming out of his house with her sixteen-year-old cousin Jazmine, his arm around her, she couldn't believe it—not her Tyrone. Not Jaz, who was family (if a distant cousin). She confronted them. Jaz looked guilty. Tyrone just shrugged.

A few hours later, she went back to Tyrone's to get the things she had left there. She had a knife because she always carried one. The neighborhood was rough.

Jaz was still at Tyrone's. They argued. When the argument turned physical, Jaz grabbed a baseball bat, Tamika her knife. Jaz struck Tamika in the head and arm, and Tamika stabbed Jaz once near her shoulder. Tamika was still sputtering with anger when the police came. She asked whether Jazmine was dead. "If she ain't dead yet, I hope she will be soon," she said.

The prosecutor made a big deal of those words at Tamika's murder trial. He said it showed that Tamika was a cold-blooded killer. Tamika testified that she had acted in self-defense. The jury didn't buy it. They convicted her of first-degree murder and sentenced her to life in prison.

•

"Delores" was a familiar sight at the local hospital emergency room. She would arrive in tears, carrying a dead, or nearly dead, baby. In the past few years, she had buried three babies, all under the age of two. To most of the hospital staff, Delores was a tragic figure who kept losing babies to Sudden Infant Death Syndrome (SIDS). But others took a less charitable view.

She was arrested shortly after the fourth baby, Kimberly Ann, was buried. The local prosecutor didn't believe in babies just dying. He believed that Delores was a serial child murderer. He rejected the idea that she had a mental illness, like postpartum depression or even Munchausen Syndrome by Proxy (a pattern of behavior in which caregivers exaggerate, fabricate, or induce health problems in others). He believed Delores did it for attention.

The month-long trial was hard fought. Expert witnesses for the prosecution and defense painted different pictures of how the six-month-old died. Delores was convicted of murder and sentenced to life.

•

After dropping out of high school, "James" tried a vocational school but couldn't stop wanting the street. He liked the money and "street cred" that came with selling drugs. He had done some things he wasn't exactly proud of and had done some jail time, but that came with the territory.

He can't remember the details of the stabbing—or doesn't want to. The prosecution accused him and another man of beating and stabbing a woman to death as payback for failing to warn a drug runner that the police were coming. The woman, a mother of three, was a crack cocaine user who sometimes worked for the same people he did. She tried to stagger home after the attack but collapsed on the stairs to her basement apartment.

He took his lawyer's advice, pled guilty to murder, and was sentenced to life in prison.

•

These are the kinds of cases that prompt what is known in criminal defense circles as the Cocktail Party Question, or simply "the Question": "How can you defend those people?" When people ask this, they are not referring to shoplifters, marijuana possessors, or drunk drivers. They are also not talking about the wrongly accused or convicted. The Question refers instead to the representation of people who have committed serious acts of violence or depravity—like a "bad seed" armed with a gun who kills his neighbor; an angry girl armed with a knife who kills another girl; an "unnatural" mother who kills her own babies; an inner-city thug who kills as payback. Why spend one second on these murderers, much less advocate on their behalf?

Ronnie, Tamika, Delores, and James all committed terrible crimes and perhaps the most terrible type of crime of all: murder. Ronnie's presentence report, which contained victim impact statements from the husband, children, and parents of the woman he killed, was agonizing to read. Their anguish was palpable. Ronnie destroyed a family.

The others destroyed families too. Tamika took a mother's only daughter. James deprived three small children of their mother, casting them into the foster care system. Delores killed a defenseless infant.

As Ta-Nehisi Coates has argued in a somewhat different context, no murder is banal; the brutal and senseless loss of life is no less painful simply because it may happen more frequently in some communities.[1] I once represented a relatively privileged white man accused of killing a homeless, mentally ill African American man. The homeless man had a substantial criminal history, had been living on the streets for years, and was estranged from family. Even so, his sister howled with grief as I began my closing argument, and had to be escorted from the courtroom.

I have represented young African American men who killed other young African American men. Most had been involved in the criminal justice system, as had their victims. The families of the decedents—and of the defendants—were no less devastated simply because their loved one had a criminal history.

The impact of a murder ripples through both family and community. The trauma lingers long after the crime. As one commentator observes, "Homicide grief may be a kind of living death. Survivors slog on, diminished, disfigured by loss and incomprehension."[2]

My partner Sally's first cousin—a wife, mother, and daughter who worked as a financial advisor to the elderly—was shot to death in a Minneapolis courthouse by a deranged female relative who believed the cousin was stealing from her. The cousin's lawyer was also shot but survived. The family has never been the same.

As a matter of law and morality, murder—generally defined as the unlawful and deliberate killing of one human being by another—stands alone. In the United States, with the exception of treason, the death penalty is reserved for certain kinds of murder only.[3] These include especially heinous killings, killings with multiple victims, contract killing, murder during another violent felony, murder by a repeat felony offender, or a murder in which the victim was a police officer, firefighter, elderly person, or child.

Murder is prohibited by the Ten Commandments for Jews and Christians (the Christian Bible proclaims "Thou shalt not kill," while the Jewish Bible tends to use the word *murder*), by the Quran for Muslims (especially killing an "innocent"), by the first of the Five Precepts (Pancasila) for Buddhists (one must not "destroy living creatures"), and by the Laws of Manu for Hindus ("He who commits murder must be considered as the worst offender").[4]

The victims of Ronnie, Tamika, Delores, and James's crimes are somewhat unusual, in that they were all female and two were children. Although cases involving women, children, and victims of mass shootings tend to receive media attention, these are not the bulk of murder victims in the United States. Instead, they comprise a mere 6 percent of the population, while black men make up nearly 40 percent of murder victims.[5] As reporter Jill Leovy writes in her excellent book *Ghettoside*, "Homicide has ravaged the country's black population for a century or more.... Every day, in every city, their bodies stacking up by the thousands, year after year."[6] Sadly, homicide remains the number-one cause of death for African American men between the ages of fifteen and thirty-four.[7]

I did not represent Ronnie and the others at trial. They had already spent many years in prison by the time I got involved. Because the bulk of Georgetown's Criminal Defense & Prisoner Advocacy Clinic's work is representing indigent defendants at trial—a demanding enough undertaking—we take on only a handful of prisoners. I confess that the criteria for taking on prisoner cases are somewhat arbitrary: some clients are referred to us by criminal defense or prisoners' rights groups, some by other clients. But mostly, we "meet" these clients through correspondence.

Prisoners are often excellent correspondents. Some write beautifully. Necessity is the mother of invention here, and letters are how prisoners connect with much of the outside world. As everyone else tweets, texts, Skypes, and Facetimes, prisoners are part of an ever-dwindling group of letter writers (along with children at summer camp and grandmothers).

A prisoner letter is easily recognized by the plain white envelope, prisoner number, and prison acronym (usually FCI for federal correctional institutions or SCI for state correctional institutions) and the dense, painstakingly neat penmanship that frequently fills entire pages.

The clinic receives a lot of mail from prisoners. Although the volume can be taxing, I believe we have a duty to reply. They are incarcerated, and we are not.

I have prison pen pals: a handful of longtime prisoners with whom I regularly correspond. Most are not, and have never been, actual clients for one reason or another. A few weeks before the 2016 presidential election, I received a letter from one of my favorite correspondents, a lifer who has served more than twenty-five years. The letter began by wishing me a happy Jewish New Year and inquiring about my work in the clinic and my writing. He then shared his thoughts on the changes he had witnessed in prison over the past quarter century, the evolution of the "war on drugs," and the election. He wrote that, if he could, he would vote for Bernie Sanders for president, because Sanders "understands the root causes of our economic and social ills and knows what we need to do to get back on track." He feared, however, that "corporate America is not going to allow Sanders a chance."

He then offered his thoughts on terrorism and gun violence:

The national discussion has turned to terrorism. But, as the *New York Times* has reported, since 9/11, in this country, 45 deaths have been attributed to jihadist terrorism, 45 deaths have been attributed to white supremacist groups, and 200,000 deaths have been attributed to conventional homicides. Obviously, radicalized Islamists and skin heads are not the real problem. The availability of guns is the problem. . . . I ramble on about this purposely to raise one point: in the national discussion about violence, we need to separate the issues—police involved killings (your Trayvon Martins and Freddie Grays), black on black violence, crazy white kids shooting up schools, jihadist inspired terrorism, domestic terrorism (abortion clinics, etc.)—all of these have different components which can't be quantified by comparison. They each need to be discussed and corrected in their own context.

This was as thoughtful and well written as any op-ed I've read on these topics. He went on to share his favorite books, television shows, and music of the year. He had good taste, even though his exposure to popular culture was limited.

The prisoners represented by the clinic must be factually guilty, have served a long sentence, and have a good case for release. The truth is, I am especially drawn to the most difficult cases—violent crimes, from which most people recoil. These tend to be murders and rapes rather than non-violent drug offenses. It is not that drug offenders—some of whom are serving absurdly long sentences—are not sympathetic or compelling. But they have had plenty of supporters lately, including prosecutors, defense lawyers, and politicians from across the ideological spectrum.[8]

It may be cliché to say that, many years later, my prisoner clients are very different from who they were at the time of their crimes. But incarceration changes people, as does time. Ronnie and Tamika were children at the time of their crimes. They literally grew up in prison. Delores and James grew old in prison.

Moreover, there has always been more to them than their crimes.

•

In some ways, Ronnie is the most inscrutable of the lot. Before he picked up that shotgun, he had never been in trouble with the law. He had had no contact with juvenile court, much less adult criminal court. He was not unduly interested in guns. He and his brothers went hunting with his dad, but these were family excursions, not celebrations of killing.

He was awkward and anxious. Kids at school called him names. He had few friends and mostly kept to himself. Girls never looked at him twice.

He didn't mean to get in trouble in school but couldn't seem to help it. When kids mocked him, he did stupid stuff—drew obscene pictures, spray-painted graffiti—for which he inevitably got caught. He tried to look tough, as if nothing mattered to him. He wore a swastika on his jacket even though he didn't really know what a Nazi was.

Every time there is a shooting by a disaffected young white man—a school, church, or theater shooting—it is bad for Ronnie. This is so, even though Ronnie's crime is different from these other shootings and happened well before the 1999 shooting at Columbine High School near Littleton, Colorado, and more than a quarter-century before the 2012 shooting at Sandy Hook Elementary School in Newtown, Connecticut. But to a parole board, Ronnie seems cut from the same cloth.

In an interesting article in the *New Yorker*, Malcolm Gladwell suggests that the phenomenon of white boys shooting up schools and churches comes from a "cultural script" that originated with Columbine. The two Columbine shooters, Eric Harris and Dylan Klebold, had a website. They wrote manifestos, recorded their "basement tapes," and made home movies in which they starred as hit men. Harris proclaimed that he wanted to "kick-start a revolution." Gladwell says that most of the mass shootings in the United States after Columbine were inspired by that event; subsequent shooters have joined the revolution.[9]

Although Gladwell acknowledges that it is nearly impossible to construct a profile that describes all or even most school shooters, he suggests that at least some might have had a mild to moderate autism spectrum disorder, or what until recently was called Asperger's syndrome.[10] The disorder is characterized by difficulties with social interaction (including an impaired ability to read social cues), narrow interests, and restricted and repetitive patterns of behavior.

But Ronnie was awkward, not autistic.

Moreover, the crime happened well before the internet. Ronnie has never surfed the web for mass shootings or right-wing extremism. He did not play violent videogames or obsessively view pornography.

When he grabbed the gun, he did not intend to fire it; he wanted it for leverage. When he pulled the trigger—once, twice, five times in all—it felt like it was happening to someone else, not him.

I met Ronnie after he had served twenty-eight years in a maximum-security prison. He was forty-four years old. He hadn't seen a lawyer in a quarter of a century. Legal fees had taken his parents' savings. Ronnie told me he had written 1,200 letters to lawyers over the years. He didn't know why he kept count.

He had been badly brutalized during the first years of his incarceration. He was then held in protective custody. After that, he made a couple of friends and learned to cope with prison life.

I saw Ronnie because a prison buddy of his wrote to me about him. This was touching: one prisoner writing about how another guy could really use a lawyer.

When I first met Ronnie, he still looked sixteen: a middle-aged teenager. His face was soft, his skin unlined and unweathered. Of course, he had barely experienced weather. He was also untattooed, an unusual thing for a white male prisoner, especially an alleged neo-Nazi. He worked in the prison factory making blue jeans, prison uniforms, and license plates.

I asked whether he had many visitors. He said his two brothers visited once a year on "family day." His mother used to come, but she had moved away some years ago and now keeps in touch mostly through letters. Phone calls are expensive, he explained. His father died shortly after he went to prison. An uncle writes to him regularly and visits when he can.

We talked about the crime, but only because Ronnie seemed to want to. He wanted me to know how sorry he was. He still cannot believe that he did what he did. He would give anything to take it back.

I told him the clinic would do what we could to help him but cautioned against being too hopeful. It was a difficult case. He understood and was grateful.

•

Tamika wrote a letter to the clinic asking for help. She said she was thirty-nine years old and had been in prison since she was fifteen for killing another girl over a boy. She had had three parole hearings and been denied each time.

I asked her to write again, sharing more about herself—her childhood and early adolescence, the crime, the trial, and her time in prison. "Dear Madam/Sir," she wrote, not knowing whether I was a man or woman. She thanked me for my interest in her case. Then she conscientiously replied to my list of questions.

Tamika was raised by her maternal grandmother. Her parents were teenagers when she was born, her mother barely fourteen and her father a couple of years older. For a time, her parents lived with her grandmother too. Then they moved out, lived on their own for several years, and had two more daughters. Tamika stayed with her grandmother. When she was nine, her parents separated, and her mother and sisters moved in with her and her grandmother.

Tamika recalled these early years as happy, especially when she lived alone with her grandmother, her "first best friend." Tamika felt safe and loved under her grandmother's care.

She described a stormy relationship with her mother, who was a drug user—heroin and crack cocaine. Her father both used and sold drugs.

Tamika's mother was not happy to move back in with her own mother. There were angry scenes about house rules. Tamika's mother insisted she was "grown" and could do as she pleased. "Not if you're living in my house," the grandmother said. Tamika's mother took out her unhappiness on Tamika. She beat her for the smallest infraction. When her grandmother discovered welts on Tamika, she kicked her daughter out.

Tamika was eleven when she found her grandmother's lifeless body on the living room couch. She tried to rouse her. "Please wake up, Grandma," Tamika cried. "Don't leave me."

After her grandmother died, she went to live with her mother and sisters. She immediately began to have problems. She was disobedient at home. She skipped school and got in fights. By the time she was twelve, she was smoking cigarettes, drinking beer, and had had sex with a boy. Her mother "disciplined" her with whatever she could get her hands on—a broom handle, a large wooden spoon, a belt. Tamika called the police after an especially bad beating and was placed in a juvenile shelter home. She was ultimately returned to her mother. On another occasion, Tamika was sent to a psychiatric hospital. By the time she was fourteen, she was drinking hard alcohol, smoking marijuana (and sometimes crack), and having sex with older boys. "It was like I was throwing myself away," Tamika wrote.

She often lay awake at night wondering why her cousin Jaz had to die. Why couldn't they just stitch her up? She admitted that, back then, she liked to fight. But she only meant to cut Jaz, not kill her. Tamika thought of the television cartoons she used to watch at her grandmother's house. An anvil would fall on a character, only to have them pop back up in the next frame. No cartoon character died and stayed dead.

Tamika went to trial on a self-defense theory, since she had been defending herself when she pulled out her knife. Plus, the only alternative was to plead guilty for a twenty-year sentence. She must have been high or still in a rage when she told the police she hoped Jaz would die soon if she wasn't dead already. She was embarrassed about this.

She never saw or heard from Tyrone again, except when he testified against her at trial.

Tamika wrote about how frightened she was to be held in a women's prison after her arrest. She was called a "boarder" because she was being held before trial. At first, she was not allowed to interact with other prisoners and was kept in a separate wing. She was not well behaved. She cried and yelled, cursed at guards, and threw things.

She was so desperate for human contact that when she learned she could take classes she was thrilled. By the time she went to trial, she had obtained her GED. When Tamika turned sixteen and was allowed to live with other prisoners, an older woman took her under her wing and taught her how to cope with prison life. Tamika was grateful. The older inmate also showed her how to control her temper.[11]

Tamika remembered little of her trial, which only took a few days. Her court-appointed lawyer had been confident about her chances. He never told her she could receive a life sentence.

Tamika wrote:

I do regret what happened, and am deeply sorry for what I did. I've always taken responsibility for my actions, and never once denied my part. If I could change the past, I would. I made a bad decision, which changed my life. I had to learn that violence isn't the answer for any problem, that there is a better and more productive way to handle situations. . . .

I am not that 15-year-old who enjoyed fighting anymore. I am a 39-year-old mature adult. I'm hoping to one day be given a second chance to prove to society that I have changed.

•

Delores was the best friend of another client—the woman I mentioned in the introduction, who was released after having served many years in prison for a crime she didn't commit.[12] The two had been in prison together for twenty-four of those years.

A colleague asked me if I knew about the "One Friend" rule. I said no. I didn't know what she was talking about. She explained, "When you represent a woman prisoner and manage to get her out, you have to make clear that you are willing to represent one friend—and one friend only."

I laughed when I heard this. But she was right. Women prisoners tend to be loyal. My other client said she could not feel free while Delores was still in prison.

Delores was happily married but lonely. Her husband, Bill, worked a lot. When he wasn't working, he was at the bowling alley or on the golf course. Delores had few friends and was mostly at home.

Delores wanted kids but couldn't seem to have any. She got pregnant several times and gave birth without incident, but the babies died. She and Bill grieved each of their losses—separately, in their own ways—and tried again. Doctors told Delores she had a genetic predisposition for SIDS. She was arrested when she was still reeling from the loss of the last baby.

Delores did not testify at her trial. Her lawyer said the case was about the sufficiency of evidence and that since Delores was already on record pleading not guilty, there was no need to say more. When the jury found her guilty, she looked at her husband in dismay.

When Delores became eligible for release after twenty years, she appeared before the parole board. Despite the fact that baby killers are especially reviled in prison and targeted for ridicule and abuse, she had served her time well. She had participated in every program she could—educational, therapeutic, and religious. For most of the twenty years, she had worked in the prison hospital as a nurse's aide. A devout Catholic, she had also worked in the chaplain's office.

She was denied parole because she showed "too little emotion" at the hearing.

Two years later, she had her next hearing. She was now on the honors floor—a privilege given to a select group of inmates with exemplary disciplinary records. She was still working in the hospital and the chaplain's office. She had continued to participate in programs. Though she had learned to bury her feelings in order to endure her incarceration, she understood from the previous hearing that she needed to reveal more. When she did, a river of grief poured out of her.

She was denied parole because she showed "too much emotion."

I took on Delores's case after her second parole hearing. I did so partly for my previous client but also because this was the kind of case I was after: a long-serving prisoner convicted of a serious crime who had done her time but might never get out.

Her account of her previous parole hearings also struck a chord: it was straight out of *The Shawshank Redemption*. In the movie, Red (played by Morgan Freeman) appears before the parole board and is routinely denied parole no matter what he says or how many years he serves. After every hearing, the word "DENIED" is stamped on his file. Finally, after forty years, the board grants him parole:

PAROLE HEARINGS MAN: Ellis Boyd Redding, your files say you've served forty
    years of a life sentence. Do you feel you've been rehabilitated?
RED: Rehabilitated? Well, now let me see. You know, I don't have any idea what
    that means.

PAROLE HEARINGS MAN: Well, it means that you're ready to rejoin society.

RED: I know what you think it means, sonny. To me it's just a made up word. A politician's word, so young fellas like yourself can wear a suit and a tie, and have a job. What do you really want to know? Am I sorry for what I did?

PAROLE HEARINGS MAN: Well, are you?

RED: There's not a day goes by I don't feel regret. Not because I'm in here, or because you think I should. I look back on the way I was then: a young, stupid kid who committed that terrible crime. I want to talk to him. I want to try and talk some sense to him, tell him the way things are. But I can't. That kid's long gone and this old man is all that's left. I got to live with that. Rehabilitated? It's just a bullshit word. So you go on and stamp your form, sonny, and stop wasting my time. Because to tell you the truth, I don't give a shit.[13]

I thought it was cruel of the parole board to stir up Delores's hopes by giving her a hearing every two years, only to deny release.

I was also moved to take Delores's case because her husband, Bill—who has stood by her all these years—paid a lawyer more than $50,000 to draft a letter to the parole board. Not only did the lawyer bill for her time; she charged for every soda and candy bar she shared with Delores during the few times they met. One itemized bill included fifty cents for half a Snickers bar. It made me feel ashamed of my profession.

We put together a parole petition and prepared Delores for the hearing, pushing her to dig deep on tough questions so the board would see she was capable of insight. We talked about "dissociation"—a state of emotional detachment triggered by trauma—which might explain why she had no clear recollection of what she was doing at the time of the baby's death. We helped her articulate what might have been going on.

This time, Delores was denied parole because she "posed a danger to society" and her release would "diminish the seriousness of her crime." Of course, these were the factors underlying the sentence she was already serving.

We appealed the parole board's decision. The appeal was denied. Other unsuccessful parole hearings and appeals followed.

•

James pled guilty to murder. He regretted his crime. He knew the woman he killed; he had once bought presents for her kids. He says it all happened so fast: a buddy picked him up saying there was trouble, they confronted the woman and a man on the street, a fight broke out, James pulled out his knife, there was a lot of blood.

James had considered going to trial. However, not only would several eyewitnesses have identified him and his codefendant—the incident happened in broad daylight—but the prosecution would have offered evidence of their prior crimes, including a prior beating of the dead woman for stealing drug money. It wouldn't have gone well.

James apologized to the woman's family and his own at the sentencing hearing. His mother and grandmother wept as he was led off in shackles.

He served twenty-five years before he got out. Most of his sentence was served at a remote prison hours away from family and community. He tried to make use of the time by reading, writing, and thinking. He found God but was quiet about it. As the years passed, he felt less and less like the callous young man who committed the crime. His favorite movie is *The Shawshank Redemption*; his favorite passage, when Red speaks about wanting to talk sense to his younger self.

Some say there are only two days in prison: the day you go in and the day you get out. Others, like James, feel every single second of their sentence.[14] "Doing time" can be literal; for many prisoners, the passage of time is all that is happening. When James faced the panel of officials who would decide whether he would be released, he said he wasn't sure he was worthy. He told them he would live with his crime for the rest of his life, whether or not he was free.

•

Ronnie, Tamika, Delores, and James happen to be convicted prisoners serving lengthy sentences instead of defendants facing trial, but I would have happily represented them at trial. Sometimes I wish I *had* represented them at trial.

Once convicted, it is very hard to get a person out of prison. This is true whether the person has gone to trial or pled guilty. The presumption of innocence only exists at trial; it is long gone by the time a convicted person files an appeal or appears before a parole board. In its place is a presumption of "finality."

Finality means that once a case is decided, it should stay decided. To accomplish this, there is enormous deference to the verdicts of judges and juries. Once a conviction is obtained, the system does everything it can to preserve and perpetuate it.

Finality is so important that one former state high court judge, Harvard law professor Charles Fried, claimed that it trumped factual innocence.[15] In other words, a wrongly convicted and imprisoned person should stay locked up so that the rest of us can feel that when a case is over, it's over.

Then-justice Fried wrote about the importance of finality in connection with a notorious Massachusetts day care child sex abuse case, *Commonwealth v. Amirault*, at a time when it was becoming clear that this particular case—along with similar cases in California, New Jersey, and North Carolina—were witch hunts with no basis in truth.[16] The family that had run the day care center—Violet Amirault; her daughter, Cheryl; and her son, Gerald—had all been convicted of ritualized sex abuse at the Fells Acres Daycare Center in Malden, Massachusetts. Fried wrote for the majority of the Supreme Judicial Court:

> The condemnation and punishments of the criminal justice system are awesome and devastating. That is why their imposition is hedged about with presumptions and procedural safeguards that heavily weight the risk of error in favor of the accused and are designed to assure both the appearance and the reality that the accused had every fair opportunity of defense. But once the process has run its course—through pretrial motions, trial, posttrial motions and one or two levels of appeal—the community's interest in finality comes to the fore. The regular course of justice may be long, but it must not be endless. . . . When a serious crime has been committed, the victims and survivors, witnesses, and the public have an interest that the guilty not only be punished but that the community express its condemnation with firmness and confidence. . . . The mere fact that, if the process were redone, there might be a different outcome, or that some lingering doubt about the first outcome may remain, cannot be a sufficient reason to reopen what society has a right to consider closed.[17]

Fried and the other members of the court acknowledge that the sudden and peculiar outbreak of child sex abuse cases in day care centers in the 1980s raised serious questions about the suggestibility of child witnesses and the credibility of their testimony. They even admitted their own doubts about the veracity of witness statements in the Amirault cases, writing, "We recognize that some of the children's statements included charges that were quite improbable."[18] Still, the court denied a new trial and reinstated convictions that had been overturned.

•

Ronnie is now in his fifties. He clings to memories of life before prison. Small, insignificant moments have become precious: walking in the field near his house, Christmas dinner, taking a bath. He longs for quiet—a place without the constant din of men speaking, shouting, snoring. He has gotten used to the sounds of surveillance: the clang of metal doors opening and shutting, the clinking of keys, and constant announcements over the PA system.

Ronnie has spent nearly forty Christmases in prison. This makes me think of a John Prine song, "Christmas in Prison," in which an inmate laments the loneliness of incarceration at Christmastime, notwithstanding the special food.[19]

In a memoir about the eight years he served for a carjacking he committed when he was sixteen, Yale Law graduate Dwayne Betts also writes about Christmas in prison and notes that being incarcerated at Christmas is especially hard for a young person. Betts recalls,

> The first cellmate I ever had was Peanut. He told me he'd spent the past five or six Christmases in a cell. Not that he'd been locked up for five years, just that the holiday season seemed to always find him in a cage. Nothing but a kid like me, but spending just as much time in a cell as at home. For fighting, for not going to school. Little stuff that you'd think someone would have helped him deal with all the time he spent locked up.[20]

Like the others, Ronnie is a model inmate. He takes college-level classes and participates in Bible study. But the parole system in the state where he is imprisoned is especially arcane. Ronnie has had only two hearings before the parole board. We submitted a thick petition documenting Ronnie's accomplishments in prison, his good behavior, and his plan to live with his two brothers if released. We urged the parole board to take note of the fact that Ronnie was only sixteen at the time of the crime and had no criminal record. We included letters of support from people who had worked with Ronnie in prison and family members who have kept in touch with him. We also included the latest research on brain development showing that the teenage brain is still developing, especially the part of the brain that controls impulses.

The parole board denied parole. Ronnie won't get another hearing for several years.

•

Over the last two decades, Tamika, who is now in her forties, has taken every course and participated in every program the prison has had to offer. She has a stack of degrees and certificates. She has taken college-level courses taught by professors from several local universities and colleges. She has been training seeing-eye dogs for nearly twenty years. She loves being part of this program, though it always breaks her heart to part from the dogs she has trained.

Tamika has rebuilt her relationship with her father, who got clean some years ago. She is glad to have him in her life. He sometimes disappoints—by not coming to see her as promised, not being the most diligent correspondent, and rarely putting money in her prison canteen account. She tries to accept him for who he is.

Tamika's mother is a changed person: she is drug-free, alcohol-free, and churchgoing. She is sorry she wasn't there for Tamika when Tamika needed her. She and Tamika have worked hard on their relationship. They are now close.

When we undertook Tamika's case, we developed an ambitious plan for obtaining parole: we would master the law of parole in that state, endeavor to figure out the politics there, and develop a list of tasks that would enable us to put together an effective petition. We would then reach out to people in positions of power to persuade them to support Tamika's release. (The clinic's prisoner advocacy consists largely of seeking parole or executive clemency. Except for parole appeals, we leave postconviction litigation to others.)

We wondered why Tamika was still locked up. It didn't make sense. If a fifteen-year-old one-time murderer, now a model inmate in her forties, wasn't worthy of parole, who was?

I consulted a law professor who had practiced criminal law in the state for many years. He suggested that I call the county prosecutor of the county where Tamika had been tried, someone whom the professor had taught in law school. The county is relatively small, the case memorable, and the prosecutor had been a public defender before working his way up in the prosecutor's office. The professor thought all this was promising. I was to drop the professor's name and assure the prosecutor that our conversation was off the record. This last thing was odd—I've never really understood what it means for something to be "off the record"—but I went along with it.

I hate making these kinds of calls. I have to rev myself up for the bowing and scraping that is a prerequisite for any meaningful help from people in power—all the while preparing myself for disappointment. After more than three decades of criminal defense, you'd think I'd be used to being rebuffed. I am used to it, but I don't especially like it.

On this occasion, I didn't give the call much thought. It was a Friday afternoon. I figured I'd leave a message with a secretary. Then I could think about exactly what I wanted to say—even prepare some notes—when the prosecutor called back the following week.

But the secretary put me right through to the prosecutor. He was friendly and seemed to get a kick out of me being a law professor. He wondered whether I was calling about jobs for my students. No, not on this occasion, I said—though I am always on the lookout for employment opportunities for students. We chatted amiably about the job market, made the connection about his former law school professor, and then I launched in.

I told him I was calling about Tamika's case and began to describe it. He interrupted me almost immediately. He said he knew the case well, because he had been the arresting officer. He had been a police officer before going to law school. In fact, he was the officer to whom Tamika had said she hoped the victim would die if she wasn't dead yet. He had been a key witness at her trial.

He was proud of his background—he had gone from being a regular patrol officer to a criminal lawyer to the county's chief prosecutor. He was the first former cop in the state to become a chief prosecutor. He said he'd been on every side of the criminal process—police officer, defender, prosecutor—and it gave him a broad perspective.

I agreed. I told him I appreciated his range of experience and, as a result, was hoping we could have a candid conversation. I started out gently. "Can we agree," I asked, "that this particular homicide is not the worst, most heinous crime you ever saw—it's a pretty ordinary homicide?" "Absolutely," he said, continuing, "It's an ordinary homicide by a very young person." I was relieved to hear it. "Are you surprised that Tamika is still in prison?" I asked. "Dumbfounded," he said. "We all figured she'd get out after around eight years."

This was my opening. If you thought eight years was enough back then, might you be willing to help me get Tamika out now—or at least not stand in the way? I asked. He said he wouldn't stand in the way but that he didn't feel he could actively help. What if the victim's family doesn't oppose release? I asked. That would make it easier for me to be more helpful, he replied.

We had a clear goal now.

•

For better or worse, homicide is an ordinary crime, at least in the United States. It occurs with alarming frequency in some jurisdictions—Detroit, Memphis, Oakland, St. Louis, Birmingham, Milwaukee, Baltimore, Cleveland, Stockton, Indianapolis.[21] In recent years, cities that had managed to reduce the killings have experienced rising murder rates: Chicago, New York, Baltimore, Philadelphia, New Orleans, Milwaukee, and Washington, DC.[22] Homicide is simply a fact of life in some places.

Firearms play an outsized role. Some 70 percent of homicides are committed with guns—usually semiautomatic ones.[23] These are essentially killing machines; it's hard to miss when you're spraying bullets. I have often thought that the difference between assault and murder—between a client doing a few years and doing life—is luck and inches. This is especially so with firearms. But it is also true of stabbings, the second most common form of homicide.

There were approximately twelve thousand murders in the United States in 2014.[24] Homicide is typically associated with gang violence, drug turf wars, "dispute resolution by gun," a "robbery gone bad," or loss of control due to momentary anger, fear, jealousy, or vengefulness. However, there are, of course, more sinister examples—murder as a hate crime, murder as a form of terrorism, murder-rape, and especially vicious killings.

When I was a young law professor, I represented a woman who survived a homicidal hate crime: a homophobic attack on the Appalachian Trail. (She was not a criminal defendant but rather a victim of crime, which was unusual for me.) She and her girlfriend, both experienced hikers, decided to set up camp for the night in a remote spot. They didn't know they were being followed by a man they had encountered earlier. He watched as they made love and then started shooting at them with a single-gauge shotgun. My client was struck in the face and neck five times but managed to make her way out of the woods in the dark in order to flag down help. Before setting out, she made a tourniquet for her girlfriend, who had been struck twice in the back and couldn't move. The girlfriend slowly bled to death.

The man didn't know these women. They had done nothing to him. He meant to kill them simply because they were gay.[25]

I have also defended people accused of hate crimes. Once, I represented a white woman charged with participating in a mob that set upon and beat a small group of African Americans whose car had broken down in a working-class white neighborhood. One of the African American women in the group had pleaded with my client, "one woman to another," to help stop the attack. My client responded by shoving the other woman down.

Later, I had as a client a young man who stabbed an openly gay teenager after calling him a "faggot."

Neither of these clients saw themselves as racist or homophobic. They just got carried away in the moment.

There are some murders so cruel and depraved they could never be called "ordinary." I think of abduction-captivity-rape-murder cases, especially brutal child abuse murders, and murder featuring gratuitous cruelty or torture. It is hard not to feel revulsion toward the perpetrators.

Sadly, there are as many ordinary murderers as depraved ones on death rows throughout the country. This is one of the problems with capital punishment. Although we profess to do so, we do not reserve the "ultimate punishment" for the worst of the worst. Prosecutors too often charge indiscriminately; all murder becomes capital murder. Jurors—especially after being "death qualified" (not opposed to capital punishment)—offer little resistance.

Moreover, there is a story behind even those who commit the most depraved murders.[26] Very few murderers were born as such.

•

We decided to reach out to Jazmine's mother. With help from our chief investigator, we found out where she was living. We also learned a few things about her: she was an African American woman in her midsixties, she lived alone, and she was active in her local church. In keeping with how we generally conduct investigations, we decided to pay her a visit without alerting her first by phone or mail. People tend to be nicer when approached in person.

I chose two people for this critical assignment: a very able clinic student who had been working on Tamika's case and the clinic office manager, who had urged me to take Tamika's case from the start and was eager to take on more responsibility in the clinic's prisoner work. Both were African

American women, one in her midtwenties and the other her midfifties. Both were appealing—the student because of her youth and sincerity and the office manager because of her maturity and faith. These qualities would be helpful in a conversation about forgiveness.

The two set out early in the morning and drove several hours to the address we had for Jazmine's mother. She wasn't home. They called me. I urged them to hang tight, go get lunch, but keep a lookout. Investigation takes time and patience.

We were lucky. Jazmine's mother came home just after lunch. The student and office manager approached her and introduced themselves. They said they were there to talk about Tamika. Jazmine's mother invited them in.

They talked and prayed. The student told Jazmine's mother about the years that Tamika had served and who she was now. She had gone from being a child to a middle-aged woman. The office manager talked about Tamika's remorse, shame, and desire to be forgiven. It was significant to Jazmine's mother that Tamika had lost her child-bearing years to the prison. She recognized this was a lot to lose.

They talked about Jazmine too. About how it feels to lose a child—and about the woman Jazmine might have become.

But Jazmine's mother did not think it diminished Jazmine's loss to forgive Tamika. She said, "It's enough time."

•

Forgiveness is an extraordinary thing—especially in the context of murder. The most remarkable recent example is the forgiveness offered by family members of those killed by Dylann Roof in South Carolina only days after his horrific crime in 2015.

Roof, then a twenty-one-year-old, boyish-looking white supremacist, shot and killed nine African Americans engaged in Bible study at the Emanuel African Methodist Episcopal Church in Charleston, South Carolina, on June 17, 2015. After they welcomed him, he spent an hour with his victims before opening fire. As President Obama said the following day, "Any death of this sort is a tragedy. Any shooting involving multiple victims is a tragedy. There is something particularly heartbreaking about the death happening in a place in which we seek solace and we seek peace, in a place of worship."

And yet that same week, at the bond hearing, the daughter of one of the victims delivered an astonishing statement to Mr. Roof: "I just want everybody to know . . . I forgive you. You took something very precious away from me. I will never talk to her ever again, I will never be able to hold her again. You hurt me. You hurt a lot of people. But God forgives you, and I forgive you." The mother of another victim said, "May God have mercy on you." The sister of another said, "We have no room for hating, so we have to forgive. I pray God on your soul."[27]

The idea of forgiveness as a key criminal defense sensibility is intriguing. I think defenders have to have a capacity for compassion—no matter what a client is accused of—and be able to appreciate and respect the client as a person, both of which might include some measure of forgiveness.

Defenders are also genuinely interested in flawed people. We need to understand them—in a forgiving sort of way. As one of his biographers noted, Clarence Darrow "sought to make even the most hideous of crimes comprehensible." For Darrow, "there were no moral absolutes, no truth, no justice. . . . Only mercy."[28] As Darrow reflected:

> Strange as it may seem, I grew to like to defend men and women charged with crime. It soon came to be something more than the winning or losing of a case. I sought to learn why one goes one way and another takes an entirely different road. I became vitally interested in the causes of human conduct. This meant more than the quibbling with lawyers and juries. . . . I was dealing with life, with its hopes and fears, its aspirations and despairs. With me it was going to the foundation of motive and conduct and adjustments for human beings, instead of blindly talking of hatred and vengeance, and that subtle, indefinable quality that men call "justice" and of which nothing really is known.[29]

But it is one thing for lawyers—who are in the forgiveness business—to forgive and quite another for victims. Given the hideous nature of the crime, the willingness of the Charleston survivors to forgive was truly astonishing.

And yet, the act of forgiving might be more than an expression of grace toward a wrongdoer. It may also be a way for devastated individuals and communities to heal. Everett Worthington, a professor of psychology at Virginia Commonwealth University, whose research examines the effects of forgiveness, had his own capacity for forgiveness tested when his mother was brutally murdered during a home invasion.

In the days after his mother's death, he employed a five-step process he had previously developed: First, you "recall" the incident, including all the hurt. Next, you "empathize" with the person who wronged you. Then you offer the "altruistic gift" of forgiveness, maybe by recalling how good it felt to be forgiven by someone you yourself have wronged. Next, you "commit" yourself to forgive publicly. Finally, you "hold onto forgiveness"—even when feelings of anger surface.

Professor Worthington found that his approach worked for him, and other studies confirmed his experience and intuition. According to research, forgiveness helps mental and physical health, while not forgiving—harboring anger and resentment—has the opposite effect.[30] This suggests that, whatever happens to Dylann Roof in the criminal justice system, the decision of some of the victims' relatives to forgive may help them to ease their pain and move on with their lives.

But it takes courage and enormous moral conviction to be generous to someone who has caused such agony and loss.

•

We filed a parole petition on Tamika's behalf, which included, among the many supporting materials, a letter from Jazmine's mother saying she did not oppose release. We shared this with the chief prosecutor. We don't know whether it sparked any action from him or not, because we never heard back from him.

We got two state senators to endorse Tamika's release. The deans of the state's two law schools also weighed in, urging the importance of second chances for young people.

We noted that people from across the political spectrum were rethinking our excessive reliance on incarceration. We quoted Attorney General Eric Holder:

Although the United States comprises just five percent of the world's population, we incarcerate almost a quarter of the world's prisoners. While few would dispute the fact that incarceration has a role to play in any comprehensive public safety strategy, it's become evident that such widespread incarceration is both inadvisable and unsustainable. It requires that we routinely spend billions of dollars on prison construction—and tens of billions more, on an annual basis, to house those who are convicted of crimes. It carries both human and moral costs that are too much to bear.[31]

We quoted Supreme Court Justice Anthony M. Kennedy, who said, "Our resources are misspent, our punishments too severe, our sentences too long."[32]

Citing the state's standards for parole, we made a strong case for Tamika. We pointed to Tamika's youth at the time of the crime, the mitigating circumstances, Tamika's accomplishments in prison, and her release plan.

The parole hearing went well. Tamika talked about how much she had grown during her years of incarceration. She expressed regret for the rash and childish behavior that had led to her taking a life at fifteen. She managed to control her nerves and be herself. We had worked hard on this—on Tamika not just reciting the "right words" but revealing her sweet nature.

The parole board issued a favorable recommendation. They were putting Tamika forward for parole. We were overjoyed.

It turned out the recommendation did not mean Tamika was getting out; it only meant she was now on a long wait list for a "risk assessment," to be performed by a mental health professional at another institution. It could be months before she was seen. We did everything we could to expedite the process. The current governor was in his last months in office, and we had made some good contacts in the administration. We hoped the governor would bypass the evaluation and grant clemency. But he took no action.

A new governor took office. We reached out to his criminal justice staff. We urged them to take a look at Tamika's case. We were told she was on the assessment wait list, and the new governor was not going to do anything about that.

It took more than a year for the assessment to happen. It consisted largely of standard psychological tests and an account of her family history. The findings emphasized her disadvantaged childhood, physical abuse by her mother, drug use, failure to complete high school, nature of her crime, and poor initial adjustment to prison and concluded that Tamika posed a low to moderate risk of reoffending.

The report noted that Tamika had some favorable qualities that might offset the findings, but it also pointed to a lingering "adolescent resentment" over not being fairly treated by the criminal justice system.

Tamika currently remains in prison, having now served twenty-eight years. She is waiting for the governor to act.

•

The fact that Tamika was convicted of murder—not manslaughter, aggravated assault, or a comparable violent felony—looms large in her case, as it does for Ronnie, Delores, and James. Murder is in a class of its own.

Murder in a small town is especially big news. Take, for instance, the 2005 murder of twenty-five-year-old photographer Teresa Halbach in Two Rivers, Wisconsin. The brutal slaying was newsworthy enough: the dead woman's charred remains were found in a burn pit on a salvage lot. But when Steven Avery was accused of the murder—a man who had spent eighteen years in prison for a rape he did not commit and for which he was exonerated—there was a media frenzy.

Partway through *Making a Murderer*, the acclaimed Netflix documentary about the case, a *Dateline NBC* reporter is seen cheerfully discussing the murder. "This is the perfect *Dateline* story," she says. "It's a story with a twist, it grabs people's attention. . . . Right now, murder is hot, that's what everyone wants, that's what the competition wants, and we're trying to beat out the other networks to get that perfect murder story."[33]

Some big-city murders are equally newsworthy or can become so. The 2014 podcast *Serial*, which examined the 1999 murder of Baltimore high school senior Hae Min Lee and the prosecution and conviction of her ex-boyfriend Adnan Syed, became a cultural sensation.[34]

I watched every episode of *Making a Murderer*, though I found it painful. The case against Avery left too many questions unanswered. The arrest, interrogation, and incompetent representation of Avery's mentally disabled nephew and alleged accomplice, Brendan Dassey, were especially troubling. I don't know what happened to Ms. Halbach, but it seemed to me the state failed to prove beyond a reasonable doubt that either Avery or Dassey was guilty. It remains disturbing that the two are serving life sentences.

However, I couldn't wait for each new installment of the radio documentary *Serial*. The credulous tone of the storytelling was peculiarly compelling; the producers were genuinely trying to understand and not judge what had happened.

Of course, these true crime stories of murder are not new. Truman Capote essentially invented the genre with his 1965 nonfiction book—sometimes called a "nonfiction novel"—*In Cold Blood*.[35] The book tells the story of the home invasion and murder of four members of the Clutter family in Holcomb, Kansas, in 1959 and the subsequent capture, trial, and execution of the perpetrators, Richard Hickock and Perry Smith.

When Capote learned of the quadruple murder, he traveled to Kansas to write about it. He was accompanied by his friend and fellow writer Harper Lee. Together they interviewed local residents and law enforcement officers. After the two killers were convicted, Capote spent hours interviewing them.

In Cold Blood was first published as a serial in the *New Yorker* and was an immediate sensation. It was then published in book form by Random House and was a best seller.

The Kansas crime was brutal, and Capote doesn't hold back in recounting it. Hickock and Smith had recently been paroled from the Kansas state penitentiary and had been told by an inmate that they would find easy money at the Clutter home. Disappointed in what they found when they got there, however, they slit Herbert Clutter's throat and shot him in the head. Then they shot his wife, Bonnie, and two children, Nancy and Kenyon, each with a single shotgun blast to the head. They came away with a small portable radio, a pair of binoculars, and less than fifty dollars.

Capote's probing examination of Hickock and Smith's psychological motivations and his brilliant writing distinguish the book from a conventional whodunit. The two murderers emerge as people—damaged and dangerous, but people.

•

After repeatedly being denied parole, we needed a new strategy for Delores. The parole board was apparently unable to see beyond her crime. All they saw was a baby killer—a monstrous person unworthy of release.

They also had difficulty with Delores herself—with what she said about the crime, how she said it, her "lack of insight," and her "shallow remorse." We had to acknowledge that this was not entirely baseless. Delores had always found it difficult to talk about her crime, especially to the parole board. She was sometimes at a loss for words or said the wrong thing. In one hearing, she seemed to blame little Kimberly Ann, describing her as a colicky baby. In another, she said she was "going through a bad time" at the time of the crime. In the beginning, she claimed to have no memory of what she had done. Ultimately, however, she admitted ending her baby's life by placing a pillow over her face. At one hearing, she said she believed that this baby would die like all the others and wanted to take her out of her misery. At another, she said she could not offer any reason for her conduct because it lacked all reason.

The parole board did not seem to appreciate Delores's double meaning here—that she had no *reason* (no explanation) because no person with *reason* (in their right mind) would have done such a thing.

We needed Delores to be evaluated by a respected mental health professional who would address both the crime and Delores. Although we could not promise Delores that this would absolutely lead to her release, we needed to change things up.

The clinic had no funds for a psychological evaluation, so Delores and Bill would have to pay. Bill was now retired and living largely on savings and Social Security. I told them a good report might make a difference but that they might also end up spending a lot of money for nothing. Moreover, there might be an emotional cost for Delores. She would need to share her life's story, as well as her deepest thoughts and feelings, with whomever we hired—to be open in a way that was difficult for her. They talked it over and decided to do it.

We found an experienced forensic psychologist who lived not too far from the prison. This was important for cutting costs. His credentials included having worked for law enforcement as well as for criminal defendants, which made him credible. When we described Delores's case, he was intrigued.

When he first met with Delores, she was anxious and guarded. She had spent much of her life burying her feelings; it was difficult to reveal them to a stranger. She sometimes used irony as a defense. But this made her seem distant—as if she were an observer, rather than a participant, in her own life. Moreover, Delores was put off by the doctor's wise-cracking "Jewish uncle" personality—something so familiar to me I barely noticed it.

The psychologist understood all of this but feared he would only scratch the surface unless he gained Delores's trust. He was concerned about the time it would take to break through. He wondered whether it might make sense to bring me in. "She trusts you," he said, and he suggested that maybe if I were present, Delores would be less wary and more forthcoming. He proposed that I join him the next time he went to the prison—that we travel there together and engage in a joint effort. I said yes, of course—so long as my presence would not compromise the integrity of his work. He assured me it would not. We scheduled a time.

•

This was not the first time I had done something unusual with a mental health professional on behalf of a client. I once represented a prisoner who was serving a lengthy sentence for the murder of her abusive husband. After having endured horrible violence at the hands of her husband, she accepted an offer by some male friends to beat him up. When she lured her husband to them, they beat him to death. She told the jury she hadn't meant for him to die.

When it looked like she would be released through clemency or parole—her case was part of a successful effort to gain the release of a handful of women state prisoners who had killed abusive partners—her chief concern was her son. He had been only five when he lost both of his parents. My client's sister had taken in the boy and had raised him with her own children. She had done this even though she was angry at her sister for bringing shame to the family. But it hadn't been her nephew's fault. And besides, the aunt received a monthly check from the state for him.

The sister had taken the boy to see his mother a couple of times early in her incarceration but hadn't done so in years. My client hadn't seen her son since he was in first grade. He was now about to enter high school.

The sister provided her nephew with the basics, but there wasn't a lot of love. Worse, she routinely bad-mouthed his mother. Whenever he misbehaved, she would say, "You'll end up like your mother, a violent criminal."

My client longed to see her son and be reunited with him. In order to prepare for this, she called her sister and asked that she bring the boy to the prison. The sister balked. She said she had asked her nephew if he wanted to see his mother and he said no. He said he was afraid of his mom—that she might kill him, too.

I reached out to the sister and proposed that the boy see a therapist. I suggested that the best way to prepare him to see his mother was to talk through his fears. I would find the therapist and arrange for funding. When the boy was ready to see his mother, I would pick him up, take him to the prison, oversee the visit, and take him back home again. She agreed.

Almost immediately, the therapist said there was a problem. What the boy really needed was family therapy with the mom present. Absent that, she believed that the boy would benefit from having someone in the room who knew his mother and could answer questions about her. The therapist asked whether I might participate in therapy—as a surrogate for my client.

I said sure.

The boy's curiosity about his mother was the most memorable part of these sessions. He wanted to know everything about her—what she looked like, how she acted, what she liked and disliked and, mostly, how she felt about *him*. I assured him his mother thought about him every single day and missed him terribly. Being separated from him was the very worst punishment she had endured. He soon overcame his fears.

When my client was released, her son came to live with her. It wasn't always easy, but they managed to make it work. They lived together until he went off to college.

•

My participation in Delores's evaluation was one of the most interesting experiences of my professional life. We worked with her for hours. She wept much of the time. She reflected hard on the questions we asked and revealed things she had never shared before. Something real and powerful had taken place.

She had had a miserable, loveless childhood. Her parents had been incapable of kindness. They ridiculed and rejected her at every turn. This continued until her parents' death. At her father's deathbed, he said to her, "At least I won't have to see *your* face again." Her mother used to chase Delores with scissors and cut her hair as a form of punishment. Delores was incarcerated when her mother was dying. She obtained permission to see her in the hospital and was taken there in shackles. When her mother saw her, she turned away and said, "I want you to go."

She had no faith in her own ability to be a mother, even though she was desperate for family. She had loved her first child, Lucy, with all her heart. Lucy was playful, bright, and affectionate. When she contracted meningitis and died, Delores was racked with grief. Within months, a younger child also died of meningitis. There was no suggestion of foul play in these deaths. But there was also no grieving process. She and Bill buried the children and said nothing more about them. They proceeded to have more children.

Delores was a traumatized person, not an evil one. The more detail she offered, the more we saw this. She recalled holding Lucy in the ambulance and sobbing, "Please God, don't take her. Don't take my child."

The psychologist had also interviewed Bill. Bill acknowledged that he hadn't done much to comfort Delores after these awful losses. He knew she was suffering; so was he. But he wasn't very good at talking about such feelings. "I'm not one for asking questions," he said.

When asked why he had stood by Delores all these years—after all, he could have divorced her and remarried and was pressed to do so by friends and family—Bill said he was old-fashioned. When he and Delores got married, he pledged to stand by Delores in good times and bad, and he meant it. Besides, he said, he still loved her.

The psychologist and I made a good team. Because it was in Delores's legal interest to open up, I did everything I could to get her to do so. I encouraged and inveigled and pushed. I confronted her when I thought she was offering an empty answer. "You can do better," I would say. "Come on, what were you really feeling?"

I had explained to Delores that we were under no obligation to share the evaluation with the parole board if it wasn't favorable. So there was no downside to candor. I reminded her of this.

At one point, Delores got angry, something she hadn't been brave enough to do before in my presence. This happened when we disparaged the idea that her life was in "God's hands." We were trying to get her to fight for herself, but maybe we were being superior in our own secularism. She said we had no right to mock her faith. We apologized.

We got her to recount in detail what she recalled about the crime. As Delores had tried to explain to the parole board, it turns out that Kimberly Ann was indeed a colicky baby. Delores had been inelegant when she said this to the board. She had not meant to blame her baby but rather to explain the context of her crime. Colicky babies can test the patience of the most loving of parents. Kimberly Ann would howl and shriek for hours at a time. She was inconsolable. Delores feared it was meningitis again. Bill wasn't there. She was alone with her terror.

A combination of grief, dread, self-loathing, and exhaustion made her do the unthinkable in the early morning hours. She still has a hard time accepting that she acted on these feelings. Immediately after she took her baby's life, she tried to undo it. She called her neighbor, a nurse. She wanted someone to bring Kimberly Ann back to life. It was too late.

"I must be a monster," Delores said. "Everyone thinks I'm a monster, so maybe I am."

I reached for her hand. "No, you're not," I said.

•

James was granted parole on his first eligibility date. This does not often happen. His winning personality might have helped, as did his early acceptance of responsibility and remorse. Moreover, as a DC prisoner, he was under the control of the United States Parole Commission, whose practices are more predictable and less politicized than state parole boards.

A childhood friend with a thriving business had a job waiting for James. The friend had kept in touch during James's incarceration and was delighted to do this. After James was released, we helped him with certain tasks that can be challenging for someone who has spent decades behind bars: getting a driver's license, opening a bank account, applying for a credit card, learning how to use a debit card. James lived with his mother for a time but got his own place as soon as he was able. He was a grown man and intended to act like one. He does not stay in touch—there is no reason to—and he has remained out of trouble.

•

Fascination with murder and murderers starts early. What child has not heard some version of a fairy tale by the Brothers Grimm? Murder and mayhem are frequent themes.

Consider *Bluebeard*, which tells the story of a rich nobleman whose pretty young wives keep dying.[36] Bluebeard takes yet another wife. Soon after their marriage, he goes away, leaving her with a ring of keys and instructions to use all but the smallest, which locks the door to a room she must never enter. Of course, she enters the room, which is filled with the remains of his murdered wives. The key becomes covered in blood, which tips Bluebeard off to her transgression. She is saved at the last minute from joining the other wives, but the image of a room full of murdered young women remains.

Or consider *The Robber Bridegroom*, in which a man looking to offload his daughter gives her to the first "gentleman" that comes along.[37] The gentleman invites his bride-to-be for a visit. The dutiful girl sets off despite a feeling of foreboding. The house turns out to be a den of cannibals. As the girl watches from behind a barrel, she sees her future husband and his friends return with a girl they've kidnapped, chop her up, cook her, and eat her. They devour all but a single finger, which the bride uses to make a case against the gentleman.

Then there is *The Singing Bone*, in which two brothers are tasked with killing a wild boar, with the successful one promised the king's daughter in marriage.[38] One brother goes out and kills the boar. When his drunken brother sees this, he murders the successful brother and takes the boar to the king to claim the princess. He is later revealed as a murderer and thief when his dead brother's bone is turned into a flute, which tattles on the killer through song. He is then put to death himself.

J. K. Rowling's wildly popular *Harry Potter* books essentially begin with a murder: when he was a year old, Harry witnessed his parents' killing by the evil wizard Lord Voldemort.[39] Voldemort attempted to kill Harry as well, but for reasons not immediately revealed, Voldemort's spell rebounded, leaving Harry with only a lightning bolt-shaped scar on his forehead. According to prophecy, Harry has the power to vanquish the "Dark Lord."

Of course, murder is a recurring theme in the Bible, as well as in the works of Sophocles, Shakespeare, Dostoyevsky, Poe, Dickens, and Dreiser, to name a few literary giants.

The most popular course ever at Amherst College was a large lecture taught by Professor Austin Sarat, which he simply called "Murder." While most classes at the small, prestigious liberal arts college had fifteen students, more than three hundred enrolled in this course, a fifth of the student body. Professor Sarat explained the course's popularity by pointing to the universal fascination with murder. "We are a killing society, awash with violence," he said. He tells students on the first day of the course that "murder is a window into American culture." He also believes that narcissism fuels an interest in "the one experience of our lives we can't experience."[40]

•

The evaluation of Delores was overwhelmingly positive, the psychologist's report persuasive. But the parole board clearly didn't read it.

The report focuses on issues raised by prior parole boards in denying parole: Delores's acceptance of responsibility for her actions, issues relating to remorse and insight, concerns about her presentation and demeanor at previous hearings, and her risk for future violent behavior.

The report carefully notes the sources of information relied upon: nearly eighteen hours interviewing Delores and administering tests; a three-hour interview of Delores's husband, Bill; police reports, the presentence report, and hearing transcripts; letters in support of Delores's release; certificates earned while Delores was incarcerated; psychological research on women who kill their babies; professional literature about the effects of long-term incarceration on women.

The report quotes at length what Delores said about her crime and her description of herself as a "sorry excuse for a mother." In the end, she felt she was sparing her child from having such a mother.

The report describes a private, reserved, and relatively unexpressive person who keeps her thoughts and feelings to herself. Nonetheless, the report finds that Delores has more insight than she is comfortable discussing with others. It notes that "emotional insulation" has been a longtime coping mechanism for Delores (exacerbated by long-term incarceration) and that Delores's presentation—her flat tone, austere appearance, and "emotional blandness"—undercuts her genuine acceptance of responsibility and enormous remorse.

Finally, the report concludes that, according to several psychological instruments used to evaluate the likelihood of future violence, Delores poses the lowest possible risk of violent reoffending. In order to counter the suggestion that she is a dangerous psychopath, she was also evaluated for "psychopathy" and was found to have none.

•

Delores remains in prison, as do Ronnie and Tamika. It is hard to say when, if ever, they will get out. Tamika has the best chance of release because of the relative ordinariness of her crime, her youth at the time, her gender, and the positive (if not terribly influential) recommendation by the parole board where she is imprisoned.

Ronnie wants desperately to be free but understands why he remains confined. He destroyed two families—his neighbor's and his own. He has found some solace in his Christian faith. He continues to hope.

Delores feels sorrow, regret, and bewilderment. She realizes this last thing is not helpful. She is now in her midseventies, as is her husband.

Ronnie, Tamika, and Delores are among the many lifers who are supposed to get out but may never do so. Though eligible for parole, they wind up serving endless sentences, contrary to the intention of the sentencing judge and contrary to basic fairness. As former Sing Sing Correctional Facility warden Lewis E. Lawes once said, "Death fades into insignificance when compared with life imprisonment. To spend each night in jail, day after day, year after year, gazing at the bars and longing for freedom, is indeed expiation."[41]

This is the new American exceptionalism: never-ending incarceration.[42] If Ronnie and the others had committed their crimes in any other Western democracy, they would have been freed long ago. Because they were juveniles at the time of their crimes, Ronnie and Tamika might even have been given new identities—truly a fresh start—in some countries.[43]

The get-tough criminal justice "reforms" of the 1980s and 1990s—including "truth in sentencing" (which requires offenders to serve 85 percent of a prison sentence), the demise of indeterminate sentencing (and with it parole), and the advent of mandatory minimums and guidelines sentencing—are largely responsible for longer sentences.[44] But the longer the sentence, the more institutionalized the prisoner and the harder reentry. We are not readying prisoners to rejoin society; we are relegating them to grow old in prison.[45]

Ronnie, Tamika, Delores, and James did something very bad many years ago. But they are all very different now.

Not every killing is the same nor is every killer. We must learn to distinguish among them. Some who kill are dangerous and require lengthy confinement. But many one-time killers have sufficiently discharged their debt to society, will never kill again, and pose no other danger to society. They've earned a second chance.

5

Guilty Clients,
Guilty Lawyers

———————————◄O►—

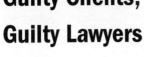

"How can you represent those people?"

Everyone asks this question.

I point to the role of the defense lawyer in the adversary system, the harshness of punishment, and pervasive racism in criminal justice.

But the truth is I like guilty people, the more flawed the better.

My clients are strong and weak, kind and cruel, hard-working and feckless, cautious and reckless... Like most people.

I represent them because they represent us.

Criminal defendants are often guilty—of something, if not exactly what they're charged with. That's the nature of criminal defense. If the criminally accused were not guilty most of the time, we would not be living in a free society.

But must criminal lawyers be guilty too? I'm not talking about what our critics say—that we are essentially our clients' accomplices. This is a ridiculous allegation. We are their advocates, not their accomplices. Nor am I talking about the hand-wringing in much of the scholarship on the ethics of criminal defense, which seems to say, "It's dirty work, but someone has to do it." There is nothing dirty about criminal defense. Our adversarial system could not function without skilled and devoted counsel checking the enormous power of the state.

Rather, I am talking about lawyers who feel guilty about the injustice we witness daily—which, for many defenders, amounts to a professional guilty conscience. Even worse, I am talking about a martyred sense of guilt— lawyers who feel that *suffering* is an essential part of the job.

This is not how I feel about my life's work. I am a very happy criminal defense lawyer. Although the work can be challenging—and sometimes heartbreaking—to me, there is nothing more rewarding than standing beside someone accused or convicted of crime.

There seems to be a trend in the other direction—toward martyrdom. Consider, for example, the 2013 documentary film *Gideon's Army*, which explores indigent criminal defense in the Deep South through the stories of three young public defenders.[1] The lawyers struggle to represent their clients in the face of huge caseloads, long hours, low pay, and the routine challenges of representing the poor accused in a dehumanizing system. The film was shown at law schools and public defender agencies after it premiered on HBO and developed a substantial following. It won an award at Sundance Film Festival and received the Nation Institute and Fertel Foundation's Ridenhour Documentary Film Prize. It continues to be shown to law students and public defenders.

One of the stars of the film, Georgia public defender Travis Williams, is the very image of a martyred defender. Tattooed on his body are the names of every single client whose case he has lost at trial. The names illustrate Williams's devotion to the work; he literally wears his commitment on his skin. As he declares in the film, "Either this is your cause or this ain't." If it is your cause, you must be all in—which presumably means you should be covered in tattoos.

Williams will have to start using a smaller font if he plans to be a career defender, because criminal defendants often lose at trial.

To Williams, all loss is the same. There is no asterisk by any of the tattooed names indicating that this might have been an especially difficult case because the evidence was overwhelming or the client insisted on going to trial contrary to advice. Apparently, the client's loss is the lawyer's loss. The lawyer must bear and *wear* that loss.

I understand this feeling, especially after a crushing defeat at trial. I often experience the client's loss as my own. Wounded by defeat—and the consequences for my client—I inevitably feel that I have failed the person I was supposed to protect. But I have no tattoos and will not be getting any in the near future.

Gideon's Army also features Georgia public defender Brandy Alexander paying for gas out of a small pile of spare change, which is all she has left of her meager paycheck. Unfortunately, Brandy also recounts stories about a former client who threatened to kill her if she lost his case and another former client who bragged about raping his twelve-year-old daughter. These are unusual stories, not at all typical defender fare. They suggest a different kind of defense lawyer suffering.

The third lawyer, Mississippi public defender June Harwick, is not featured as prominently as the other two, perhaps because she doesn't seem to suffer as much. She diligently tries to represent her clients with limited resources while juggling the demands of family.

The image of the public defender as all-sacrificing and long-suffering, captured by Travis Williams's tattoos and Brandy Alexander's spare change, is not an anomaly. To many, it is the norm. This is not a good thing. It leads law students and young lawyers to revere criminal defense martyrs but resist criminal defense for themselves. Those with the interest and aptitude—but who also want children, a family, or any outside pursuits—are often intimidated by the great sacrifice such a career implies.

Unfortunately, various commentators—in both the legal profession and the academy—perpetuate this image. Jonathan Rapping, founder of the indigent defense organization Gideon's Promise and who appears in the film as a charismatic leader of a new wave of public defenders in the South, lauds the "great personal sacrifice" and "nobility" of indigent criminal defense and calls the lawyers in *Gideon's Army* "Sisyphean . . . heroes . . . pushing forward, only to slip back under the crushing weight of the system."[2] He emphasizes the "heroic" role that public defenders play in the criminal justice system as part of a movement to reclaim equal justice.[3]

Harvard law professor Charles Ogletree might have laid the intellectual groundwork for this model of indigent defense in an oft-cited 1993 law review article in which he argues that "empathy" and "heroism" are the two central and sustaining motivations for public defenders.[4] The article became mandatory reading for many would-be defenders and more experienced ones.

Ogletree's notion of empathy as a boundless connection between lawyer and client tends to invite the suffering I'm worried about. The empathy he describes goes beyond the standard definition—the ability to understand and feel compassion for another person. It goes beyond the ability to *imagine* another person's life and circumstances no matter how different from one's own, a quality I believe is essential for defense lawyers.

Ogletree's idea of empathy goes even beyond Professor Charles Fried's influential but much criticized 1976 law review article, which argues that a lawyer is a special interest "friend."[5] Ogletree ratchets up Fried's lawyer-as-friend to lawyer-as-best-friend. This best-friendship between lawyer and client is unlimited in duration, in what the lawyer does for the client (so long as it's lawful), and in the level of devastation the lawyer feels when a case is lost. The lawyer-client relationship is personal as well as professional: conventional boundaries don't apply.

I worry that this depiction of the lawyer-client relationship is so idealized it cannot exist in real life. The client is inevitably romanticized; if you are a truly devoted criminal lawyer, you will *love* all your clients no matter what. I worry that the first time a young defender finds a client loathsome or merely unpleasant, he or she will think, *I guess I'm not cut out for this work.*

In the idealized version of the lawyer-client relationship, lawyers do everything for their clients cheerfully and nonjudgmentally. Of course, indigent defenders ought not to be unduly judgmental; our clients get judged enough by everyone else. But it's impossible to never have a feeling of distaste or disapproval. Our clients—no matter how much we feel for them—sometimes do awful things.

Plus, lawyer-client relationships, like any other relationship, can be complicated and trying. Sometimes good, devoted lawyers fight *with* their clients as well as fighting *for* them. When calm counsel fails to achieve its desired outcome, we rant and rave and implore. We do this out of professional responsibility and because we care. But thankfully, there are some bounds to the lawyer-client relationship that are established by the rules and standards of the profession.

Ogletree's concept of heroism is also a harbinger of the martyred defender. When he was a staff attorney at the Public Defender Service (PDS) for the District of Columbia, Ogletree saw himself as a "sort of Robin Hood figure who can conquer what others cannot and . . . does not always have to conform to the moral rules society reserves for others."[6] The nonconformist outlaw as a model for (typically male) criminal defense lawyers has been recognized by others,[7] and it has become part of the popular culture through characters like James Woods's Eddie Dodd, the pony-tailed, marijuana-smoking lawyer in the movie *True Believer*; Al Pacino's idealistic and increasingly indignant Arthur Kirkland in the movie *And Justice for All*; Mickey Haller in Michael Connelly's Lincoln Lawyer novels (who works out of his Lincoln Town Car rather than an office); and any number of television shows featuring (usually male) criminal defense lawyers who thumb their noses at authority.

The heroic aspect of Robin Hood—the good-looking guy in tights who robs from the rich and gives to the poor—is at once altruistic and grandiose. The grandiosity might be a necessary part of trial lawyering, which requires a certain amount of confidence, if not swagger. Waxing on about his own heroics as a defender, Ogletree exalts the David versus Goliath challenge of fighting the state, the "thrill of the trial," and the "battle of wits" with both prosecutors and judges.[8]

Ogletree's notion of the heroic defender is focused almost entirely on winning, notwithstanding the fact that criminal defense lawyers often lose. Moreover, in a system dominated by guilty pleas, we seldom even go to trial.[9] There is something disturbing and presumptuous about thinking of oneself as a hero. As my good friend and fellow criminal lawyer David Stern says, "I'm offended by the notion that we're heroes. Not only are there very few heroic moments, but thinking you're a hero makes you act in ways that are not helpful to clients."[10]

What about when the everyday demands of the work—combing through police paperwork and body camera footage, endlessly waiting around in court, the random delays and postponements, dealing with unfriendly and unhelpful court staff—feel more tedious than heroic? Or when dire circumstances cannot be altered? Or when clients get in trouble again, making the thrill of victory fleeting at best? The intractable and interwoven problems of family dysfunction, poverty, drug abuse, mental illness, and crime can make it impossible to be anybody's Robin Hood.

Empathy and heroism might be motivations for short-term criminal lawyers. Some elite public defender's offices seem to embrace this model by hiring talented young lawyers from prestigious law schools to work themselves to the bone for a couple of years before moving on to lucrative law firms or other more high-profile jobs. Maybe this is because it is cost-effective: it is cheaper to have a cadre of junior lawyers who leave after two or three years. But it hurts both the quality of representation and office morale to not maintain a critical mass of seasoned defenders. Too much attrition means career defenders will have little incentive to mentor younger ones or to stick around themselves.

•

The most troubling sacrifice recounted in Ogletree's article is his taking on a murder case shortly after his beloved sister, Barbara, was found stabbed to death in her home. This was not something he was required to do; he took the case as an expression of his commitment to criminal defense.

Ogletree describes his efforts to solve the murder, which helped him come to terms with his own loss. He reviewed the evidence, met with local police, conducted investigation, and even looked for suspects among the mourners at the funeral. No arrest was ever made.

After some soul-searching, Ogletree returned to PDS and was appointed to represent a man accused of raping and murdering a woman around his sister's age. The man had raped before and was currently on parole for rape. Ogletree accepted the appointment and disclosed his recent tragedy with the client in case he wished to obtain different counsel. The client did not.

There was substantial evidence of guilt, including the defendant's wallet being found at the scene of the crime. Nonetheless, Ogletree reports that he worked harder on this case than he had on any other. He got to know the client and came to see him as more than his criminal conduct, prepared the case thoroughly, and tried the case skillfully. The jury was out for a long time before returning a guilty verdict on all counts. Ogletree says he was "devastated."[11]

I admire Ogletree's dedication and ability to compartmentalize. I have often wondered whether I would be able to carry on my work if someone I loved was the victim of a serious crime. Petty crime doesn't spark this question for most defenders. My friend Shelley Stark, a devoted state and federal public defender who died young after a stroke, used to routinely have her car broken into but never called the police—even when she caught the culprit red-handed.

· Still, what Ogletree did on the heels of his sister's murder asks too much. He was entitled to take some time to grieve. The new case was too close to what happened to his sister. No doubt Ogletree's client benefitted from having him as counsel, but he was not the only excellent lawyer in town.

Ogletree's taking this case might reflect the culture of this particular public defender's office. In a well-known essay on indigent criminal defense, Randy Bellows, another alumnus of PDS (who left the office to become a career federal prosecutor shortly after writing the article), describes his own "feverish" work on behalf of his clients as "a holy mission."[12] Another PDS alumna, Stanford law professor Barbara Babcock, refers to criminal defense as her "religion."[13]

However, as Professor Margaret Raymond points out, criminal defense fervor and self-sacrifice are not limited to this one office. She refers to a broad and "impassioned literature produced by writers who are one-hundred percent committed, with almost religious fervor, to indigent criminal defense."[14]

•

Of course, criminal defenders have many motivations; one size can never really fit all. Among the universal traits uniting defenders are a commitment to civil libertarianism, a deep feeling of camaraderie among defenders, and possessing the peculiar defender "personality."

Defenders are civil libertarians because they uphold the Bill of Rights—especially the First, Fourth, Fifth, Sixth, and Eighth Amendments—as well as its underlying values and principles, including individual autonomy, dignity, and freedom.

By camaraderie, I mean that most defenders like the *crowd*, the community of defenders. Former defenders everywhere require only the slightest prompting to rhapsodize about their erstwhile colleagues—the best bunch of people they've ever known. Maybe this is true of everyone who has ever worked anywhere. But there is a special esprit de corps among criminal defenders.

Then there's the question of personality. Many people believe there is an identifiable "defender personality." My favorite rendering of the defender personality is by Mary Halloran, the former executive director of the

Colorado Criminal Defense Bar. She calls criminal defense lawyers "a breed unto themselves" and describes them as "profane, argumentative, insecure, eccentric" and "ill at ease with people who are not themselves criminal defense lawyers." She adds, "They can't complete a sentence that doesn't include the F-word, and the more frequently and creatively it's used, the more effectively they feel they've communicated." Halloran allows that defenders have a few positive qualities. "Oddly," she notes, they "make loving parents."[15]

Professor Barbara Babcock famously said that "criminal defense work takes a peculiar mind-set, heart-set, soul-set."[16] My friend and former colleague Stu Glovin says that all defenders have the same "defective gene" and defenders "understand each other but no one understands us."[17]

I believe there is a defender prototype. "Natural defenders" are antiauthoritarian, nonconformist, irreverent, skeptical, slightly voyeuristic, slightly exhibitionist, and resilient. But defenders—including career defenders—may also be contrary to type. There are defense lawyers who need to get along with everybody, even judges and prosecutors. These lawyers don't thrive on antiauthoritarianism or nonconformism; they believe they can play by the rules, be well-liked, and still persuade others to their point of view. There are defenders who are respectful and sometimes downright pious, not irreverent or skeptical. Some defenders are basically shy and avoid attention in their "regular lives" but manage to advocate—passionately, publicly—on behalf of another. It can probably be said that most defenders are curious about the complexities of life and crime, if not exactly voyeuristic. And defenders must be resilient if they are to carry on.

Still, having a commitment to civil liberties, loving one's colleagues, or possessing a quirky personality are not necessarily sustaining motivations for criminal defense. Protecting individual rights can feel like an abstraction when the going gets rough. The pull of camaraderie doesn't always win out over competing pulls. Although I like to think I have pretty good "defendar"—the radar-like ability to recognize a kindred defender spirit, like "Jewdar" for Jews and "gaydar" for gays—I have seen too many naturals carry their defender personality off to other jobs.

•

I prefer an amalgam of motivations that productively addresses the lawyer's relationship to the client, to oneself, and to the system. I have come to believe that three things—respect for the client, dedication to professional craft, and a powerful sense of outrage—form the best model for long-term defenders.

Respect

Aretha Franklin (and Otis Redding, who wrote the song) captures what I mean by respect.[18] I mean R-E-S-P-E-C-T, in capital letters, spelled out, as an anthem of empowerment—an expression of deep regard for the humanity, dignity, and autonomy of those I represent. The respect I have in mind recognizes that every client has life experiences, values, and interests that must be considered and that *matter*.

I believe that respect, as the core bond between lawyer and client, is more sustaining than empathy or friendship and more fundamental. As the defense lawyer in Tom Wolfe's *The Bonfire of the Vanities* says to his client, "What did I tell you the first time you walked into this office? . . . I told you, '. . . I'm not gonna be your friend. I'm gonna be your lawyer. But I'm gonna do more for you than your friends.'"[19]

For indigent criminal defendants, respect is more important than friendship because they get so little of it. Zealous defense is an act of respect. Standing beside a client when everyone else is piling on, sitting together as a team at counsel table, rising together for the verdict—these are all acts of respect.

Respect offers cleaner lines to clients. It is preferable to offers of friendship that are impossible to live up to. Writer and former public defender James Kunen recounts a conversation he had with a client when he was a law student at New York University's criminal defense clinic. The exchange captures his struggle with the nature of his relationship with indigent clients. As he was walking from court with a client, the client suddenly asked, "How do you know how I feel?" Kunen replied, "I don't. All I know is what you tell me." Kunen then writes:

> We walked on in silence. Then, as we got on the elevator at 50 Lafayette, he said, "All you wealthy people. . . ." And smiled, looked at the floor, shook his head.
>
> "What about us wealthy people," I asked. "We don't know how it is?"
>
> He laughed. "How's it feel to have all that money?"
>
> I thought of saying I didn't have that much money. "It feels lucky," I said.[20]

Kunen is right: we are lucky. I feel lucky every time I'm on the other side of a prison gate. I feel lucky about the family I was born into and every advantage I have had. Not everyone is so lucky.

When you respect a client, you don't have to feel responsible for all his or her choices or be crushed by every setback. I am not urging detachment; good, respectful lawyers often become fiercely attached to their clients. But appropriate professional distance promotes good judgment and the ability to last.

A young lawyer in Georgetown's Prettyman Fellowship Program learned to appreciate respect the hard way. She was drawn to criminal defense out of a deep connection to clients. It was important to her that she like her clients and they like her. Then she was appointed to represent one of the most difficult clients ever seen by the program. He was accused of unlawfully entering certain government buildings (a charge he strongly denied). He was smart, articulate, and mentally ill (which he also strongly denied). He did not like the young lawyer and made this clear from the start. He seemed irritated by everything about her, from her youth and gender to her Southern accent. He was determined to fire her. The fellow was crushed by this. She did all she could to win him over, but he would yell at her for hours in her office. Sometimes I intervened to calm him down. At the client's insistence, she finally filed a motion to withdraw, but the motion was denied, as was a motion that he be allowed to represent himself. Ultimately, the fellow learned to toughen up a little and set some limits, and she worked hard on the client's behalf out of respect. He might have come to respect her as well.

Craft

Defenders should take pride in their professional craft. There is craft—and sometimes even art—in every aspect of defending. Defending the accused and convicted requires a serious and sophisticated set of abilities that includes ingenuity, nimbleness, and grit.

The craft of defending includes trying the hell out of cases, making arguments that keep juries out for a couple of hours when they would have otherwise convicted in twenty minutes, litigating creative motions, keeping juveniles at home instead of in institutions, and persuading judges or prosecutors that hapless clients deserve a second chance.

Caring about the quality of the work and giving a poor client the same quality representation that a rich person would have are a craft. Even high-volume defending is a craft—juggling several cases on the same day, having back-to-back trials, doing hearing after hearing, soundly counseling one client after another.

Volume may be the single most difficult aspect of indigent defense. In some places, defender caseloads range as high as 3,500 misdemeanors and 900 felonies a year, when national standards suggest they should consist of no more than 400 misdemeanors and 150 felonies.[21] A St. Louis public defender once lamented to a colleague of mine that her caseload made her feel more like a pallbearer than a lawyer. "Meet 'em and plead 'em" is the extent of representation in far too many jurisdictions.

In 2015, the problem reached crisis proportions in Louisiana, which has the highest incarceration rate in the nation. Caseloads were approaching one thousand felonies in some public defender's offices, more than half of local offices were facing insolvency, and most offices were restricting services, leaving many poor accused to fend for themselves. The Lafayette Parish Public Defender's Office laid off more than two-thirds of its fifty-two attorneys and imposed a significant salary cut for those who remained. "It's a nightmare," said chief Louisiana Public Defender James Dixon. "You have people in jail that don't have lawyers. It's that basic."[22]

Because there were not enough experienced lawyers, one young defender in New Orleans began representing people facing mandatory life sentences the same week she passed the bar. Her caseload was so high she was not able to meet minimal ethical standards:

> I miss filing important motions . . . I am unable to properly prepare for every trial . . . I have serious conversations about plea bargains with my clients in open court because I did not spend enough time conducting confidential visits with them in jail. I plead some of my clients to felony convictions on the day I meet them. If I don't follow up to make sure clients are released when they should be, they can sit in jail for unnecessary weeks and months.[23]

I acknowledge that it is impossible to ply one's craft under these circumstances. Public defenders, like all lawyers, owe "total loyalty" to each client in each case.[24] As Monroe Freedman has argued, when defenders counsel clients to plead guilty with virtually no factual or legal investigation, or manage their caseload by triage based on the nature of the charge or a claim of innocence, it creates a conflict of interest that contravenes their duty of loyalty.[25] This is harsh—especially for committed defenders in far-flung places doing everything they can to provide zealous representation under difficult circumstances. But an excessive caseload invariably creates a risk that a defender's ability to effectively represent one client will be materially limited because of responsibilities to other clients—the definition of conflict of interest.

Excessive volume is a systemic problem requiring a systemic solution. Restraint in charging decisions, greater use of diversionary programs (and programs that actually divert cases from the system instead of requiring a guilty plea), and decriminalization of some conduct would help. Bail reform would help. Fully funding the directive of *Gideon v. Wainwright* would also help. Some legal organizations have brought these kinds of challenges.[26]

Still, for most defenders, craft is essential for effectual defense. Developing a viable defense theory; challenging the credibility of government witnesses and making points consistent with your theory in cross-examination; effectively preparing defense witnesses; making powerful and persuasive arguments—all these are part of the craft. There is nobility in the effort and, of course, in doing it well. You don't have to be a hero, but you need to hone your craft.

Outrage

Outrage is an essential driving force for defenders. By outrage, I do not mean the feeling that leads some to throw their hands up in despair at the difficulties of defending. These defenders don't last. I mean a sense of shared moral and political outrage. My friend Ilene, a career poverty lawyer and clinical law professor, regularly says to students, "If you're not outraged, you're not paying attention." What she means is that you cannot represent the poor without finding occasion for outrage.

Defenders bear witness to the pervasiveness of injustice and the randomness of justice. Too much depends on the luck of the draw, including the assignment of a judge, prosecutor, and defender.

I have been defending the poor for more than thirty years, and I still come back from court outraged.

Sadly, too often there is a lack of outrage from clients. The poor become accustomed to maltreatment. I can't tell you the number of clients who have comforted *me* upon being incarcerated, saying, "I'll be all right. Don't worry about me." In a familiar courtroom ritual, they empty their pockets of the trappings of freedom—wallet, keys, cell phone, coins—before a bailiff takes them into captivity.

Far too many people live with the feeling that incarceration is inevitable. According to the most recent data, more than half of state and federal prisoners are parents of a minor, resulting in nearly two million children with an incarcerated parent. This cruel effect of mass incarceration falls especially hard on African American families. Appallingly, one in fifteen black children has a parent in prison.[27] Many of these children end up in the foster care system, the juvenile justice system, and sometimes the penitentiary.

With outrage as a motivation, the struggle is everything. It says to clients, their families, and their communities, "This person is worth fighting for." It says to the system, "Hold your horses, not so fast—not without a fight." It stops the conveyor belt—at least for a moment. When respect, craft, and outrage come together, they create a synergy that keeps defenders going.

•

But maybe we do need criminal defense heroes and martyrs. I understand the desire for heroes; they inspire. I have some of my own: Nelson Mandela, Eleanor Roosevelt, Rosa Parks, Martin Luther King, Jr., Sandy Koufax, Arthur Ashe, Billie Jean King. The sports heroes seem wildly out of place next to the others—except that, like the others, they showed courage in the face of adversity, challenged the status quo, and contributed to social change.

But maybe sports heroes are less surprising than one would think. Many people have sports heroes. My friend Larry—an accomplished psychologist who presented his work all over the world before his untimely death in 2017—used to cry at the mere mention of Willie Mays. Mays was the defining figure of Larry's childhood.

No doubt my heroes reflect my own cultural generation. All are from the twentieth century.

The only lawyer on my list is Nelson Mandela. But he is there for many reasons other than being a lawyer. I do have two rather conventional lawyer heroes: Clarence Darrow and Atticus Finch. One is real, the other fictional, and both are flawed. The fact that they are flawed makes them easier to relate to.

Darrow has been played by Orson Welles and Spencer Tracy in film. Paul Muni, Melvyn Douglas, and Henry Fonda played him on stage. He is generally portrayed as a superstar who took on impossible causes and won—the country's first celebrity defense lawyer. In some ways, Darrow the superstar is as much a fictional character as Finch.

The real Darrow was a talented trial lawyer, ardent civil libertarian, and champion of workers as well as of the criminally accused. He was interested in socialism, was skeptical of religion, and despised capital punishment. He was brilliant and witty. But he was also arrogant, sloppy, a womanizer, and accused of once bribing a jury (a charge for which he was acquitted). He was an oddly ambivalent feminist who went from being a fierce advocate for women's rights to a less than enthusiastic supporter of women's suffrage. He once remarked that women should be public defenders because they don't need the money.[28]

Atticus Finch, the defender of a falsely accused black man in 1930s Alabama, is perhaps the single most revered lawyer in popular culture. Few books are more celebrated than *To Kill a Mockingbird*.[29] It won the Pulitzer Prize, was made into an acclaimed movie starring Gregory Peck, continues to sell a million copies each year, and is required reading at most American high schools.[30] Oprah Winfrey calls the book her favorite of all time[31] and "our national novel."[32] The American Film Institute selected Atticus Finch as the greatest movie hero of all time. He has inspired generations of lawyers and would-be lawyers.

Still, Atticus has taken a beating in recent years. First, a group of commentators and scholars questioned whether he deserved to be so revered. Among the detractors are writer Malcolm Gladwell, who describes Atticus as a paternalistic racial "accommodator,"[33] and legal scholars Monroe Freedman and Steven Lubet, who argue that Atticus is a racist and anti-Semite (Freedman) and an exploiter of sexism and class bias (Lubet).

Gladwell likens Atticus to James ("Big Jim") Folsom, a Southern liberal who was governor of Alabama for most of the 1950s and who believed in changing "hearts and minds" one by one rather than through massive legal and social reforms.[34] Freedman, the earliest and most prophetic of the critics, assails Atticus for being conscripted to represent defendant Tom Robinson instead of volunteering, for not challenging Jim Crow, and for making light of the virulent anti-Semitism and racism of the Ku Klux Klan by calling it a "political organization."[35] Lubet criticizes Atticus for a sexist theory of defense (that complainant Mayella Ewell "wanted it" when she asked Tom Robinson to help her move a chifforobe) and for a class-based slap at Mayella's credibility as "unwashed and illiterate" poor white "trash."[36]

Another commentator concludes that both the book and its central figure have lost their luster over time:

> To Kill a Mockingbird, it appears, is not getting better with age, and each
> time . . . new readers revisit the streets of Maycomb, those streets look less
> insightful and less heroic. Hardest hit by these revisionary readings is the
> novel's purported hero, Atticus Finch. For forty years the source of continuous
> accolades. . . . Nowadays, many readers of the novel are like as not to empha-
> size Finch's complicity with, rather than his challenges to, the segregationist
> politics of his hometown, and as a result Lee's novel is beginning to lose its
> iconic status. Never in all its years has the song of the mockingbird sounded so
> unsweet.[37]

It almost makes you want to tell Atticus's daughter, Scout, to sit back down in the most memorable scene in the book, when—in what Gladwell calls "one of American literature's most moving passages"[38]—after the jury finds the accused Tom Robinson guilty, Atticus quietly gathers his belongings and walks out of the courtroom. Scout recounts:

> Someone was punching me, but I was reluctant to take my eyes from the peo-
> ple below us, and from the image of Atticus's lonely walk down the aisle.
> "Miss Jean Louis?"
> I looked around. They were standing. All around us and in the balcony on
> the opposite wall, the Negroes were getting to their feet. Reverend Syke's voice
> was as distant as Judge Taylor's:
> "Miss Jean Louise, stand up. Your father's passin.'"[39]

I still shed a tear when I read this passage. Atticus deserves this recognition no matter the postmodern postmortems, some of which are more persuasive than others. Atticus should be revered for unflinchingly defending a man accused of interracial rape in the Depression-era South, for literally putting himself between a lynch mob and his client, and for insisting on justice for his poor black client when injustice was inevitable.

Atticus is not an activist but a criminal lawyer representing an indigent defendant charged with a capital offense. That he is a man of his time and place—who prefers to see the best in people, even those with "blind spots,"[40] and who plays on peoples' prejudices to defend his client instead of working to end all prejudice—does not make him less of a hero. Moreover, there is no shame in accepting an appointment to represent an indigent defendant rather than volunteering, downplaying the Klan to young children who feared for their father's safety, putting forward the only viable theory of defense in a rape case—a combination of consent and fabrication—or even in displaying a certain amount of "accommodation" as a trial lawyer. That Atticus might not be perfect does not make him less of a hero.[41]

Then came the much-publicized release of Harper Lee's *Go Set a Watchman* in 2015. The book, a long-buried sequel to *Mockingbird* (though written before it), did further damage to the heroic image of Atticus Finch.

Most of the coverage of *Watchman* was about the circumstances underlying the book's publication—whether it was suddenly discovered when thought lost; whether Lee really wanted it released or was manipulated by her lawyer and publisher; whether the increasingly frail Lee, who died seven months after the book's release, could provide informed consent.

I am among the skeptics of Lee's having wanted this book published. My view is based on the thirty-fifth-anniversary edition of *To Kill a Mockingbird*. When this special edition was released in 1995, it had the original jacket design but was emblazoned with a gold band that boasted, "A New Foreword by the Author." For the millions of readers who loved *Mockingbird*, the prospect of a few more words from its reclusive author was thrilling. Since *Mockingbird*, Lee had written nothing else and had barely uttered a word in public.

But the promised new foreword was nothing of the kind. Instead, the publisher reprinted part of a letter Lee had written two years earlier, rejecting a British publisher's request for an introduction to the novel:

> Please spare "Mockingbird" an Introduction. As a reader I loathe Introductions. To novels, I associate Introductions with long-gone authors and works that are being brought back into print after decades of internment. Although "Mockingbird" will be 33 this year, it has never been out of print and I am still alive, although very quiet. Introductions inhibit pleasure, they kill the joy of anticipation, they frustrate curiosity. The only good thing about Introductions is that in some cases they delay the close to come. "*Mockingbird*" still says what it has to say; it has managed to survive the years without preamble.

Those hundred words say a lot about how Lee felt about *Mockingbird*. She had said what she wanted to say in the book, was proud of how it had stood the test of time, and didn't want to muck it up with more words. If she didn't want to write a brief addendum to her celebrated book, it seems to me she would hardly be inclined to publish a sequel.

That said, what should we make of Atticus Finch in *Watchman*, either in addition to his character in *Mockingbird* or as a completely different man? In *Watchman*, the future erstwhile champion of an innocent black man is a member of a white "Citizens' Council," or, in the words of *New York Times* book critic Michiko Kakutani, a "racist" and "bigot."[42]

I appreciated that Harvard law professor Randall Kennedy began his review of *Watchman* in the *New York Times Book Review* with a nod to Monroe Freedman for exposing the subtle faults of *Mockingbird* Atticus that are now unambiguous in *Watchman*.[43] I acknowledge that I found this new portrayal painful. Still, I prefer University of Chicago law professor Richard McAdam's cool-headed interpretation of Atticus as a brave and able lawyer but no anti–Jim Crow "radical." McAdams calls Atticus a typical Southern white liberal in both books. He was "liberal" in the sense that he opposed lynching and was humane, if paternalistic, in his dealings with black people. But like other Southern liberals, he did not oppose racial segregation, black disenfranchisement, or laws prohibiting interracial marriage. McAdams is not surprised by any of this. "Those who cannot remember the past are condemned to being shocked by the most ordinary things," he writes.

Still, criminal lawyers should not disown Atticus. Though Atticus accepts a criminal appointment in *Watchman* for an insidious reason—to prevent the NAACP from taking the case instead—it is understood he will represent his client well.[44] *Watchman* does nothing to diminish Atticus's exemplary efforts on behalf of Tom Robinson, a case he undertook because Robinson was innocent and "he could not for the life of him let the black boy go to prison because of a half-hearted, court-appointed defense."[45]

It is noteworthy that the criminal case Atticus undertakes in *Watchman* is very different from that of the innocent Tom Robinson. The black defendant in *Watchman* is factually guilty: he was driving fast when he ran over a drunken white man. It turns out Atticus represents the guilty and innocent alike.

•

Why do we need heroes when we seem to enjoy debunking them more than embracing them?

Many people seem to think that icons and heroes are important. The cover of *Time* magazine on June 14, 1999, trumpeted the "100 Heroes and Icons of the Twentieth Century," including twenty who exemplified "courage, selflessness, exuberance, superhuman ability and amazing grace," such as Rosa Parks (one of mine), Harvey Milk, and Che Guevara (two very fine additions).[46]

Of course, we choose heroes based on our own needs and values. Atticus Finch meets mine—or at least, he did when I read *To Kill a Mockingbird* in my youth. He gave me my first image of the trial lawyer as champion. I am now the same age as Atticus, more or less. After rereading the book, I admire him even more.

As Ernest Hemingway once wrote, "As you get older, it is harder to have heroes, but it is sort of necessary."[47] Bernard Malamud explains, "Without heroes, we are all plain people, and don't know how far we can go."[48]

But to regard *oneself* as a hero is something else entirely. To be charitable, maybe this is how some people motivate themselves. For instance, Charles Schultz's alter ego Charlie Brown desperately wants to be a hero. In one famous strip, Charlie Brown's baseball team is one out away from the championship. He is on the mound, pitching:

SCHROEDER: "Get this last man out, Charlie Brown, and the championship is ours!"

VIOLET: "You can do it, Charlie Brown . . . we're all behind you!"

LUCY: "That's right, Charlie Brown . . . we're with you . . . pitch it to 'im, boy! Strike him out. You blockhead!"

GANG: "It's a high fly ball! Catch it Charlie Brown! Catch it and the championship is ours!"

"Have you got it, Charlie Brown?"

"Don't miss it!"

"Get under it, Charlie Brown!"

"Isn't this exciting?"

"What if he drops it?"

"If he drops it, let's all kick him!"

"If Charlie Brown catches this fly ball, we'll win the championship!"

"Just think of it . . . we'll be champions!"

"We'll all get our names in the paper!"

"And they'll give a gold cup!"

"And pins and buttons and pennants."

"DON'T DROP IT!!!" "It's coming down!"

"The fly ball is coming down!"

CHARLIE BROWN: "If I catch it, we'll win the championship and I'll be the **HERO!** If I miss it, I'll be the **GOAT!** I can hear it now. . . . 'Charlie, the Goat, Brown!' Good Grief! How did I ever get into this?!"

The fly ball comes down, lands in Charlie Brown's glove . . . and drops out on the ground.

GANG: **"AAUGH!"**

CHARLIE BROWN: "So I drop the fly ball and we lose the championship! I could have been the hero. . . . Instead, I'm the **GOAT.** The other team is carrying their manager home on their shoulders. . . . Heroes ride. . . . Goats walk. . . . I wanted so much to be the hero. . . . But I always end up being the **GOAT!** No matter how hard I try, I always end up being the **GOAT!"**[49]

The quest for heroism doesn't work out for Charlie Brown. It's too much pressure; all or nothing, hero or goat.

For some, the desire to be a hero is more primal. Ernest Becker argues in his Pulitzer Prize–winning book, *The Denial of Death*, that the quest for heroism is a way of fending off mortality and being part of something eternal, which, in turn, gives life meaning. To Becker, the quest is mostly based in fear. As he writes in the beginning of the book, "The idea of death, the fear of it, haunts the human animal like nothing else; it is a mainspring of human activity—activity designed largely to avoid the fatality of death, to overcome it by denying in some way that it is the final destiny for man."[50]

Not surprisingly, Becker's book captured filmmaker Woody Allen's imagination. In *Annie Hall*, the death-obsessed Alvy Singer (Allen) buys *The Denial of Death* for his new girlfriend, Annie (Diane Keaton). He wants her to understand his view of life—that life is divided into the "horrible" and "miserable." The horrible, he explains, consists of "terminal cases," "the crippled," and other people like that who, amazingly, "get through life." The miserable consists of everybody else, who should be thankful they are only miserable.[51]

Whatever its genesis, believing you are a hero can lead to a toxic combination of self-sacrifice and self-importance in criminal defenders. Nothing can compete with the urgency of the work and no one is more important than the lawyer. This is not a supportable professional or personal model.

Monroe Freedman says that "the lawyers we should hold up as role models are those who earn their living in the kinds of practices that most lawyers pursue—corporate, trusts and estates, litigation, even teaching—but who also volunteer a small but significant amount of their time and skills to advance social justice."[52] He may be on to something, even if Freedman is only suggesting that these pedestrian lawyers are worthy of respect.[53]

But if what Freedman means is that he admires ordinary people who manage to cope with whatever is thrown at them and work hard without losing their appreciation for life, the model seems less pedestrian. Aren't these the people most of us are drawn to, unsung though they may be? It is about such people that the writer and poet Marge Piercy writes in *To Be of Use*, one of my very favorite poems.[54]

Stephen Stept, the producer of a public television movie on Clarence Darrow, preferred the flawed version of the man to the heroic one for good reason, saying, "If he was just a hero, a knight in shining armor, it'd be really boring." He called Darrow a "beautifully flawed character. . . . A man with great passion [and] a profound sense of justice . . . [but] who was, in his own right, kind of cynical and . . . somewhat vain." Stept found "personal heroism" in Darrow's "perseverance" and in his "believing in [himself] and pulling [himself] up and moving on and doing even greater work."[55]

Acknowledging that people you admire have flaws doesn't mean you can't look up to them. Among the contemporary criminal defense lawyers I admire are Stephen Bright, Bryan Stevenson, Judy Clarke, and David Bruck. They are all talented and committed capital defense lawyers who undoubtedly have their faults. A former fellow and I once "anointed" a handful of criminal lawyers—including Bright, Stevenson, and Sister Helen Prejean—"criminal defense prophets and saints."[56] We probably shouldn't have used the word "saint" (or "prophet," for that matter), even though we did so in a paper about the Judeo-Christian influence in criminal defense. We wanted to recognize the extraordinary work of these people, not deify them.

When hero-lawyers morph into "moral saints," the work becomes more a *burden* than a blessing. Philosopher Susan Wolf describes the moral saint as so devoted to a "moral imperative" that he or she essentially lacks "an identifiable, personal self" and has a "life strangely barren."[57] Moral saints have either no personal life or a tattered one. This is because the moral imperative of the work leaves no room for anything else. As legal ethics scholar Bradley Wendel says, there is something "unsettling about a person who was so single-mindedly committed to doing good that he or she had no other projects, passions, and commitments," and we would "recoil from this kind of hero."[58] Or as billionaire real estate tycoon George Wade (Hugh Grant) says to cause lawyer Lucy Kelson (Sandra Bullock) in the movie *Two Weeks Notice*, "No one wants to live with a saint. Saints are boring."[59]

There is such a thing as too much commitment.

•

I admit I have my own guilt, or at least things I feel bad about. Career defender Stu Glovin says public defenders "live in the land of broken toys" and there is "something broken about all of us."[60] Bryan Stevenson uses similar language in explaining why he represents people on death row, writing, "My life is filled with brokenness. . . . I don't do what I do because I have to, because I've been trained to. I do what I do because I'm broken too. You cannot defend condemned people without being broken. You recognize this community of the broken. That makes it not about them, but about you—I'm trying to save *my* life. When they're executed, a part of me dies. When they're exonerated, I feel their freedom."[61]

This is startlingly similar to Clarence Darrow, who defended more than a hundred men who were facing the death penalty, of whom not a single one was executed. This was a good thing, according to Darrow, because if one had been executed, he feared he might not survive it. "It would almost, if not quite, kill me," he said. Darrow knew his own limits:

> I had a strongly emotional nature which has caused me boundless joy and infinite pain. I had a vivid imagination. Not only could I put myself in the other person's place but I could not avoid doing so. My sympathies always went out to the weak, the suffering, and the poor. Realizing their sorrows I tried to relieve them in order that I myself might be relieved.[62]

The deep connection between both Stevenson and Darrow and their clients sounds a lot like the empathy Charles Ogletree describes. But Stevenson and Darrow do what they do not only out of concern for their clients but because there is something in it for *them* too.

We are all flawed. At our best, we recognize our failings and struggle to overcome a least some of them.

I often say that if I had been born as disadvantaged as most of my clients and remained trapped in poverty, I would probably be a shoplifter. It's not that I believe stealing is OK. It's that I'm a shopper and, if I lacked the means, I would probably still be a shopper. I am reminded of Rosa Lee Cunningham, about whom I wrote in the first chapter of this book. She was a misdemeanant version of my Jewish grandmother. When Rosa Lee's grandchildren needed new winter coats, she went to a local Washington, DC, department store and boosted them. When my siblings and I needed new coats, my grandmother took us to Marshall Fields in Chicago and bought them.

Of course, shoplifting is hardly the sole province of the poor. My partner Sally's Grandma Annie was a compulsive thief—perhaps a kleptomaniac. All manner of things could be found in her massive pocketbook, including steak. Apparently, her behavior was well known: her son had an arrangement with the small grocery store in her apartment building that they bill him rather than call the police. No one was safe from Grandma Annie's sticky fingers. Sally's mother would buy cartons of cigarettes—Montclair Menthol Gold 100s. Whenever Grandma Annie stopped by, several packs would go missing. Afterward, when Sally's mom paid her mother a call, Grandma Annie would proudly present her with a pack of her own cigarettes, announcing, "Betty, I have your brand!"

My friend Susan's grandfather routinely hid things at Filene's Basement until the price went down. This is not exactly shoplifting, but close. A more embarrassing shoplifting incident at the Filene's Basement flagship store in downtown Boston involved former Massachusetts Supreme Judicial Court justice Ruth Abrams. In 1992, she was arrested for switching the price tag on a twelve-dollar wallet with a lower-priced one. She denied wrongdoing and was never formally charged, but it was a front-page story in the *Boston Globe*.

I don't feel guilty about my own inner shoplifter. But I would *be* guilty.

I do, however, feel guilty about two things as a lawyer: getting it wrong and losing my cool.

But lawyers get it wrong all the time, especially trial lawyers. I sometimes describe trial work as mistake management because mistakes are inevitable, and you have to manage them. Trials happen at a fast and furious pace. Lawyers are bound to miss some things or not address them as cogently as they would like. One of my favorite *New Yorker* cartoons features a lawyer leaving a courthouse with a thought balloon above his head that says, "I wish I had said . . . I wish I had said . . . I wish I had said. . . ." The caption is "The Defense Never Rests."

A good friend and career public defender in Rochester, New York, says the real reason criminal trial lawyers like to win at trial is so no one will ever see the trial transcript with all the idiotic things we said and did.[63]

We don't want to make mistakes. We want to be perfect. "An actor may fumble his lines," Clarence Darrow once wrote, "but a lawyer needs to be letter-perfect."[64] Amazingly, Darrow always spoke without notes. I rely on compulsively detailed outlines for trials and hearings to make sure I don't miss a thing. Still, I screw things up.

I once represented a young man I'll call Manny. He called the clinic after having shot a man in the chest during an argument. Manny saw the man reaching for an object in his waistband, thought it was a gun, and shot out of fear. He wanted to turn himself in. The case against him was strong: he was unlawfully carrying a firearm; he shot an unarmed man (who had been reaching for a wallet in the waistband of his sweatpants so it wouldn't fall down during a fist fight); and, although Manny fired only once, the man was hospitalized for two weeks and lost a piece of his lung.

To make matters worse, the complainant turned out to be a member of the National Guard with no prior record. Manny had a prior conviction for selling drugs and was on probation. Although this was his only conviction, and he was doing well on probation, the conviction would make it difficult for Manny to testify at trial. Plus, the gun charge alone was a probation violation.

When Manny met with us at the clinic, he made no excuses. He felt awful about what had happened and was worried about the other man's condition. But he was also worried about the time he was facing and the effect it would have on his family. He had a longtime girlfriend with whom he had two young children. He had not been involved in drugs since being placed on probation. The reason he was carrying a gun that day was because he heard that someone was after him.

He asked about cooperating with the government. He had information about unsolved homicides, which he was willing to share if it could cut some of the time he would have to be away from his family. Manny understood this would put him at risk. But it was worth it if he could see his kids grow up.

He pled guilty and was held without bail. He was interrogated by police and prosecutors and given polygraph exams. He provided crucial information in several "cold" murder cases. He testified before grand juries and trial juries. He helped resolve several cases.

When it was time for Manny's sentencing, I was cautiously optimistic, as was the fellow working with me. Manny had been locked up for more than a year. The probation judge agreed to terminate Manny's probation without further incarceration. We got Manny accepted into a rigorous, five-year residential program in California that specialized in working with young men with criminal backgrounds but who showed promise. To our relief, the presentence investigator also recommended this program and that Manny receive a "split sentence" of jail time and probation. The time he had already served in jail would suffice.

We told Manny that, under all the circumstances, we had a decent chance of getting the sentence we were seeking: time served and probation, with the condition that he successfully complete the five-year out-of-state program. We told him that he should prepare himself for the worst, which, in my judgment, was a sentence that would require him to serve five or six years in prison instead of the program, followed by a period of supervision overseen by the sentencing judge.

On the day of the sentencing, the courtroom was filled with Manny's neighbors, friends, and family, who had written letters of support attesting to his good prospects for rehabilitation. We had submitted a lengthy sentencing memorandum, which included a letter from Manny to the judge. He wrote,

> Your Honor, I am truly sorry for what I have done. I have disappointed my family and my kids. . . . This is the longest time I have ever been incarcerated. I hate to say it, but I needed to come to jail to really see how it feels to be away from my family. Now I see it's no place for me, and while I'm here I am taking the first real steps to changing my life for the better forever. . . . I want to be a positive role model for my children and my nieces and nephew.

As the hearing was about to begin, the complainant strode into the courtroom in full National Guard uniform. He gave a victim impact statement about how it felt to be shot, to collapse on the street, to be rushed into surgery, to be on a respirator. He said he almost lost his life, and for no reason. He was Manny's age.

I made the sentencing argument, acknowledging the seriousness of the complainant's injury but emphasizing Manny's contrition and promise. He was a family man, a good man. His substantial assistance to law enforcement was already part of the (sealed) record, confirmed by the prosecution.

It was significant that the presentence investigator—who essentially worked for the court—agreed that a rehabilitative program rather than a lengthy sentence was in order.

Then it was Manny's turn to speak. He began by apologizing to the victim. "I'm sorry, man," he said. "I didn't mean to do it." The judge erupted in rage. "You didn't mean to? You didn't *mean* to? You armed yourself with an illegal gun, went into the community, took the gun out and fired it. You shot an unarmed man serving our country." Manny tried to explain what he meant—that he didn't know the other man was unarmed, he reacted out of fear, it was an honest mistake—but the judge cut him off. "You're not taking responsibility, young man."

The judge sentenced Manny to thirty-six years. This was not a split sentence. Under applicable sentencing law, Manny would likely serve thirty years before he was released by the United States Parole Commission.

The fellow and I were crushed. Manny did not deserve to be in a cage for three decades. He had done everything he could during his year of incarceration to help the government and show he was worthy of redemption. Had it all been for nothing?

We went to see Manny at the DC jail the next morning at around 6:00 a.m. This might have been the earliest lawyer-client meeting in the history of the jail. I wasn't sleeping anyway and neither was the fellow working with me. I thought Manny might refuse to see us, but he came right away and wouldn't let us apologize. He said, "I'm not mad at y'all. You did everything you could. I'm the one who had that gun."

His kindness made us feel worse. We told him we weren't giving up. We would file a motion asking the judge to reconsider the sentence. We would ask the prosecutor to join our motion, as it was not in the government's interest to have cooperators clobbered at sentencing. The prosecutor had only asked for a sentence within the "guidelines." He was as surprised as we were by the judge's sentence.

I had a hard time coping with what happened. I had failed our client in so many ways: I knew this judge was volatile and should have anticipated the problem with Manny's word choice. I should have foreseen that the complainant would appear in uniform. I should have prepared Manny for the worst-case scenario no matter our optimism.

My faith in my lawyerly judgment was shattered. When students and fellows sought my advice, I wanted to send them elsewhere. "Why are you asking me?" I wanted to say. "I clearly know nothing."

I felt wretched. I couldn't sleep or eat. I couldn't find my sense of humor.

My friend Ilene, the civil poverty lawyer, chided, "Are you so narcissistic you never make mistakes?" "Good point," I said (even though I was tempted to say that, apparently, I *was* so narcissistic). "Yes, I do make mistakes," I said. "But not this big." "Come on," she said. "The best any of us can do is the best we can do." "I know," I said. "But I have to be able to rely on my judgment, and my judgment is what failed me—to the tune of *thirty years*." She thought about this. "I once had a case in which I made a serious miscalculation," she said, "I had a hard time getting over it, too. Thank God it was only money."

I met with the trial prosecutor, his supervisor, and the chief of the office's violent crimes division. I spoke to him candidly. I was asking for help under unusual circumstances. The judge would never change Manny's excessive sentence based on a defense motion only; we needed to file a joint motion. I told him about Manny's scant record and the circumstances of the crime. But mostly I talked about his cooperation, which had been provided based on assurances that it would be a significant factor at sentencing. I told him that what happened to Manny would send a message to other criminal defendants: if you cooperate, not only will you be in peril as a "snitch," but the government will not come through for you. When word gets around, no defense lawyer will advise a client to cooperate.

The division chief got it. I didn't have to beg. He joined our motion, signaling to the judge that this case was equally important to the government. It made a difference. Unfortunately, Manny wasn't sent to the program, but his sentence was reduced to six years in prison, which was at least in line with our advice to him. Manny was grateful. He would get out in time to be a father to his children.

The truth is, I don't believe in "doing the best you can." I have a higher standard for criminal defense lawyers. Some lawyers' "best" is slim comfort to the client. I believe in providing the kind of representation my clients would receive if they were able to pay for the best lawyer in town. I try to instill this ethos in my students and fellows.

But as Ilene pointed out, there is narcissism in perfectionism. I make mistakes. My students and fellows make mistakes. Hopefully we learn something from our errors and make new and different ones next time.

•

It is helpful for criminal lawyers to become good at forgetting. Edward Feathers, the central character in English writer Jane Gardam's novel *Old Filth*, is a barrister who spent most of his professional life in Hong Kong. (His nickname, "Filth," stands for "Failed in London Try Hong Kong.") Before becoming a judge, he was a terrific advocate who tried lots of cases, was appointed Queen's Counsel ("took silk"), and was known for his wit. He learned the importance of forgetting early on:

> Filth had always said—of his Cases—"I am trained to forget." "Otherwise," he said, "how could I function?" Facts, memories, the pain of life—of lives in chaos—have to be forgotten. Filth had condemned men to death. Had seen innocent men convicted. As a Silk he reckoned that fifty percent of his Cases had gone wrong.[65]

Thank goodness 50 percent is higher than my experience. But cases do go wrong. And it can be hard to carry on afterward, especially if you feel responsible for the loss. Defense lawyers—at least conscientious ones—often feel responsible.

How to forget but not entirely forget? Not only would the latter be impossible, but it's probably not desirable. There is a small drawer in the back of my brain where I put painful court experiences. The memories aren't gone; they are carefully tucked away. Some things should not be entirely forgotten.

No one ever told me to develop an ability to forget when I was a young public defender. I wish they had. How else to get over some of the terrible things that happen and to start anew? Persistence and passion are also helpful, according to psychologist and "grit" expert Angela Duckworth.[66] But a little forgetting is indispensable.

We should teach that to defenders.

•

I confess that I have become less good-tempered as I head into my fourth decade in criminal defense.

I can always tell when I need a few days away. I fear I might cross over from fantasy to reality and grab a prosecutor by the shirt collar and throttle him or her. Or I might become Al Pacino in the movie *And Justice for All* and give a judge a piece of my mind—"*You're* out of order! *You're* out of order! The *whole trial* is out of order! *They're* out of order!"[67]

I do what I can to hold my tongue for both tactical and ethical reasons. First, a temper tantrum is not usually persuasive. Second, lawyers have an ethical obligation to "demonstrate respect for the legal system and for those who serve it, including judges, other lawyers and public officials"[68] and to avoid conduct that is "prejudicial to the administration of justice."[69] There is a little leeway, though. As part of our duty to the client, the legal profession, and the justice system, lawyers are allowed to confront and challenge the "rectitude of official action."[70]

But an angry outburst at prosecutors or judges—unless strategically done—probably isn't smart.

Yet even when I hold my tongue, my true feelings sometimes slip out in facial expressions. Once, during a misdemeanor assault trial in which I was supervising a student lawyer, a judge made so many terrible evidentiary rulings—always against the defense—that I showed my dismay. The judge called me up to sidebar. "Ms. Smith," he said, "Your facial expressions are conveying your dislike of this court's rulings." "With all due respect, Your Honor," I replied, "that's *restraint*." This did not go over well.

I tried to explain to the judge that I may be a professor, but I'm also defense counsel, and lawyerly zeal is part of the package. I quoted one of my favorite lines from a federal appeals court: "A criminal trial is not a minuet."[71] The judge was not mollified. I later realized I had blown a rare opportunity to quote Mae West. During her trial on indecency charges, she took every opportunity to mock the proceedings. When the trial judge confronted her—"Miss West, are you trying to show contempt for this court?"—she replied, "On the contrary, Your Honor. I was doing my best to hide it."

The final straw in the student assault trial was when the judge ruled that bystanders who happened upon the incident were biased simply because they were called by the defense. This was absurd, and we did not hold back in arguing that these witnesses, like all witnesses, must be evaluated on their merits, not on who called them. (The judge was later rebuked by the appeals court for this ruling.)

When I was a young public defender in Philadelphia, I cited a United States Supreme Court case at a preliminary hearing. At the time, preliminary hearings were held in police station courtrooms in the neighborhoods where the crime was alleged to have occurred. This one was in South Philly. The judge looked at me as if I had lost my mind. "Ms. Smith," he scowled, "Are you citing a U.S. Supreme Court case in this courtroom? Do you know where you are?" Apparently, the judge thought South Philadelphia was his own personal fiefdom, immune to federal constitutional law.

A former fellow had a similar experience in a trial in the Bronx. He objected to the introduction of certain evidence under the Confrontation Clause of the Sixth Amendment, citing the well-known United States Supreme Court case *Crawford v. Washington*.[72] The judge was not impressed. "You're going to need to cite a New York Court of Appeals case," she said.

A good friend—a lawyer and law professor who specializes in family law and domestic violence—was recently ordered by a judge not to talk to her client during a civil trial. This was apparently to stop my friend from advising her client (who was currently on the witness stand) about the content of the client's testimony.[73] Stunned, she adhered to the judge's order. When she regained her equilibrium, she explained to the judge that he could not order her to violate core ethical responsibilities—communicating with a client, giving advice, and providing competent representation—and that her client also had a due process right to confer with her.

This kind of judicial behavior is a central challenge in trial work. It is especially shocking to young lawyers, who think judges are going to be like their smartest law professors—knowledgeable about and engaged in the law. Alas, this is seldom the case. (My old friend and public defender colleague Cookie Ridolfi, who attended parochial schools throughout her childhood, was afraid that, as a new lawyer, she would look up at the judge in his or her black robe and say, "Yes, Sister.")

It is hard to strike the right tone before a judge who is often wrong but never in doubt. Self-righteous incredulity—getting on one's high horse—is seldom effective. You must instead swallow your pique, do what you can to convince the judge, and at the very least, leave a decent record.

•

Along with learning how to forget, criminal defense lawyers have to learn how to take a punch. The system is full of bullies.[74] Criminal defendants are regular targets, and so are their lawyers. Getting slapped down, dressed down, and put down is part of the job.

A judge who apparently didn't like having to deal with my (admittedly frequent) objections to his (often insane) rulings said to me, "Ms. Smith, every time you talk, this poor man"—pointing to the court reporter—"has to transcribe it. And he's not getting any younger." (This particular court reporter was sort of ancient.)

Another judge yelled at me throughout the entire jury selection process. He conducted the bulk of the questioning of prospective jurors and allowed the attorneys to ask follow-up questions. But every time I asked a question, he became enraged (all the while incorporating many of my questions). Out of the presence of jurors, he finally exploded. "Ms. Smith," he said, "You are making this process take much longer than it should." "Your Honor," I demurred, "I'd like to see the transcript. I bet you yelling at me is taking much more time than my questions."

I have to watch myself. Judges and prosecutors do not always appreciate my sense of humor.

I tried a misdemeanor police assault case with a fellow that lasted several days because the judge kept interrupting the trial to hear other matters. One day was particularly frustrating. We were scheduled to begin first thing in the morning, only to have the case called for trial at ten minutes before the luncheon recess. We were told we would resume promptly at 2:00 p.m., but other matters again got in the way. When the trial was eventually reconvened, we got through maybe fifteen minutes of testimony before adjourning for the day.

When the judge said we would resume first thing the next day, I was anxious. I inquired whether the trial might be put off until the following day instead. I explained that my last legal ethics class of the semester was scheduled for the next day, there were nearly one hundred students in it, and the class could not be rescheduled. The judge asked what time the class was. I told him 3:30 p.m.

"That is ridiculous, Ms. Smith," he said. "What makes you think we won't be finished with this trial by tomorrow afternoon?" I swallowed hard and said, "I guess I have a little PTSD from today." The judge—who was known for having a temper with lawyers—lost it. I am not sure I have ever received such a dressing down by a judge. He found my remark "outrageous" and "disrespectful." He refused to hear anything further from me, would not accept an apology, and stormed off the bench.

I don't know why my tongue-in-cheek comment set him off. I had appeared before him many times, and he was a big supporter of the Georgetown clinical program. I thought our relationship was solid enough to withstand a little teasing. Clearly, I had overstepped.

I prostrated myself before him. I sent an email expressing my regret. I acknowledged that my remark was a poor attempt at humor. I said I had nothing but respect for the court and trusted he would not hold this unfortunate incident against my students, fellows, or clients. This last thing was a pressing concern; we were still in trial.

I received no reply. The next day, when the case was called for trial, I asked to approach the bench to make sure all was well. It wasn't. In the presence of the fellow and prosecutor, the judge rejected the suggestion that my comment was meant in humor and launched into another rebuke. In truth, I have repressed the substance (or it is tucked away in that small drawer) because it was so shaming. I felt about an inch tall.

An article in the *New York Times Magazine* called "How to Take a Punch" is instructive. It quotes seventeen-year-old Claressa Shields, the first American woman to win an Olympic gold medal in boxing, in 2012. She says you should never shut your eyes when you're about to be punched and should try to avoid even blinking. Instead, you should "watch the fist come in and learn from it." To counter a swing to the face, you should duck your head to the side, a tactic called "slipping." This is because, even if it doesn't hurt, a blow to the face looks bad. Whatever you do, Shields counsels, don't get angry—and don't let yourself be overtaken by fear, spite, or rage. "If you get hit, tell yourself: 'It's just one punch.'"[75]

It was just one punch, I said to myself as we went forward to trial. *I can take it. I've taken worse.* I also said to myself, *I did what I could to protect the client. This is not about me.* The client was ultimately acquitted. Nothing heals a punch quicker.

One judge literally took a punch at a public defender. Brevard County, Florida judge John C. Murphy, angered by Andrew Weinstock's refusal to waive his client's right to a speedy trial, said, "If I had a rock, I would throw it at you right now," and then threatened to "go out back" and "beat [Weinstock's] ass." The judge made good on the threat by going out into the hall and punching Weinstock in the head. A videotape of the incident went viral, leading to (surprisingly lenient) discipline: the judge was suspended (with pay) for a short while, sent to anger management classes, and then returned to the bench.[76] Only after extensive bad press was he later removed.[77]

Taking a (metaphorical) punch includes handling the routine disappointments that come with being counsel for the defense: objections overruled, motions denied, arguments rebuffed. You take it unblinkingly and learn a little something. You jump back into the ring when the bell dings, eager for more.

•

You can be an excellent, committed defender and also have a full life. It is not all guilt, sacrifice, and suffering. As legal ethics scholar Alice Woolley notes, not only do criminal lawyers have perfectly good lives, but their lives are made especially rich and meaningful by helping those who need them most—"people down on their luck, underdogs, people whom everyone else has thrown on the dust heap"—and by contributing to a "world that is compassionate and fair and holds people in authority to account."[78]

Even capital defenders, who carry a particularly heavy weight, can have fun. Sometimes the mirth is unexpected; it is literally gallows humor. My old friend and colleague Marc Bookman, a death penalty lawyer and writer, manages to find the humor—macabre though it sometimes is—in death penalty cases. In one article, he shares examples of pathetic, shameful lawyering from ten capital cases—situations that, as he says, "would be funny were they not so deadly serious." They include a lawyer who parked his car during critical testimony; one who cut and pasted a former client's appeal to that of his current client without changing the name of the judge, trial lawyer, or trial exhibits; and a lawyer who "strategically slept" through much of a capital trial.[79]

Having a sense of humor is essential in criminal defense. When asked whether most of her clients are guilty, career public defender Arlene Popkin replied, "Not if I can help it!"[80]

Defenders have to be brave, bold, and intrepid. I do not mean to make light of what is required; the work is consuming and can be grueling. But it is a recipe for disaster to become a martyr for the work, forsaking family, friends, and oneself.

There is more than enough guilt to go around. But not enough shared responsibility. Too often we fail to see ourselves in people who commit crime, preferring instead to see them as the "other," a "criminal," or a "bad person" who needs to be caged and cast off. Ferdinand von Shirach, a German criminal defense lawyer and writer, puts it this way:

> We chase after things, but they're faster than we are, and in the end we never catch up. I tell the stories of people I've defended. They were murderers, drug

dealers, bank robbers, and prostitutes. They all had their stories, and they weren't so different from us.

All our lives, we dance on a thin layer of ice; it's very cold underneath, and death is quick. The ice won't bear the weight of some people and they fall through. That's the moment that interests me. If we're lucky, it never happens to us and we keep dancing. If we're lucky.[81]

There is some sacrifice in criminal defense work, as there is in any important work. But one need not be a martyr. For me, the work is a privilege. There is nothing more stimulating, fun, challenging, heartbreaking, and rewarding than representing people accused or convicted of crime.

Acknowledgments

I wrote much of this book while caring for my parents in South Florida. I was supposed to be on sabbatical in Australia. But my mother's cancer returned with a vengeance as my father became increasingly diminished from dementia. So I went to live with them for a few months.

It is remarkable that I did any writing at all during that time. I was at my parents' beck and call. I don't think I've heard my name called more times in a single day. I was driver, cook, and all-around errand runner. People at the local Walgreens and Publix knew me by name.

I would read passages to Mom from time to time. When she decided to stop chemotherapy—well after I had returned home—she called me on the phone. "I want you to send me the manuscript of your new book right away," she said. Then she read it, calling me every few hours to share her thoughts. This was an extraordinary act of devotion.

I owe many debts to many people. (Please forgive me for omitting anyone.)

To the fellows, students, staff, and faculty at Georgetown's Criminal Defense & Prisoner Advocacy Clinic and E. Barrett Prettyman Fellowship Program, who worked with me on many of the cases recounted in the book or helped me talk through ideas: Hannah Ackerman, Ty Alper, Zawadi Baharanyi, Jordan Barnett, Eboni Blenman, Jordan Blumenthal, Carmen Brooks, Barbara Butterworth, Tucker Carrington, Moses Cook, John Copacino, Lindsay Dressler, Samuel Eilers, Andrew Ferguson, Ryan Ferguson, Alejandro Fernandez, Eduardo Ferrer, Alison Flaum, Corrine

Fletcher, Cynthia Frezzo, Jessica Gingold, Joe Goldstein-Breyer, Zach Goodman, Vincent Haskell, Sophia Heller, Kris Henning, Paul Holland, Seana Holland, Jacob Howard, Camilla Hsu, Sai Iyer, Vida Johnson, Ashley Jones, J. D. King, Eric Klein, Yaniv Kot, Jacob Lemon-Strauss, Michael Marks, Nate Mensah, William Montross, Texys Morris, Katie Moss, Olinda Moyd, Brandi McNeil, Wally Mlyniec, Barrie Newberger, Eli Northrup, Alaric Piette, Devin Prater, Teruko Richardson, Kari Ridgeway, Mitchell Schwartz, Ben Schiffelbein, Ben Shaw, Alison Siegler, Patrick Simmons, Jiseon Song, Cassandra Snyder, Robin Walker Sterling, Viraj Talwar, Chidinma Ume, Lindsey Webb, Sarah Young, and James Ziegler.

To my excellent research assistants: Charlotte Berschback, Joyce Dela Pena, Christopher Duffner, Andrea Fenster, Claire Mauksch, Holly Travis, and Juliana Wishne.

To Helen Garner, Sally Greenberg, Betsy Kuhn, Barbara Pizer, and Ilene Seidman, who generously read an early draft of the manuscript, or portions of it, and made helpful suggestions.

To the friends and family who cheered me on: Jane Aiken, Nan Aron, Bernie Arons, Vivian Aston, Barbara Babcock, Hallie Baker, Laurie Barron, Louise Bowen, Shelley Broderick, John Beranbaum, Marc Bookman, Christina Bradley, Susan Brooks, Jennifer Brown, Debbie Butler, Paul Butler, Carmia Caesar, Mal Catt, Elizabeth Chadis, Laura Cohen, Brad Colbert, Cathryn Crawford, Angela Jordan Davis, Karen Delacy, Maryellen Delacy, Sindi Deisen, Amy Deutsch, Terri Doane, Steven Drizin, Barbara Eichner, Jules Epstein, Monroe Freedman, Karen Friedman, Stuart Glovin, Danny Greenberg, Ellen Greenlee, Bonnie Hardy, Jeannie Hess, Sandra Horwich, Tracey Hughes, Catherine Klein, Kevin Kramp, Carrie Lamson, Lex Lasry, Ben Lerner, Felicia Eichner Levin, Helen Levin, Judy Levin, Mark Levine, Richard Lubin, Marc Margolius, Joe Margulies, Allegra McLeod, James McKown, Loni Smith McKown, Paul Messing, Esperanta Moise, Sherally Munshi, Avis Murray, Alyson Myers, Karen Nelson, Gary Nixon, Nick Olcott, Jill Paperno, Sarah Park, Gary Peller, Nancy Radner, Cookie Ridolfi, Martha Rappoli, Ann Roan, Sandra Rosenthal, Tanina Rostain, David Rudovsky, Kathy Schultz, Stuart Schuman, Analie Seide, Kate Seidman, Larry Seidman, Mike Seidman, Lauren Eckhouse Silva-Pinto, Marilyn Silverstein, David Singleton, Anita Smith, David Smith, Gail Smith, Glenn Smith, Tiki Srieud, Robin Steinberg, Lauren Stempler, David Stern, Pam Smith Stern, Jean Sternlight, Leslie Eichner Storch, Dean Strang, Phyllis Subin, Karen Tokarz, David Udell, Kim Vaeth, Earl Ward,

Chuck Watson, Nancy Weintrub, Tim Westmoreland, Steve Wizner, Alice Woolley, Ellen Yaroshefsky, and Steven Zeidman.

To my son, Joe Greenberg, who inspires me every day and who, together with my fellows and students, makes me hopeful for the next generation.

To my Welsh terrier, Hapus, my beloved companion for the past sixteen years and who has kept me company through every writing project.

I am also grateful to Peter Matson, my literary agent at Sterling Lord Literistic, and Ellen Adler at the New Press, who introduced me to Micah Kleit, director of Rutgers University Press. I couldn't be happier to be an RUP author. Micah, who is also my wonderful editor, believed in this book from the start. Elisabeth Maselli at Rutgers and Josh Wilkerson also provided essential guidance at various stages of the publishing process.

Finally, I want to thank Dean William Treanor of the Georgetown University Law Center, who knew me when I was a *Yale Daily News* cartoonist and supported this book project in every possible way.

Notes

Introduction

1 See Abbe Smith, *Case of a Lifetime: A Criminal Defense Lawyer's Story* (New York: St. Martin's Press, 2009).

2 Alan Dershowitz, *The Best Defense* (New York: Random House, 1982), xiv.

3 The Innocence Project was founded in 1992 by Barry Scheck and Peter Neufeld. See "About," Innocence Project, accessed October 4, 2015, http://www .innocenceproject.org/free-innocent. Scheck made the remark at a 2009 conference at Hofstra University School of Law. Scheck is a friend. See Abbe Smith, "In Praise of the Guilty Project: A Criminal Defense Lawyer's Growing Anxiety about Innocence Projects," *University of Pennsylvania Journal of Law and Social Change* 13, no. 3 (2009–2010): 321. As of August 2015, more than three hundred people in the United States have been exonerated by DNA testing, including twenty who served time on death row. See "Exonerate the Innocent," Innocence Project, accessed July 23, 2018, https://innocenceproject.org/exonerate.

4 See generally Smith, "In Praise of the Guilty Project," 315–330. For essential reading on mass incarceration, see Michelle Alexander, *The New Jim Crow: Mass Incarceration in the Age of Color Blindness* (New York: New Press, 2010); Marie Gottschalk, *Caught: The Prison State and the Lockdown of American Politics* (Princeton: Princeton University Press, 2015).

5 David Cole, "Punitive Damage," *New York Times*, May 18, 2014, 24. See also Katie Rose Quandt, "Watch John Oliver Explain the Insanity of Our Prison System with Puppets," Mother Jones, last modified July 21, 2014, http://www.motherjones.com/ mixed-media/2014/07/john-oliver-prison-system-sesame-street-puppets; and James Q. Whitman, *Harsh Justice: Criminal Punishment and the Widening Divide between America and Europe* (Oxford: Oxford University Press, 2005).

6 Pew Charitable Trusts, "Punishment Rate Measures Prison Use Relative to Crime," Pew Charitable Trusts Public Safety Performance Project, March 23, 2016, http://www.pewtrusts.org/en/research-and-analysis/issue-briefs/2016/03/the

-punishment-rate (finding that the United States became 165 percent more punitive from 1983 to 2013, a period during which the imprisonment rate soared).

7   As of the latest Justice Department data, more than two million people are incarcerated in the United States. Danielle Kaeble and Mary Cowhig, "Correctional Populations in the United States, 2016," Bureau of Justice Statistics Bulletin, April 2018, 1, https://www.bjs.gov/content/pub/pdf/cpus16.pdf (reporting that, although the number of incarcerated persons has been declining, there are currently 2,162,400 people incarcerated in the United States). See also Peter Wagner and Bernadette Rabuy, "Mass Incarceration: The Whole Pie 2015," Prison Policy Initiative, last modified December 8, 2015, http://www.prisonpolicy.org/reports/pie2015.html (reporting that in 2015, the U.S. criminal justice system held more than 2.3 million people in 1,719 state prisons, 102 federal prisons, 2,259 juvenile correctional facilities, 3,283 local jails, and 79 Indian Country jails, as well as in military prisons, immigration detention facilities, civil commitment centers, and prisons in the U.S. territories); "Incarceration," Sentencing Project, accessed October 4, 2015, http://www.sentencingproject.org/template/page.cfm?id=107 (reporting that more than 2 million people are incarcerated in the United States).

8   "Too Many Laws, Too Many Prisoners: Never in the Civilised World Have So Many Been Locked Up for So Little," *Economist*, last modified July 22, 2010, https://www.economist.com/briefing/2010/07/22/too-many-laws-too-many-prisoners.

9   See David Cole, "Can Our Shameful Prisons Be Reformed?," *New York Review of Books*, last modified November 19, 2009, https://www.nybooks.com/articles/2009/11/19/can-our-shameful-prisons-be-reformed/ (noting that the incarceration rates in these two countries are both 40 percent less than in the United States).

10 See E. Ann Carson, "Prisoners in 2014," Bureau of Justice Statistics Bulletin, September 2015, 1, https://www.bjs.gov/content/pub/pdf/p14.pdf (reporting that in 2014 there was a 1 percent decrease in the number of prisoners in state and federal correctional facilities); Carl Hulse and Jennifer Steinhauer, "Sentencing Overhaul Proposed in Senate with Bipartisan Backing," *New York Times*, October 2, 2015, A19 (reporting about a bipartisan measure that would cut mandatory prison sentences for nonviolent offenders, promote early releases, institute effective reentry programs, and allow young offenders to seal their criminal records); Timothy Williams, "Police Leaders Join Call to Cut Prison Rosters," *New York Times*, October 21, 2015, A1 (reporting that more than 130 police chiefs, prosecutors, and sheriffs who believe that "too many people are behind bars that don't belong there" have formed an organization to call for fewer criminal prosecutions and an end to mandatory minimum sentences). But some scholars and commentators are not so sanguine that things are changing. See generally Gottschalk, *Caught*, 7–21, 48–78 (discussing reform efforts and the entrenched resistance to reform, which Gottschalk calls "carceral clawback").

11 "Racial Disparity," Sentencing Project, accessed October 13, 2015, http://www.sentencingproject.org/template/page.cfm?id=122 (reporting that more than 60 percent of people in prison are racial and ethnic minorities and, for black males in their thirties, one in ten is in prison or jail on any given day).

12 Lauren E. Glaze and Erinn J. Herberman, "Correctional Populations in the United States, 2012," Bureau of Justice Statistics Bulletin, December 2013; Gottschalk, *Caught*, 1 (calling the reach of the criminal justice system "truly breathtaking" and noting that more than eight million people—or one in twenty-three adults—are under some form of state control).

13 "Too Many Laws."
14 Livia Luan, "Profiting from Enforcement: The Role of Private Prisons in U.S. Immigration Detention," Migration Policy Institute, last modified May 2, 2018, https://www.migrationpolicy.org/article/profiting-enforcement-role-private-prisons-us-immigration-detention (reporting that during 2016, approximately 353,000 immigrants identified for detention or removal by U.S. Immigration and Customs Enforcement passed through one of more than two hundred immigration detention facilities, a growing number of which are private jails and prisons. This rate is up from 209,000 in 2001); Doris Meissner et al., "Immigration Enforcement in the United States: The Rise of a Formidable Machinery," Migration Policy Institute, January 2013, https://www.migrationpolicy.org/research/immigration-enforcement-united-states-rise-formidable-machinery (documenting the vast machinery of U.S. immigration enforcement, including detention). See also Michiko Kakutani, "When History Repeats," New York Times, July 15, 2018, SR1 (noting that the Pentagon is preparing to house as many as twenty thousand "unaccompanied alien children" on American military bases).
15 See Ashley Nellis, Life Goes On: The Historic Rise in Life Sentences in America (Washington, D.C.: Sentencing Project, 2013), 1, https://sentencingproject.org/wp-content/uploads/2015/12/Life-Goes-On.pdf. The Sentencing Project reports that the population of prisoners serving life without parole (LWOP) has risen more sharply than the population of "ordinary lifers," with an increase of 22.2 percent since 2008. Approximately 10,000 lifers have been convicted of nonviolent offenses, nearly half are African American, more than 10,000 lifers were convicted of crimes that occurred before they were eighteen years old, and more than 5,300 are female. As Marie Gottschalk reports, the total life-sentenced population in the United States is approximately 160,000—roughly twice the size of the entire incarcerated population in Japan (Gottschalk, Caught, 170).
16 See "Nursing Homes behind Bars," New York Times, updated September 29, 2014, http://www.nytimes.com/2014/09/29/opinion/nursing-homes-behind-bars.html (noting that the number of inmates who are fifty-five and older has nearly quadrupled since 1995, and that this age group is expected to account for a third of all prisoners by 2030).
17 See Robert A. Ferguson, Inferno: An Anatomy of American Punishment (Cambridge, Mass.: Harvard University Press, 2014), 131–137 (describing the horrors of the private prison industry); see also Gottschalk, Caught, 68–69 (describing the private corrections industry as "too big to fail").
18 Ferguson, Inferno, 131. As of 2016, the Department of Justice will no longer send federal prisoners to private prisons. Charlie Savage, "U.S. to Start Phasing Out Use of Private Prisons to House Federal Inmates," New York Times, August 19, 2016, A11. It is too soon to say whether this development will have any effect on the much larger state prison system.
19 Alexis de Tocqueville, Democracy in America, trans. Henry Reeve (London: Saunders and Otley, 1835), accessed October 5, 2015, http://www.gutenberg.org/files/816/816-h/816-h.htm.
20 Adam Liptak, "U.S. Prison Population Dwarfs That of Other Nations," New York Times, April 23, 2008, http://www.nytimes.com/2008/04/23/world/americas/23iht-23prison.12253738.html.
21 See generally Bryan Stevenson, Just Mercy: A Story of Justice and Redemption (New York: Spiegel & Grau, 2014), recounting the efforts to vindicate Walter

McMillian, an Alabama man convicted of capital murder and sentenced to death—notwithstanding an ironclad alibi and questionable evidence of guilt as a result of police coercion and perjury.

22 See Barry Scheck et al., *Actual Innocence: When Justice Goes Wrong and How to Make It Right* (New York: New American Library, 2001).

23 See Carol S. Steiker and Jordan M. Steiker, "The Seduction of Innocence: The Attraction and Limitations of the Focus on Innocence in Capital Punishment Law and Advocacy," *Journal of Criminal Law and Criminology* 95, no. 2 (Winter 2005): 619.

24 Gottschalk, *Caught*, 39–45 (discussing the degrading conditions of confinement endemic to U.S. prisons and jails).

25 Gideon v. Wainwright, 372 U.S. 335 (1963).

26 Anthony Lewis, *Gideon's Trumpet: How One Man, a Poor Prisoner, Took His Case to the Supreme Court—and Changed the Law of the United States* (New York: Random House, 1964), 215.

27 Paul Butler, *Let's Get Free: A Hip-Hop Theory of Justice* (New York: New Press, 2009), 30.

28 Mary Jordan, "If Clinton Wins, Thomas Perez Does Too. Only Question: What Job Does He Get?," *Washington Post*, July 5, 2016, https://www.washingtonpost.com/ national/if-clinton-wins-thomas-perez-does-too-only-question-what-job-does-he -get/2016/07/05/d7e38480-4184-11e6-88d0-6adee48be8bc_story.html?noredirect =on&utm_term=.b9f194771fd7.

29 "Clarence Darrow Is Dead in Chicago," *New York Times*, March 14, 1938, accessed October 5, 2015, http://www.nytimes.com/learning/general/onthisday/bday/0418 .html.

30 *Adam's Rib*, directed by George Cukor (Hollywood: Metro-Goldwyn-Mayer, 1949), DVD. The classic courtroom romantic comedy featured Spencer Tracey as a prosecutor and was written by Ruth Gordon and Garson Kanin.

31 See Butler, *Let's Get Free*, 26: "The biggest threat to freedom in the United States comes not from some foreign or terrorist threat but rather from our dysfunctional criminal justice system. It is out of control. We define too many acts as crimes, punish too many people far longer than their crimes warrant, and therefore have too much incarceration. Some people deserve to be in jail, but not two million. . . . The two million Americans in prison represent the most urgent challenge to democratic values since the civil rights era."

32 See Liliana Segura, "Throwaway People: Teens Sent to Die in Prison Will Get a Second Chance," *The Nation*, last modified May 9, 2012, http://www.thenation .com/article/throwaway-people-teens-sent-die-prison-will-get-second-chance/; see also Jill Loevy, *Ghettoside: A True Story of Murder in America* (New York: Spiegel & Grau, 2015), 37 (referring to the diminishment of young black homicide victims as "gang members," "at risk" youth, and "throwaway people").

Chapter 1 Petty Criminals

1 See generally Alexandra Natapoff, *Punishment Without Crime: How Our Massive Misdemeanor System Traps the Innocent and Makes America More Unequal* (New

York: Basic Books, 2018); Issa Kohler-Hausmann, *Misdemeanorland: Criminal Courts and Social Control in an Age of Broken Windows Policing* (Princeton, N.J.: Princeton University Press, 2018). See also Robert C. Boruchowitz, Malia N. Brink, and Maureen Dimino, *Minor Crimes, Massive Waste: The Terrible Toll of America's Broken Misdemeanor Courts* (Washington, D.C.: National Association of Criminal Defense Lawyers, 2009), https://www.nacdl.org/reports/misdemeanor/; Eisha Jain, "Proportionality and Other Misdemeanor Myths," *Boston University Law Review* 98 (May 2018): 953–980; Issa Kohler-Hausmann, "Misdemeanor Justice: Control Without Conviction," *American Journal of Sociology* 119, no. 2 (2013): 351–393; Alexandra Natapoff, "Misdemeanors," *Southern California Law Review* 85 (2012): 101–163; Alisa Smith and Sean Maddan, *Three Minute Justice: Haste and Waste in Florida's Misdemeanor Courts* (Washington, D.C.: National Association of Criminal Defense Lawyers, 2011), http://www.nacdl.org/reports/threeminutejustice/; and Jenny Roberts, "Why Misdemeanors Matter: Defining Effective Advocacy in the Lower Criminal Courts," *University of California at Davis Law Review* 45, no. 2 (2011): 277–372.

2 Steve Borgia, *Courtroom 302: A Year behind the Scenes in an American Criminal Courtroom* (New York: Alfred A. Knopf, 2005), 40.

3 See generally Robert M. Bohm, "'McJustice': On the McDonaldization of Criminal Justice," *Justice Quarterly* 23, no. 1 (March 2006): 127–146.

4 See Smith and Maddan, *Three Minute Justice*, 9.

5 Smith and Maddan, 14.

6 Paul Butler, *Let's Get Free: A Hip-Hop Theory of Justice* (New York: New Press, 2009), 16–17.

7 Butler, 1.

8 Megan Stevenson and Sandra Mayson, "The Scale of Misdemeanor Justice," *Boston University Law Review* 98 (2018): 731, 737, 744–747 (calculating that there are 13.2 million misdemeanor cases filed in the United States in 2016). See also Natapoff, "Misdemeanors," 103; and Alexandra Natapoff, "Misdemeanor Decriminalization," *Vanderbilt Law Review* 68, no. 4 (May 2015): 1063 (noting that every year in the United States, just over two million felony cases are filed compared to ten million misdemeanors). Professor Natapoff calls the misdemeanor the "paradigmatic U.S. criminal case" because "most cases are misdemeanors, most of what the system does is generate minor convictions, and most Americans who experience the criminal system do so via the petty offense process" ("Misdemeanor Decriminalization," 1063).

9 Natapoff, "Misdemeanors," 116–138.

10 Natapoff, 1, 116–138.

11 See generally Erica Hashimoto, "The Problem with Misdemeanor Representation," *Washington and Lee Law Review* 70, no. 2 (Spring 2013): 1019.

12 U.S. Const. amend. VIII ("Excessive bail shall not be required, nor excessive fines imposed, nor cruel and unusual punishments inflicted").

13 Nick Pinto, "The Bail Trap," *New York Times Magazine*, August 13, 2015, https://www.nytimes.com/2015/08/16/magazine/the-bail-trap.html.

14 Pinto, "Bail Trap." New York City courts use bail far less than in many jurisdictions, and yet roughly forty-five thousand people are jailed each year simply because they can't pay bail. Even though the city's courts set bail much lower than the national average, only one in ten defendants is able to pay it at arraignment. Even when bail

is comparatively low—$500 or less, as it is in one-third of nonfelony cases—only 15 percent of defendants are able to come up with the money to avoid jail.

15 See "Frequently Asked Questions," The Plea, PBS Frontline, accessed October 18, 2015, http://www.pbs.org/wgbh/pages/frontline/shows/plea/faqs/.

16 Natapoff, "Misdemeanor Decriminalization," 1063.

17 *Annie Hall*, directed by Woody Allen (Burbank, Calif: United Artists, 1977), DVD.

18 See Butler, *Let's Get Free*, 132 (noting that the expression "I caught a case"— popularized through hip-hop culture—reflects the arbitrary nature of criminal justice: a person catches a case in the same way as he or she might catch a cold).

19 See generally Katherine R. Kruse, "Fortress in the Sand: The Plural Values of Client-Centered Representation," *Clinical Law Review* 12, no. 2 (Spring 2006): 369–440 (discussing the history, development, and theory of client-centered lawyering).

20 See Leon Dash, *Rosa Lee: A Mother and Her Family in Urban America* (New York: Basic Books, 1996).

21 Dash, 9.

22 Dash, 251.

23 Dusky v. United States, 362 U.S. 402 (1960).

24 See generally Jenni Gainsborough, *Mentally Ill Offenders in the Criminal Justice System: An Analysis and Prescription* (Washington, D.C.: Sentencing Project, 2002), http://www.sentencingproject.org/doc/publications/sl_mentallyilloffenders.pdf.

25 Nicholas Kristoff, "Inside a Mental Hospital Called Jail," *New York Times*, February 9, 2014, New York ed., SR1.

26 Doris J. James and Lauren E. Glaze, *Mental Health Problems of Prison and Jail Inmates* (Washington, D.C.: U.S. Department of Justice, Office of Justice Programs, Bureau of Justice Statistics, 2006), 1, http://www.bjs.gov/content/pub/pdf/mhppji.pdf; see also Kevin Johnson, "Mental Illness Cases Swamp Criminal Justice System," *USA Today*, last updated July 21, 2014, http://www.usatoday.com/story/news/nation/2014/07/21/mental-illness-law-enforcement-cost-of-not-caring/9951239/ (reporting that about 1.2 million people in state, local, and federal custody reported some kind of mental health problem according to a 2006 Justice Department study).

27 See Nicholas Turner, "Stop Placing the Mentally Ill in Jails," *New York Times*, last updated February 26, 2015, http://www.nytimes.com/roomfordebate/2015/02/26/would-we-be-safer-if-fewer-were-jailed/stop-placing-the-mentally-ill-in-jails (reporting that nationally, 14.5 percent of men and 31 percent of women in jails have a serious mental illness, and 68 percent have problems with substance abuse; the rates are even higher in New York City); and Kristoff, "Inside a Mental Hospital Called Jail" (reporting that the number of inmates at the Cook County Jail suffering from serious mental illness can run as high as 60 percent).

28 Kristoff, "Inside a Mental Hospital Called Jail."

29 Butler's own description of his arrest and prosecution is well worth reading in full. See Butler, *Let's Get Free*, 5–16.

30 Butler, 16.

31 Butler, 14.

32 Butler, 15.

33 Butler, 15.

34 Butler, 17.

35 See David Remnick, "Back Issues: Henry Louis Gates Jr.," *New Yorker*, July 22, 2009, http://www.newyorker.com/online/blogs/newsdesk/2009/07/back-issues-henry-louis-gates-jr.html (noting that a Cambridge, Massachusetts, police officer put Harvard professor Henry Louis Gates in handcuffs "rather than believe his lying eyes: that Gates was, in fact, the legitimate resident"—essentially arresting him for "being black while at home").

36 See Matt Stevens, "Starbucks CEO Apologizes after Arrests of 2 Black Men," *New York Times*, April 15, 2018, https://www.nytimes.com/2018/04/15/us/starbucks-philadelphia-black-men-arrest.html (reporting about two black men waiting to meet a third man at a Starbucks, who were arrested for trespass).

37 Butler, *Let's Get Free*, 11.

38 See Misdemeanor Jury Trial Act of 2002, D.C. Code §16-705(b)(1)(A) (2012).

39 Butler, *Let's Get Free*, 1.

40 Butler, 17–18.

41 See Erik Eckholm, "A State Cuts Jail Time for Probation Violators, and Costs," *New York Times*, September 12, 2014, New York ed., A14 (reporting that in response to the revelation that half of prison admissions were for probation violators, many with no new crimes, North Carolina instituted a policy that seeks to avoid probation revocation); see also Gina Barton, "No New Conviction, but Sent Back to Prison," *Milwaukee Journal Sentinel*, January 17, 2015, http://archive.jsonline.com/watchdog/watchdogreports/no-new-conviction-but-sent-back-to-prison-b99420782z1-288939871.html (reporting that more than half of the people sent to Wisconsin's prisons in 2013 were locked up for violating probation or parole).

42 Smith and Maddan, *Three Minute Justice*, 9.

43 For an article on the imposition of the death penalty based not on the crime but on the quality of counsel, see Stephen B. Bright, "Counsel for the Poor: The Death Sentence Not for the Worst Crime but for the Worst Lawyer," *Yale Law Journal* 103, no. 7 (May 1994): 1835–1884.

44 See *Model Rules of Professional Responsibility*, Rule 3.8, Comment 1 (Chicago: American Bar Association, 2016): "A prosecutor has the responsibility of a minister of justice and not simply that of an advocate."

Chapter 2 Ordinary Felons

1 "Canon 2," *Model Code of Judicial Conduct*, Rule 2.11(A)(2)(a) (A)(2)(c) (American Bar Association Center for Professional Responsibility, 2010).

2 For a thorough and interesting analysis of this epithet, see Nancy Isenberg, *White Trash: The 400-Year Untold History of Class in America* (New York: Viking Press, 2016).

3 Sentencing Project, *Women in the Criminal Justice System: Briefing Sheets* (Washington, D.C.: Sentencing Project, 2007), http://www.sentencingproject.org/wp-content/uploads/2016/01/Women-in-the-Criminal-Justice-System-Briefing-Sheets.pdf.

4 Todd D. Minton and Daniela Golinelli, *Jail Inmates at Midyear 2013—Statistical Tables* (Washington, D.C.: U.S. Department of Justice, Office of Justice Programs,

Bureau of Justice Statistics, 2014), 1, https://www.bjs.gov/content/pub/pdf/jim13st
.pdf.

5 *Orange Is the New Black*, 7 seasons, directed by Andrew McCarthy (New York: Astoria Studios / Netflix, 2013–2018); Piper Kerman, *Orange Is the New Black: My Year in a Woman's Prison* (New York: Spiegel & Grau, 2010).

6 Sentencing Project, *Briefing Sheets*.

7 Women in Prison Project, *Women in Prison Fact Sheet* (New York: Correctional Association of New York, 2002), 1, http://www.prisonpolicy.org/scans/Fact_Sheets _2002.pdf.

8 Lawrence A. Greenfeld and Tracy L. Snell, *Women Offenders* (Washington, D.C.: Department of Justice, Office of Justice Programs, Bureau of Justice Statistics, 2010), 9, http://bjs.gov/content/pub/pdf/wo.pdf.

9 Sentencing Project, *Briefing Sheets*.

10 Kevin Liptak, "Obama Reducing 102 Inmates' Sentences," *CNN Politics*, October 7, 2016, http://www.cnn.com/2016/10/06/politics/obama-reducing-prison-sentences -announcement/index.html; see also David Cole, "Why Hasn't Obama's Clemency Initiative Helped More Nonviolent Drug Offenders?," *New Yorker*, July 4, 2016, http://www.newyorker.com/news/news-desk/why-hasnt-obamas-clemency -initiative-helped-more-nonviolent-drug-offenders.

11 John Pfaff, "For True Penal Reform, Focus on the Violent Offenders," *Washington Post*, July 26, 2015, https://www.washingtonpost.com/opinions/for-true-penal -reform-focus-on-the-violent-offenders/2015/07/26/1340ad4c-3208-11e5-97ae -30a30cca95d7_story.html.

12 John F. Pfaff, "The Micro and Macro Causes of Prison Growth," *Georgia State University Law Review* 28, no. 4 (Summer 2012): 1270.

13 Pfaff, "For True Penal Reform."

14 Peter Baker, "Obama Calls for Effort to Fix a 'Broken System' of Criminal Justice," *New York Times*, July 14, 2015, A18.

15 Barack Obama, "Remarks by the President at the NAACP Conference," The White House, July 14, 2015, https://www.whitehouse.gov/the-press-office/2015/07/14/ remarks-president-naacp-conference.

16 Patrick A. Langan and David J. Levin, *Recidivism of Prisoners Released in 1994* (Washington, D.C.: Department of Justice, Office of Justice Programs, Bureau of Justice Statistics, 2002), 1, https://www.bjs.gov/content/pub/pdf/rpr94.pdf.

17 Langan and Levin, *Recidivism*, 1.

18 Maggie Astor, "California Voters Remove Judge Aaron Persky, Who Gave a 6-Month Sentence for Sexual Assault," *New York Times*, June 6, 2018, https://www .nytimes.com/2018/06/06/us/politics/judge-persky-brock-turner-recall.html.

19 Liam Stack, "Outrage over Sentencing in Rape Case at Stanford," *New York Times*, June 6, 2016, A15.

20 Pfaff, "For True Penal Reform."

21 Marie Gottschalk, *Caught: The Prison State and the Lockdown of American Politics* (Princeton: Princeton University Press, 2015), 165–166; Marie Gottschalk, "Raze the Carceral State," *Dissent*, Fall 2015, https://www.dissentmagazine.org/article/ criminal-justice-reform-minimum-sentencing-mass-incarceration. See also Katrina vanden Heuvel, "The Moral and Political Case for Reforming the Criminal Justice System," *Washington Post*, November 18, 2014, https://www.washingtonpost.com/ opinions/katrina-vanden-heuvel-the-moral-and-political-case-for-criminal-justice

-reform/2014/11/17/3eedc60c-6e7a-11e4-8808-afaa1e3a33ef_story.html?noredirect =on&utm_term=.b70a1eddc65e.

22 Dylan Thomas, "Do Not Go Gentle into That Good Night," in *The Poems of Dylan Thomas* (New York: New Directions, 1952), 193–194.

23 William M. Adler, *Land of Opportunity: One Family's Quest for the American Dream in the Age of Crack* (New York: Atlantic Monthly Press, 1995).

24 Charles Dickens, *Oliver Twist* (London: Richard Bentley, 1838).

25 Client to Abbe Smith, in the author's possession.

26 Timothy Williams, "A '90s Legacy That Is Filling Prisons Today," *New York Times*, July 4, 2016, A1; "Justice 4 Lenny," Justice 4 Lenny, accessed July 7, 2016, http:// www.justice4lenny.org/.

27 Christopher Uggen, Sarah Shannon, and Jeff Manza, *State-Level Estimates of Felon Disenfranchisement in the United States, 2010* (Washington, D.C.: Sentencing Project, 2012), 2, http://sentencingproject.org/wp-content/uploads/2016/01/State -Level-Estimates-of-Felon-Disenfranchisement-in-the-United-States-2010.pdf; Jeff Manza and Christopher Uggen, *Locked Out: Felon Disenfranchisement and American Democracy* (Oxford: Oxford University Press, 2008).

28 Vann R. Newkirk II, "Polls for Prisons: Incarcerated People Voted in Primaries in Vermont, Puerto Rico, and Maine. Why Can't They Vote Anywhere Else?," *Atlantic*, March 9, 2016, http://www.theatlantic.com/politics/archive/2016/03/inmates -voting-primary/473016/.

29 Brian C. Kalt, "The Exclusion of Felons from Jury Service," *American University Law Review* 53, no. 1 (October 2003): 67; Darren Wheelock, "A Jury of One's 'Peers': The Racial Impact of Felon Jury Exclusion in Georgia," *Justice System Journal* 32, no. 3 (2011): 335.

30 See Darren Wheelock, "Collateral Consequences and Racial Inequality: Felon Status Restrictions as a System of Disadvantage," *Journal of Contemporary Criminal Justice* 21, no. 1 (February 2005): 82–90; and Sarah B. Berson, "Beyond the Sentence—Understanding Collateral Consequences," *National Institute of Justice Journal*, no. 272 (September 2013): 25–28.

Chapter 3 Rapists

1 Paul Butler, *Let's Get Free: A Hip-Hop Theory of Justice* (New York: New Press, 2009), 132 (noting that the expression "I caught a case" reflects the arbitrary nature of criminal justice—a person catches a case in the same way he or she might catch a cold). See D.C. Code §16-2307 (2009).

2 See generally Dusky v. United States, 362 U.S. 402 (1960) (holding that in order to be competent to stand trial, a defendant must have a "sufficient present ability to consult with his lawyer with a reasonable degree of rational understanding" and a "rational as well as factual understanding of the proceedings against him"; internal quotations omitted).

3 Most state transfer statutes create a presumption in favor of adult prosecution if this is "in the interest of the public welfare and protection of the public security and there are no reasonable prospects for rehabilitation." See, for example, D.C. Code §§16-2307, 16-2301 (2009).

4 Contrary to my usual practice of saying *alleged rapist* instead of *rapist* and *complainant* or *alleged victim* instead of *victim*, here I will sometimes refer to *rapists* and *rape victims* (and/or *rape survivors*). I do so even though, of course, not everyone accused of rape is guilty. I mean to confront the reality of what it means to represent guilty rapists. There is some controversy over using the term *victim* versus *survivor*. See Stephen J. Schulhofer, "The Trouble with Trials, the Trouble with Us," *Yale Law Journal* 105, no. 3 (December 1995): 851 ("The victims, once pitied or despised for what was seen as weakness or masochism, are now 'survivors,' with status that brings respect").

5 Harper Lee, *To Kill a Mockingbird* (New York: HarperCollins, 1960).

6 Lee, 215. For a critical analysis of Atticus Finch's cross-examination of Mayella Ewell, arguing that Finch employed sexist strategies and "tortured" Mayella, see Steven Lubet, "Reconstructing Atticus Finch," *Michigan Law Review* 97, no. 6 (May 1999): 1348. For an excellent rejoinder, see Randolph N. Stone, "Atticus Finch, in Context," *Michigan Law Review* 97, no. 6 (May 1999): 1378–1381.

7 John Henry Wigmore, *Evidence in Trials at Common Law*, ed. James H. Chadbourn, vol. 5, §1367 (1904; repr., Boston: Little, Brown, 1974), 32.

8 Wigmore, 32.

9 United States v. Wade, 388 U.S. 218, 256–258 (1967) (White, J., dissenting in part and concurring in part; internal citations omitted).

10 See "Crime in the United States 2011," Federal Bureau of Investigation, accessed January 7, 2016, http://www.fbi.gov/about-us/cjis/ucr/crime-in-the-u.s/2011/crime-in-the-u.s.-2011/offenses-known-to-law-enforcement/standard-links/national-data (revealing that rape happens once every 6.3 minutes, murder every 36 minutes, robbery every 1.5 minutes, and aggravated assault every 42 seconds).

11 "Facts and Figures: Ending Violence against Women," U.N. Women, accessed March 9, 2016, http://www2.unwomen.org/en/what-we-do/ending-violence-against-women/facts-and-figures.

12 Stone, "Atticus Finch, in Context," 1378–1379.

13 Lee, *To Kill a Mockingbird*, 214, 112.

14 Alice Sebold, *Lucky* (New York: Scribner, 1999), 128.

15 Alice Sebold, *The Lovely Bones* (New York: Little, Brown, 2002).

16 Alice Sebold, "HERS; Speaking of the Unspeakable," *New York Times Magazine*, February 26, 1989, http://www.nytimes.com/1989/02/26/magazine/hers-speaking-of-the-unspeakable.html.

17 Sebold, *Lucky*, 22.

18 Sebold, 111.

19 Patricia Weaver Francisco, *Telling: A Memoir of Rape and Recovery* (New York: HarperCollins, 2000), 25–26.

20 Barbara Brotman, "From Silence to Eloquence: In Brutal Detail, 'Lucky' Author Alice Sebold Writes about Her Rape," *Chicago Tribune*, November 24, 1999, http://articles.chicagotribune.com/1999-11-24/features/9911240355_1_smart-aleck-alice-sebold-emily-dickinson.

21 Sebold, *Lucky*, 16–18.

22 Jessica Stern, *Denial: A Memoir* (New York: HarperCollins, 2010), 216.

23 See Angela Harris, "Race and Essentialism in Feminist Legal Theory," *Stanford Law Review* 42, no. 3 (February 1990): 598–601 (pointing out that historically, rape was something that happened to white women, not black women, and it "signified the

terrorism of black men by white men, aided and abetted, passively [by silence] or actively [by 'crying rape'], by white women"); Dorothy E. Roberts, "Rape, Violence, and Women's Autonomy," *Chicago-Kent Law Review* 69, no. 2 (December 1993): 362–369 (discussing the racialized meaning of rape); and Jennifer Wriggins, "Rape, Racism, and the Law," *Harvard Women's Law Journal* 6, no. 1 (1983): 103 ("The history of rape in this country has focused on the rape of white women by Black men. From a feminist perspective, two of the most damaging consequences of this selective blindness are the denials that Black women are raped and that all women are subject to pervasive and harmful sexual coercion of all kinds").

24   Sebold, *Lucky*, 32–33.

25   Sebold, 203, 206.

26   See Abbe Smith, "Representing Rapists: The Cruelty of Cross Examination and Other Challenges for a Feminist Criminal Defense Lawyer," *American Criminal Law Review* 53, no. 2 (Spring 2016): 255–309.

27   See Marie Gottschalk, *Caught: The Prison State and the Lockdown of American Politics* (Princeton: Princeton University Press, 2015), 196–214; and Allegra M. McLeod, "Regulating Sexual Harm: Strangers, Intimates, and Social Institutional Reform," *California Law Review* 102, no. 6 (December 2013): 1153–1621.

28   Kansas v. Hendricks, 521 U.S. 346, 350 (1997).

29   Gottschalk, *Caught*, 196.

30   Jim Loney, "Nowhere to Go, Miami Sex Offenders Live under Bridge," *Reuters*, February 4, 2008, http://www.reuters.com/article/domesticNews/ idUSN0515234320080205.

31   Sarah Stillman, "The List," *New Yorker*, March 14, 2016, http://www.newyorker .com/magazine/2016/03/14/when-kids-are-accused-of-sex-crimes; see also "Raised on the Registry: The Irreparable Harm of Placing Children on Sex Offender Registries in the U.S.," Human Rights Watch, May 2013, https://www.hrw.org/sites/ default/files/reports/us0513_ForUpload_1.pdf.

32   Stillman, "The List."

33   J. J. Prescott and Jonah E. Rockoff, "Do Sex Offender Registration and Notification Laws Affect Criminal Behavior?," *Journal of Law and Economics* 54, no. 1 (February 2011):161–206.

34   Andrew J. Harris et al., "Sex Offending and Serious Mental Illness: Directions for Policy and Research," *Criminal Justice and Behavior* 37, no. 5 (May 2010): 596–612; Amy Norton, "Sex Offenders Have Higher Rate of Mental Illness," *Reuters*, May 17, 2007, http://www.reuters.com/article/2007/05/17/us-sex-offenders -idUSCOL76032420070517.

35   18 U.S. Code §4248 (2015) (federal statute on civil commitment of a "sexually dangerous person").

36   Susan J. Brison, *Aftermath: Violence and the Remaking of a Self* (Princeton: Princeton University Press, 2002), 46 (referring to rape as a "social murder"—a crime that causes "a temporary social death, one from which a self can be resurrected only with great difficulty and with the help of others").

37   See Rose Corrigan, *Up against a Wall: Rape Reform and the Failure of Success* (New York: New York University Press, 2013), 65–116 (arguing that the attitudes of medical personnel, police, and prosecutors continue to have a significant effect on rape reporting, charges brought, and conviction rate, notwithstanding efforts of the feminist antirape movement).

38 Stern, *Denial*, 16, 19.
39 Stern, 63.
40 Helen Garner, *This House of Grief: The Story of a Murder Trial* (Melbourne: Text Publishing, 2014), 244.
41 Brison, *Aftermath*, 108, 109.
42 Sebold, *Lucky*, 181–182.
43 Janet Malcolm, *The Crime of Sheila McGough* (New York: Alfred A. Knopf, 1999), 26.
44 Malcolm, 67.
45 Sebold, *Lucky*, 152.
46 Sebold, 152–153.
47 Larry S. Pozner and Roger J. Dodd, *Cross-Examination: Science and Techniques*, 2nd ed. (New York: LexisNexis, 2004); Steven Lubet and J. C. Lore, *Modern Trial Advocacy: Analysis and Practice*, 5th ed. (Boulder, Colo.: LexisNexis / National Institute for Trial Advocacy, 2015); Thomas A. Mauet, *Trial Techniques and Trials*, 9th ed. (New York: Aspen, 2013).
48 Stephen J. Schulhofer, *Unwanted Sex: The Culture of Intimidation and the Failure of Law* (Cambridge, Mass.: Harvard University Press, 1998), 260.
49 Eva Nilsen, "The Criminal Defense Lawyer's Reliance on Bias and Prejudice," *Georgetown Journal of Legal Ethics* 8, no. 1 (1994–1995): 1–44.
50 Sebold, *Lucky*, 191, 192, 199, 201.
51 Sebold, 192.
52 Johnson v. United States, 333 U.S. 10, 14 (1948).
53 See generally Radley Balko and Tucker Carrington, *The Cadaver King and the Country Dentist: A True Story of Injustice in the American South* (New York: Public Affairs, 2018) (recounting the wrongful rape and murder convictions of two innocent men in rural Mississippi). See also *When They See Us*, directed by Ava DuVernay (Los Gatos, Calif.: Netflix, 2019) (television miniseries about five teens from Harlem falsely accused of a brutal sexual assault in Central Park in 1989).
54 "Government Misconduct," Innocence Project, last accessed January 20, 2016, https://www.innocenceproject.org/causes/government-misconduct/.
55 Samuel L. Gross et al., "Exonerations in the United States: 1989 through 2003," *Journal of Criminal Law and Criminology* 95, no. 2 (2004–2005): 529 (finding that 73 percent of all DNA exonerations between 1989 and 2003 overturned rape convictions).
56 Brady v. Maryland, 373 U.S. 83 (1963) (requiring prosecutors to disclose exculpatory evidence to the defense as a matter of due process); *Model Rules of Professional Conduct*, Rule 3.8(d) (Chicago: American Bar Association, 2014).
57 Janet Malcolm, *The Journalist and the Murderer* (New York: Alfred A. Knopf, 1990), 42.
58 Butler, *Let's Get Free*, 4.
59 Elizabeth Schneider, "Feminism and the False Dichotomy of Victimization and Agency," *New York Law School Law Review* 38 (1993): 397.
60 Roberts, "Rape, Violence, and Women's Autonomy," 365; Kimberle Crenshaw, "Race, Gender, and Sexual Harassment," *Southern California Law Review* 65, no. 3 (March 1992): 1469; Wriggins, "Rape, Racism, and the Law," 117–123.
61 *13th*, directed by Ava DuVernay (Los Gatos, Calif.: Kandoo Films / Netflix, 2016) (documentary film on the long history of racism in criminal justice).

62 Interestingly, a Georgetown colleague who has come to know Mr. Horton says he was never called "Willie," only "William."
63 Jeffrey J. Pokarak, "Rape as a Badge of Slavery: The Legal History of, and Remedies for, Prosecutorial Race-of-Victim Charging Disparities," *Nevada Law Journal* 7, no. 1 (Fall 2006): 38–43.
64 Coker v. Georgia, 433 U.S. 584 (1977).
65 Brief Amici Curiae of the American Civil Liberties Union, the Center for Constitutional Rights, the National Organization for Women Legal Defense and Education Fund, the Women's Law Project, the Center for Women Policy Studies, the Women's Legal Defense Fund, and Equal Rights Advocates, Inc., Coker v. Georgia, 433 U.S. 584 (1977) (No. 75-5444), 1976 WL 181482.

Chapter 4 Murderers

1 See generally Ta-Nehisi Coates, *Between the World and Me* (New York: Spiegel & Grau, 2015).
2 Jill Leovy, *Ghettoside: A True Story of Murder in America* (New York: Spiegel & Grau, 2015), 35.
3 Kennedy v. Louisiana, 554 U.S. 407 (2008) (holding the death penalty unconstitutional for child sexual assault that does not result in the death of the victim).
4 See also "The Five Precepts: Pañca-sila," Access to Insight, Barre Center for Buddhist Studies, updated November 30, 2013, http://www.accesstoinsight.org/ptf/dhamma/sila/pancasila.html. Chapter 10 of the *Dhammapada* (a collection of Buddha's verses) states, "Everyone fears punishment; everyone fears death, just as you do. Therefore do not kill or cause to kill."
5 Leovy, *Ghettoside*, 5.
6 Leovy, 6.
7 Jennifer Gonnerman, "Jill Leovy's 'Ghettoside,'" *New York Times*, January 21, 2015, https://www.nytimes.com/2015/01/25/books/review/jill-leovys-ghettoside.html.
8 Prosecutors, defense lawyers, and politicians have all signed on to this project. See Michael S. Schmidt, "U.S. to Release 6,000 Inmates from Prisons," *New York Times*, October 7, 2015, A1 (reporting that the Justice Department is preparing to release roughly six thousand federal prisoners starting at the end of October 2015 as part of an effort to roll back the harsh penalties given to nonviolent drug dealers in the 1980s and 1990s); Peter Baker, "Obama Plans Broader Use of Clemency," *New York Times*, July 4, 2015, A1 (reporting that Clemency Project 2014—a consortium of lawyers that includes the American Bar Association, the American Civil Liberties Union, the National Association of Criminal Defense Lawyers, Families Against Mandatory Minimums, fifty law firms, and more than twenty law schools—is preparing applications for clemency from President Obama on behalf of federal prisoners who are nonviolent drug offenders); and Carl Hulse and Jennifer Steinhauer, "Sentencing Overhaul Proposed in Senate with Bipartisan Backing," *New York Times*, October 2, 2015, A19 (reporting on a bipartisan measure largely focusing on nonviolent offenders).
9 Malcolm Gladwell, "Thresholds of Violence: How School Shootings Catch On," *New Yorker*, October 19, 2015, http://www.newyorker.com/magazine/2015/10/19/thresholds-of-violence.

10 Gladwell, "Thresholds of Violence."

11 See R. Dwayne Betts, *A Question of Freedom: A Memoir of Learning, Survival, and Coming of Age in Prison* (New York: Avery, 2010), 186 ("[I came to] realize . . . that prison wasn't like they say in the papers. Sometimes it was worse, but sometimes what people said missed every one of those kind moments that kept me from losing that last bit of sense I had. I watched older people pull young folks under their wing for no other reason than they could, and there was always the rumor of someone helping someone else beat a case").

12 See Abbe Smith, *Case of a Lifetime* (New York: Palgrave Macmillan, 2008).

13 *The Shawshank Redemption*, directed by Frank Darabont (Los Angeles: Castle Rock Entertainment, 1994), DVD. The movie is based on a Stephen King novella. Stephen King, "Rita Hayworth and Shawshank Redemption: Hope Springs Eternal," in *Different Seasons* (New York: Viking Press, 1982).

14 See Betts, *Question of Freedom*, 186 ("I felt every second that I was behind the walls and bars of the prisons that held me").

15 Commonwealth v. Amirault, 424 Mass. 618 (1997); see also Dorothy Rabinowitz, "'Finality' for the Amiraults," *Wall Street Journal*, updated June 30, 1999, http://www.wsj.com/articles/SB930693023496478111.

16 See generally Richard Beck, *We Believe the Children: A Moral Panic in the 1980s* (New York: Public Affairs, 2015); Debbie Nathan and Michael Snedeker, *Satan's Silence: Ritual Abuse and the Making of a Modern American Witch Hunt* (San Jose, Calif.: Authors Choice Press, 2001); and Richard A. Gardner, *Sex Abuse Hysteria: Salem Witch Trials Revisited* (Cresskill, N.J.: Creative Therapeutics, 1990). But see Ross E. Cheit, *The Witch-Hunt Narrative: Politics, Psychology, and the Sexual Abuse of Children* (New York: Oxford University Press, 2014) (arguing that skeptics went too far in in calling the prosecution of alleged sexual abuse of children a witch hunt, as many children have been sexually abused).

17 *Amirault*, 424 Mass. at 637.

18 *Amirault*, 424 Mass. at 648.

19 John Prine, "Christmas in Prison," in *Sweet Revenge* (Atlantic Records, New York, NY, 1973).

20 Betts, *Question of Freedom*, 24.

21 Daniel Fisher, "America's Most Dangerous Cities: Detroit Can't Shake No. 1 Spot," *Forbes*, October 29, 2015, http://www.forbes.com/sites/danielfisher/2015/10/29/americas-most-dangerous-cities-detroit-cant-shake-no-1-spot/.

22 Monica Davey and Mitch Smith, "Murder Rates Rising Sharply in Some Cities," *New York Times*, September 1, 2015, A1.

23 See "Crime in the United States 2014," Federal Bureau of Investigation, accessed January 22, 2016, https://www.fbi.gov/about-us/cjis/ucr/crime-in-the-u.s/2014/crime-in-the-u.s.-2014/offenses-known-to-law-enforcement/violent-crime/violent-crime.

24 "Crime in the United States," FBI.

25 See Abbe Smith, "On Representing a Victim of Crime," in *Law Stories*, ed. Gary Bellow and Martha Minow (Ann Arbor: University of Michigan Press, 1996), 149–168. See also Claudia Brenner, *Eight Bullets: One Woman's Story of Surviving Anti-gay Violence* (Ithaca, N.Y.: Firebrand Books, 1995) (a surviving victim telling her story).

26 For a thoughtful discussion of what capital defense entails, see William R. Montross Jr. and Meghan Shapiro, "Wrecking Lives: When the State Seeks to Kill," in

How Can You Represent Those People?, ed. Abbe Smith and Monroe H. Freedman (New York: Palgrave Macmillan, 2013), 113–120.

27 Matt Schiavenza, "Hatred and Forgiveness in Charleston," *Atlantic*, June 20, 2015, http://www.theatlantic.com/national/archive/2015/06/dylann-roof-manifesto -forgiveness/396428/.

28 John A. Farrell, *Clarence Darrow: Attorney for the Damned* (New York: Doubleday, 2011), 9.

29 Clarence Darrow, *The Story of My Life* (New York: Scribner, 1932), 75–76.

30 Schiavenza, "Hatred and Forgiveness."

31 See Jacob Sullum, "Eric Holder Condemns Mass Incarceration (Again)," *Forbes*, November 22, 2013, http://www.forbes.com/sites/jacobsullum/2013/11/22/eric -holder-condemns-mass-incarceration-again.

32 "Justice Criticizes Lengthy Sentences," *New York Times*, August 10, 2003, http://www.nytimes.com/2003/08/10/us/justice-criticizes-lengthy-sentences .html (quoting Justice Kennedy's remarks at a 2003 American Bar Association meeting).

33 *Making a Murderer*, directed by Laura Ricciardi and Moira Demos (Los Gatos, Calif.: Synthesis Films / Netflix, 2015); see also Kathryn Schultz, "Dead Certainty: How 'Making a Murderer' Goes Wrong," *New Yorker*, January 25, 2016, http://www .newyorker.com/magazine/2016/01/25/dead-certainty.

34 *Serial*, season 1, produced by Sarah Koenig and Julie Snyder, podcast, MP3 audio, https://serialpodcast.org/season-one.

35 Truman Capote, *In Cold Blood* (New York: Random House, 1966).

36 Charles Perrault, "Bluebeard," in *Histoires ou contes du temps passé* (Paris, 1697), 57–80.

37 Jacob & Wilhelm Grimm, "The Singing Bone" in *The Original Folk and Fairy Tales of the Brothers Grimm: The Complete First Edition*, 89–91 (Jack Zipes ed. and trans., Princeton University Press, 2014) (1812).

38 Jacob & Wilhelm Grimm, "The Robber Bridegroom" in *The Original Folk and Fairy Tales of the Brothers Grimm: The Complete First Edition*, 135–137 (Jack Zipes ed. and trans., Princeton University Press, 2014) (1812).

39 See generally J. K. Rowling, *Harry Potter and the Philosopher's Stone* (London: Bloomsbury, 1998).

40 Fox Butterfield, "A Course Called 'Murder' (and It's Tough, Too)," *New York Times*, March 19, 1995, http://www.nytimes.com/1995/03/19/us/a-course-called-murder -and-it-s-tough-too.html.

41 Lewis E. Lewes, "Why I Changed My Mind," in *Voices against Death: American Opposition to Capital Punishment, 1787–1975*, ed. Philip E. Mackey (New York: Burt Franklin, 1976), 194.

42 Marie Gottschalk, *Caught: The Prison State and the Lockdown of American Politics* (Princeton: Princeton University Press, 2015), 170–195 (discussing the deep commitment to life sentences in the United States and noting that forty years ago, a life sentence used to mean just over ten years but now is "death in slow motion"); see also Sharon Dolovich, "Creating the Permanent Prisoner," in *Life without Parole: America's New Death Penalty*, ed. Charles J. Ogletree and Austin Sarat (New York: New York University Press, 2012), 96–137.

43 See Gitta Sereny, *Cries Unheard: Why Children Kill; The Story of Mary Bell* (New York: Henry Holt, 1999).

44 Paula M. Ditton and Doris James Wilson, "Truth in Sentencing in State Prisons," U.S. Department of Justice, Bureau of Justice Statistics Special Report, accessed February 8, 2016, http://bjs.gov/content/pub/pdf/tssp.pdf.
45 Gottschalk, *Caught*, 171–172.

Chapter 5 Guilty Clients, Guilty Lawyers

1 *Gideon's Army*, directed by Dawn Porter (New York: HBO Documentary Films, 2013). The three defenders are Travis Williams, Brandy Alexander, and June Hardwick.
2 Jonathan A. Rapping, "The Revolution Will Be Televised: Popular Culture and the American Criminal Justice Narrative," *New England Journal on Criminal and Civil Confinement* 41, no. 1 (Winter 2015): 6–7, 22–25.
3 Jonathan A. Rapping, "Reclaiming Our Rightful Place: Reviving the Hero Image of the Public Defender," *Iowa Law Review* 99, no. 5 (July 2014): 1893–1904.
4 Charles J. Ogletree, "Beyond Justifications: Seeking Motivations to Sustain Public Defenders," *Harvard Law Review* 106, no. 6 (April 1993): 1239.
5 Charles Fried, "The Lawyer as Friend: The Moral Foundations of the Lawyer-Client Relation," *Yale Law Journal* 85, no. 8 (July 1976): 1060–1090. For an example of the criticism, see Arthur A. Leff and Edward A. Dauer, "Correspondence: The Lawyer as Friend," *Yale Law Journal* 86, no. 3 (January 1977): 573–588, http://digitalcommons.law.yale.edu/fss_papers/2816.
6 Ogletree, "Beyond Justifications," 1275.
7 James M. Doyle, "It's the Third World Down There: The Colonialist Vocation and American Criminal Justice," *Harvard Civil Rights-Civil Liberties Law Review* 27, no. 1 (Winter 1992): 71–126. In an interesting twist, career criminal defense lawyer James M. Doyle identifies and critiques what he calls "the White Man's vision," in which mostly white men act as lawless imperialists on behalf of both defendants and victims in the criminal justice system.
8 Ogletree, "Beyond Justifications," 1276.
9 Lafler v. Cooper, 132 S. Ct. 1376, 1388 (2012) (noting that in the United States, "criminal justice today is for the most part a system of pleas, not a system of trials").
10 Abbe Smith, "Too Much Heart and Not Enough Heat: The Short Life and Fractured Ego of the Empathic, Heroic Public Defender," *University of California at Davis Law Review* 37, no. 5 (June 2004): 1237.
11 Ogletree, "Beyond Justifications," 1266.
12 Randy Bellows, "Notes of a Public Defender," in *The Social Responsibilities of Lawyers: Case Studies*, ed. Philip B. Heymann and Lance Liebman (Westbury, N.Y.: Foundation Press, 1988), 71.
13 Barbara Babcock, "'Defending the Guilty' after 30 Years," in *How Can You Represent Those People?*, ed. Abbe Smith and Monroe H. Freedman (New York: Palgrave Macmillan, 2013), 1–2.
14 Margaret Raymond, "Criminal Defense Heroes," *Widener Law Journal* 13, no. 1 (2003): 170.
15 Mary Halloran, "An Ode to Criminal Lawyers," *California Lawyer*, June 1998, 96.

16 Barbara Babcock, "Defending the Guilty," *Cleveland State Law Review* 32, no. 2 (1983–1984): 175.

17 Smith, "Too Much Heart," 1264.

18 David Remnick, "Soul Survivor: The Revival and Hidden Treasure of Aretha Frank-lin," *New Yorker*, April 4, 2016, https://www.newyorker.com/magazine/2016/04/04/aretha-franklins-american-soul.

19 Tom Wolfe, *The Bonfire of the Vanities* (New York: Bantam Books, 1988), 382.

20 James Kunen, *How Can You Defend Those People? The Making of a Criminal Lawyer* (New York: Random House, 1983), 9.

21 Donald J. Farole Jr., "A National Assessment of Public Defender Office Case-loads," Bureau of Justice Statistics, October 28, 2010, http://www.jrsa.org/events/conference/presentations-10/Donald_Farole.pdf.

22 Bill Quigley, "Public Defender Meltdown in Louisiana," *Huffington Post*, Feb-ruary 25, 2016, http://www.huffingtonpost.com/bill-quigley/public-defender-meltdown_b_9318494.html.

23 Tina Peng, "I'm a Public Defender. It's Impossible for Me to Do a Good Job Representing My Clients," *Washington Post*, September 3, 2015, https://www.washingtonpost.com/opinions/our-public-defender-system-isnt-just-broken-its-unconstitutional/2015/09/03/aadf2b6c-519b-11e5-9812-92d5948a40f8_story.html.

24 *General Standard Relating to the Defense Function* 4–3.5 (Chicago: American Bar Association, 2018), https://www.americanbar.org/groups/criminal_justice/standards/DefenseFunctionFourthEdition/.

25 Monroe H. Freedman, "An Ethical Manifesto for Public Defenders," *Valparaiso University Law Review* 39, no. 4 (Summer 2005): 911–924.

26 The ACLU has brought lawsuits challenging defective indigent criminal defense systems in several states, including New York, Louisiana, Utah, and Idaho. See "Indigent Defense," ACLU, last accessed August 23, 2017, https://www.aclu.org/issues/criminal-law-reform/effective-counsel/indigent-defense. There has been an accompanying legislative reform effort as well. But see Joel Stashenko, "Cuomo Vetoes Bill for State Takeover of Indigent Criminal Defense Costs," *New York Law Journal*, January 1, 2017, http://www.newyorklawjournal.com/id=1202775891579/Cuomo-Vetoes-Bill-for-State-Takeover-of-Indigent-Criminal-Defense-Costs. Cuomo promised to introduce his own "groundbreaking" reforms to New York's indigent criminal defense system, including a guarantee of counsel at first appearance for indigent defendants everywhere in the state and improvements in the quality of representation.

27 "Parents in Prison," Sentencing Project, September 27, 2012, https://www.sentencingproject.org/publications/parents-in-prison/; Lauren E. Glaze and Lauren M. Maruschak, "Parents in Prison and Their Minor Children," U.S. Depart-ment of Justice, Bureau of Justice Statistics Special Report, revised March 30, 2010, http://www.bjs.gov/index.cfm?ty=pbdetail&iid=823.

28 Geoffrey Cowan, *The People v. Clarence Darrow: The Bribery Trial of America's Greatest Lawyer* (New York: Times Books, 1993); Clarence Darrow, *The Story of My Life* (New York: Scribner, 1932); John A. Farrell, *Clarence Darrow: Attorney for the Damned* (New York: Doubleday, 2011); Andrew E. Kersten, *Clarence Darrow: American Iconoclast* (New York: Hill and Wang, 2011); Irving Stone, *Clarence Dar-row for the Defense* (New York: Doubleday, 1941).

29 Harper Lee, *To Kill a Mockingbird* (New York: HarperCollins, 1960).

30 Charles J. Shields, *Mockingbird: A Portrait of Harper Lee* (New York: Henry Holt, 2006), 271 (noting that, according to a 1988 National Council of Teachers of English survey, *Mockingbird* was taught in 74 percent of the nation's public schools, and only *Romeo and Juliet*, *Macbeth*, and *Huckleberry Finn* were assigned more often); Maria Puente, "'To Kill a Mockingbird': Endearing, Enduring at 50 Years," *USA Today*, accessed July 12, 2010, http://www.usatoday.com/life/books/news/2010-07-08-mockingbird08_CV_N.htm.

31 "15 Years of Summer Reading," Oprah.com, accessed April 23, 2016, http://www.oprah.com/book/Summer-Reading-To-Kill-a-Mockingbird?editors_pick_id=58371.

32 "'Mockingbird' Moments: 'Scout, Atticus, and Boo,'" National Public Radio, July 8, 2010, http://www.npr.org/templates/story/story.php?storyId=128387104.

33 Malcolm Gladwell, "Courthouse Ring: Atticus Finch and the Limits of Southern Liberalism," *New Yorker*, August 10, 2009, 27.

34 Gladwell, "Courthouse Ring," 27.

35 Monroe H. Freedman, "Atticus Finch, Esq., R.I.P.," *Legal Times*, February 24, 1992, 20; Monroe H. Freedman, "Finch: The Lawyer Mythologized," *Legal Times*, May 18, 1992, 25; Monroe H. Freedman, "Atticus Finch—Right and Wrong," *Alabama Law Review* 45, no. 2 (Winter 1994): 473–482.

36 Steven Lubet, "Reconstructing Atticus Finch," *Michigan Law Review* 97, no. 6 (May 1999): 1353, 1342.

37 Christopher Metress, "The Rise and Fall of Atticus Finch," *Chattahoochee Review* 24, no. 1 (Fall 2003).

38 Gladwell, "Courthouse Ring," 27.

39 Lee, *To Kill a Mockingbird*, 242.

40 Lee, 168.

41 For a longer treatment of the criticism of Atticus Finch in *To Kill a Mockingbird*, see Abbe Smith, "Defending Atticus Finch," *Legal Ethics* 14, no. 1 (2011): 143–167.

42 Michiko Kakutani, "Review: Harper Lee's 'Go Set a Watchman' Gives Atticus Finch a Dark Side," *New York Times*, July 10, 2015, https://www.nytimes.com/2015/07/11/books/review-harper-lees-go-set-a-watchman-gives-atticus-finch-a-dark-side.html.

43 Randall Kennedy, "Harper Lee's *Go Set a Watchman*," *New York Times*, July 14, 2015, https://www.nytimes.com/2015/07/14/books/review/harper-lees-go-set-a-watchman.html.

44 Harper Lee, *Go Set a Watchman* (New York: HarperCollins, 2015), 149–159.

45 Lee, 109.

46 See "Time 100: Heroes and Icons of the 20th Century," *Time*, June 14, 1999, accessed April 24, 2016, http://content.time.com/time/covers/0,16641,19990614,00.html.

47 Lillian Ross, "The Moods of Ernest Hemingway," *New Yorker*, May 13, 1950, http://www.newyorker.com/magazine/1950/05/13/how-do-you-like-it-now-gentlemen.

48 Bernard Malamud, *The Natural* (New York: Harcourt, Brace, 1952), 148.

49 Charles Schultz, *Peanuts*, June 9–13, 16, 17 (1958), accessed June 28, 2016, http://peanuts.wikia.com/wiki/June_1958_comic_strips.

50 Ernest Becker, *The Denial of Death* (New York: Simon & Schuster, 1973), ix.

51 *Annie Hall*, directed by Woody Allen (Burbank, Calif.: United Artists, 1977).

52 Freedman, "Atticus Finch, Esq., R.I.P.," 20.

53 *Model Rules of Professional Conduct*, Rule 6.1 (Chicago: American Bar Association, 2016). The rule states that "every lawyer has a professional responsibility to provide legal services to those unable to pay. A lawyer should aspire to render at least (50) hours of pro bono publico legal services per year." Comment [1] to the rule states, "Every lawyer, regardless of professional prominence or professional workload, has a responsibility to provide legal services to those unable to pay, and personal involvement in the problems of the disadvantaged can be one of the most rewarding experiences in the life of a lawyer. . . . Services can be performed in civil matters or in criminal or quasi-criminal matters for which there is no government obligation to provide funds for legal representation, such as post-conviction death penalty appeal cases."

54 Marge Piercy, "To Be of Use," in *Circles on the Water: Selected Poems of Marge Piercy* (New York: Alfred A. Knopf, 1982), 106.

55 Bill Steigerwald, "Darrow, Flaws and All: A PBS Biography Focuses on the Man behind the Lawyer," *Los Angeles Times*, December 29, 1990, http://articles.latimes .com/1990-12-29/entertainment/ca-6505_1_clarence-darrow.

56 Abbe Smith and William Montross, "The Calling of Criminal Defense," *Mercer Law Review* 50, no. 2 (Winter 1999): 497–509; see also Richard Zitrin, "Five Who Got It Right," *Widener Law Journal* 13, no. 1 (2003): 209–234 (Zitrin eschews the idea of the "lawyer-hero" and prefers that of ordinary people who are "each extraordinary, conducting their professional lives in a way that makes them worthy of the highest praise").

57 Susan Wolf, "Moral Saints," *Journal of Philosophy* 79, no. 8 (August 1982): 420–424.

58 W. Bradley Wendel, "Our Love-Hate Relationship with Heroic Lawyers," *Widener Law Journal* 13, no. 1 (2003): 7.

59 *Two Weeks Notice*, directed by Marc Lawrence (Hollywood: Warner Brothers, 2002).

60 Smith, "Too Much Heart," 1264.

61 Ben Beaumont-Thomas, "Bryan Stevenson: 'I Don't Do What I Do Because I Have To. I Do What I do Because I'm Broken Too,'" *Guardian*, February 6, 2015, http:// www.theguardian.com/membership/2015/feb/06/bryan-stevenson-i-dont-do-what -i-do-because-i-have-to-i-do-what-i-do-because-im-broken-too; Bryan Stevenson, *Just Mercy: A Story of Justice and Redemption* (New York: Spiegel & Grau, 2014), 290 ("There is a strength, a power even, in understanding brokenness, because embracing our brokenness creates a need and desire for mercy, and perhaps a corresponding need to show mercy. When you experience mercy, you learn things that are hard to learn otherwise. You see things you can't otherwise see; you hear things you can't otherwise hear. You begin to recognize the humanity that resides in each of us").

62 Jill Lepore, "Objection: Clarence Darrow's Unfinished Work," *New Yorker*, May 23, 2011, http://www.newyorker.com/magazine/2011/05/23/objection.

63 Jill Paperno, a career defender at the Monroe County Public Defender's Office in Rochester, New York, is the source of this terrific line.

64 Lepore, "Objection."

65 Jane Gardam, *Old Filth* (New York: Europa Editions, 2006), 221.

66 Angela Duckworth, *Grit: The Power of Passion and Perseverance* (New York: Scribner, 2016).

67 *. . . And Justice for All*, directed by Norman Jewison (Burbank, Calif.: Columbia Pictures, 1979).

68 *Model Rules of Professional Conduct*, Preamble [5] (Chicago: American Bar Association, 2016).

69 *Model Rules*, Rule 8.4 (d).

70 *Model Rules*, Preamble [5].

71 Taylor v. United States, 413 F.2d 1095, 1096 (D.C. Cir. 1969).

72 Crawford v. Washington, 541 U.S. 36 (2004).

73 See Geders v. United States, 425 U.S. 80 (1976) (holding that a trial court's order prohibiting attorney-client communication during a trial violated a criminal defendant's Sixth Amendment right to counsel); but see Perry v. Leeke, 488 U.S. 272 (1989) (allowing such a prohibition during a brief recess when a defendant is on the stand but cautioning that prohibiting lawyer-client consultation should not be automatic).

74 For an excellent "memoir" by a retired University of Chicago law professor that documents bullying and lying by a highly regarded federal appeals court judge, see Albert W. Alschuler, "How Frank Easterbrook Kept George Ryan in Prison," *Valparaiso University Law Review* 50, no. 1 (Fall 2015): 7–88.

75 Malia Wollan, "How to Take a Punch," *New York Times Magazine*, May 15, 2016, 33.

76 "Brevard Judge Tells Attorney, 'I'll Beat Your Ass,' Allegedly Throws Punches," WFTV.com, last updated June 3, 2014, http://www.wftv.com/news/local/brevard-judge-accused-punching-public-defender_ngcgc/107406474; Jacob Gershman, "Public Defender Quits after Judge in Courtroom Fight Returns to Bench," *Wall Street Journal*, July 8, 2014, http://blogs.wsj.com/law/2014/07/08/public-defender-quits-after-judge-in-courtroom-fight-returns-to-bench/.

77 Fred Barbash, "Florida's 'Fighting Judge,' Whose Videotaped Brawl in the Hall Went Viral, Is Removed from the Bench," *Washington Post*, December 18, 2015, https://www.washingtonpost.com/news/morning-mix/wp/2015/12/18/floridas-fighting-judge-whose-videotaped-brawl-in-the-hall-with-a-public-defender-went-viral-is-removed-from-the-bench/?utm_term=.8d4c0ce76f7c (reporting that the Florida Supreme Court found that the judge's "egregious conduct," which had become "a national spectacle and an embarrassment to Florida's judicial system," made him unfit to remain on the bench).

78 Alice Woolley, "Not Only in America: The Necessity of Representing 'Those People' in a Free and Democratic Society," in *How Can You Represent Those People?*, ed. Abbe Smith and Monroe H. Freedman (New York: Palgrave Macmillan, 2013), 207, 208; Alice Woolley, "Context, Meaning and Morality in the Life of the Lawyer," *Legal Ethics* 17, no. 1 (June 2014): 1–22.

79 Marc Bookman, "10 Ways to Blow a Death Penalty Case," Mother Jones, April 22, 2014, http://www.motherjones.com/politics/2014/04/10-death-penalty-cases-bad-lawyering.

80 See Zitrin, "Five Who Got It Right," 225.

81 Ferdinand von Schirach, *Crime*, trans. Carol Brown Janeway (New York: Alfred A. Knopf, 2011), ix.

Index

Abrams, Ruth, 156
actual innocence. *See* factual innocence
Adam's Rib, 5
addict, 27, 28, 85
adjournment in contemplation of dismissal, 8
Adler, William, 50
adversarial system, 71, 89, 94, 135–36
African Americans: disenfranchisement of, 64–65, 84; and disproportionate imprisonment, 5; and excessive surveillance, 35; in food service, 11; and guns, 56; as jurors, 46, 65; and mass incarceration, 5, 147; and murder, 104–5; and poverty, 27; and rape, 75, 83–84, 99. *See also* Emanuel African Methodist Episcopal Church; people of color; white supremacy
aging in prison, 3, 85, 100, 107, 109, 111, 116, 117, 121, 133–34
alcohol, 9–10, 50–51
Alexander, Brandy, 137
Allen, Woody, 24, 153
American Civil Liberties Union, 99
American Dream, 50
Amherst College, 132
Amirault family (Violet, Cheryl, and Gerald), 115
And Justice for All, 139, 161

Annie Hall, 24, 57, 153
Appalachian Trail, 119
Ashe, Arthur, 147
assault, 9, 12, 19, 33, 38, 43; on a police officer, 29, 31, 32, 164
autism / Asperger's syndrome, 108
Avery, Steven, 125

Babcock, Barbara, 141, 142
bail: bail jumping, 17; excessive bail, 20; and guilty pleas, 20–21; reform, 146
Baltimore, Maryland, 48, 119, 125
Barnes, Monique's story (pseudonym), 40–41
battered women, 27, 128
Becker, Ernest, 153
Belarus, 2
Bellows, Randy, 141
bench warrant, 17
Betts, Dwayne, 116
Birmingham, Alabama, 119
B. J.'s story, 28
black and brown people. *See* African Americans; people of color
"black on black" violence, 104–6
Bluebeard, 131
Bonfire of the Vanities, The, 143
Bookman, Marc, 166
Boston, Massachusetts, 50, 156

Perez, Tom, 4
petty criminals, 36. *See also* misdemeanors
Pfaff, John, 47
Philadelphia, Pennsylvania, 40, 48, 59, 71,
    76, 119, 162
Piercy, Marge, 154
Poe, Edgar Allen, 132
police: and aggression, 32; informants, 33;
    mocking a public defender, 59; shootings,
    48, 106; and truth, 94
police and prosecutors: and misconduct, 3,
    94; power of, 6, 94
Popkin, Arlene, 166
postgraduate fellows, 12–13, 32, 38, 42, 49,
    50, 51, 56, 58, 60, 61, 69, 80, 85–86, 97–98,
    144, 154, 158, 163, 164–65. *See also* E. Bar-
    rett Prettyman fellows
posttraumatic stress disorder (PTSD), 63.
    See also competency; trauma
Prejean, Sister Helen, 154
presidential election (2016), 106
presumption of innocence, 3, 114
Prine, John, 116
prisoners, 3–5, 47, 105–7, 110–11, 114, 116,
    123, 128, 134
prisons: cost of, 123–24; population reduc-
    tion, 3, 48; prison labor, 58, 109, 117; pri-
    vate prisons/jails, 3; and reform, 47; state
    vs. federal, 47. *See also* Lorton correc-
    tional complex; Nottoway Correctional
    Center; Sing Sing Correctional Facility;
    St. Cloud Prison
probation, 8, 11, 42
prosecutors: and criminal justice reform,
    146; in Manny's story, 159–60; overcharg-
    ing, 53; preparing their witnesses, 93–94;
    in Tamika's story, 118–19, 123; as unbudg-
    ing, 9, 34, 39, 41, 98
prostitution, 24, 27
public defenders. *See* criminal defense law-
    yers / public defenders
Public Defender Service for the District of
    Columbia (PDS), 139–41

racism, 27, 93, 99–100, 135, 150–51
rape: advocacy strategy, 93–94; as a capital
    offense, 75, 99–100; cross-examination of
    complainants, 71–72, 75–76, 77, 90–91,

92–95; DNA exonerations, 94; not always
a fluid act, 82–83; not always as it seems,
93; and race, 75, 83–84, 99; sentences,
88, 99; in *To Kill a Mockingbird*, 75, 149;
victims of, 68–72, 75, 77–78, 79, 84, 88,
89–90. *See also* child sex abuse; feminism;
Jamal's story; rapists; sexual assault; sexual
violence
rapists: as ashamed, 69, 81–82, 88; befriend-
ing their victims, 81; repeat sex offenders,
75, 78–79, 100; representing rapists,
70–72, 86–88, 94, 95–99, 100 (*see also*
feminism). *See also* child sex abuse; clients; Jamal's story; rape; sex offenders;
sexual assault; sexual violence
Rapping, Jonathan, 137
Raymond, Margaret, 141
recidivism, 48
Red (character in *The Shawshank Redemption*), 112–13, 114
Redding, Otis, 143
reentry, 134
reform (criminal justice), 47, 134, 146
rehabilitation, 69–70, 85, 112–13, 158–59
religion, 1, 75, 105–6, 132, 133, 154
repeat offenders, 22, 139
Ridolfi, Cookie, 163
Rise and Fall of the Third Reich, The, 102
Robber Bridegroom, The, 131
robbery: in Capitol Hill rape case, 89;
"grab-and-dash" robberies, 58; gunpoint
robbery story, 54–55; and homicides, 119;
in Wilton Marley's story, 51
Roberts, Michele, 34
Robinson, Tom, 75, 148–49, 151
Rogers, Amy (pseudonym), 11, 13
Ronnie's story (pseudonym), 102, 107–9,
116, 133
Roof, Dylann, 121–23
Roosevelt, Eleanor, 147
Rosa Lee, 27
Rowling, J. K., 132
Russia, 2

Sally (partner), 105, 156
Sanders, Bernie, 106
Sandy Hook Elementary School, 108
Sarat, Austin, 132

About the Author

ABBE SMITH is an American criminal defense attorney, professor of law at Georgetown University, and director of Georgetown's Criminal Defense & Prisoner Advocacy Clinic. She is the author of *Case of a Lifetime: A Criminal Defense Lawyer's Story* and *Carried Away: The Chronicles of a Feminist Cartoonist.*